TELL IT ON THE MOUNTAIN

TELL IT ON THE MOUNTAIN

by William R. Lasky

with James F. Scheer

DOUBLEDAY & COMPANY, INC.
GARDEN CITY, NEW YORK
1976

ISBN: 0-385-11366-8
Library of Congress Catalog Card Number 76–2998

PRINTED IN THE UNITED STATES OF AMERICA

FIRST EDITION

With Love
Dedicated to my son
Ronald Charles Lasky

And
to
Carolyn C. Scheer

Preface

I had thought of or tried every possible way. Now, alone in my room, I found nowhere to turn. Never have I known such despair, such utter hopelessness. I couldn't bring myself to die, and I didn't want to live.

In that moment, I remembered Mademoiselle Branche, my childhood nurse, her last good-by, and the little ivory statue of the baby Jesus, which she had given me, and what she had said about the Jesus child loving me. And then I remembered the whole world was in his hands.

I was on my knees. I prayed out loud in the only prayer I knew how: "Now I lay me down to sleep. I pray the Lord my soul to keep. If I should die before I wake, I pray the Lord my soul to take."

Then, looking up, I heard myself saying, "*Jesus, help me!*"

Since that time, as a result of increased appearances to give my Christian testimony, I have received numerous suggestions from individuals that I put in more permanent form some of the incidents that witness to the truth and love of Our Lord Jesus.

"You should write a book about your parents and your life."

Although I had procrastinated in starting such an ambitious project, I found that the Lord had plans for me. He put my new friend and Christian brother James F. Scheer in my path.

The meeting and friendship with my coauthor, Jim Scheer, and his wife, Carolyn, their enthusiasm for, and concern with, the writing of this book as a witness for Our Lord, I believe, have all been in His plan for my life.

The Lasky family motto, "Always go to the top," which started with my grandfather Ike Lasky, has been a focus that Jim and I have followed in the book's writing. Without *The Man* at the top and His constant help, this book could not have been written.

Without divine guidance, my uncle Samuel Goldwyn's acid comment about my name, William, shortly after my birth, "Every Tom, Dick, and Harry is named Bill," would have remained just another Goldwynism. The fact that it is more than that is proof that all things can serve the Lord.

Perhaps through this book, many whose life directions have been random will find some value in the Lasky family credo.

Only in a few of the book's incidents, where it was felt that someone mentioned might possibly be embarrassed, have we used substitute names.

William R. Lasky

In Gratitude

I would like to express my gratitude to the following Christian leaders without whose example, maturing influence, and guidance this book would never have been written:

Billy Graham
Pat Robertson
Oral Roberts
David Wilkerson
George Otis
Brant Baker
Kathryn Kuhlman
Bob Harrington
Jimmy Swaggart
Ralph Wilkerson
Bill Gothard
Demos Shakarian
Bill Bright
Pastor Leroy Sanders
Rex Humbard
Pat Boone

Contents

List of Illustrations

TELL IT ON THE MOUNTAIN

1

In the Beginning, There Was Every Tom, Dick, and Harry

I've always wanted to know the answers and so does almost everyone else.

Many times in the long years between our first and last breath, we are puzzled by the mysteries locked within three questions:

"Who am I?"

"Why am I living on earth?"

"What am I supposed to be doing here?"

Even when we're not aware of searching for answers, the questions keep nudging our minds for attention.

Strangely, the answers were always waiting for me, as they are for anyone who *really* wants to know. And when they do come, it's the beginning of a whole new life—one of unlimited beauty and horizons of opportunity, inconceivable peace, love, and understanding.

As a very little boy, I had a built-in and insatiable curiosity about all living things: butterflies ("What makes them come in such amazing colors? Why are they similar but each a little different? Where do they come from? Where are they going?"); bees ("Why do they buzz and what are they doing way deep inside of sweet-smelling flowers?"); and hummingbirds ("How can they flutter their wings so fast?").

An all-encompassing passion to know everything about birds, fish, insects, reptiles, and animals led me from one exploration and answer-seeking study to another.

At that time I could not possibly have understood that my searching was aimed beyond all living things and toward the discovery of ultimate truth. Who or what had brought them about, or did they just happen?

Then, eventually, I got around to asking myself about myself—Bill Lasky—and trying to find out why I was around. That posed real problems.

Several decades ago, before anyone conceived the term "identity crisis," I had just that. This dilemma was aggravated by the fact that I didn't even know what an identity crisis was or what I could do about it.

The identity question has concerned me throughout my life. Perhaps it bothered me most when I started my motion picture career as an office boy at Goldwyn Studios. In the years to follow, it was still present as I climbed from apprentice film editor to assistant director, production manager, director, cameraman, assistant producer, producer, writer, actor, and whatever other category was necessary to ensure that the show would go on—along with my pay checks.

"Who am I?"

I was inclined to answer with typical show business flippancy:

"I'm William R. Lasky, and I have a birth certificate to prove it."

The equally basic question, "Why am I living on earth?" posed no greater problem:

"My father, Jesse L. Lasky, one of the founders of the Hollywood film industry and of Paramount Pictures, and my mother, Bessie Lasky, artist and poet, were married. And I happened to be the second son resulting from that marriage."

Question three was a little bit tougher than the others:

"Am I doing what I'm supposed to be doing here?"

There was a constant tug of war going on inside me. I was completely dedicated to zoology—my career choice—but I had been born into the motion picture industry, so it was a constant battle between choice and inheritance. But more about this later.

To cover my confusion, I would often answer: "Sure, I'm doing what I'm supposed to be doing. I'm handling my consequential and inconsequential work in the best way I know how and, like billions on the face of the earth, these career activities, thoroughly mixed with meaningful and meaningless social activities, add up to the script for my life until the final fade-out."

These two-dimensional show-business answers to three-dimensional questions gave me only limited satisfaction.

But I'm getting ahead of my story.

I was born on March 24, 1921. That year was in the middle of a peak period in Hollywood's silent motion picture era.

My mother told me in later years that I arrived on the scene with a dramatic flourish and "in a tremendous rush to be out in the wide world."

The initial "R" in the name of William R. Lasky does not stand for "Rocket." It was for Raymond, the Americanized front name of Ramon Novarro, one of my father's Latin film stars in the romantic Rudolph Valentino mold.

Even more pertinent is my first name, William, and the bit of Hollywood history connected with it. I was named after director William DeMille, and besides, my father always wanted a son named "Bill."

One can't select parents, but if I had a choice, I would have chosen the same parents. This is because in the package deal—over and above a wonderful father and mother—I drew a most colorful uncle, film producer Samuel Goldwyn. All of us in the United States have one Uncle Sam. I was blessed with two.

When Uncle Sam Goldwyn finished his role on earth some years ago, he left more than a shelf gleaming with Academy Award statuettes. He left a legacy of Goldwynisms—brilliant, askew observations in his own brand of perfectly mangled English:

"Include me out."

"Two words—I'm . . . possible."

"A verbal agreement isn't worth the paper it's written on."

One of the Goldwynisms vitally concerned me.

A few minutes after my debut in the maternity ward of Los Angeles' Good Samaritan Hospital, my father, given to exuberance over the least little thing and proud over his half of the accomplishment, burst into the office of his brother-in-law, Samuel Goldwyn.

"Guess what, Sam? Bessie has had our second baby, and it's another son!"

"Dot's good, Jesse," responded Goldwyn in his rich Russian-Jewish accent. "Vot are you going to call him?"

"*Bill!*" Dad replied.

Goldwyn screwed up his face in obvious distaste: "Vyfore you call him Bill? Every Tom, Dick, and Harry is named Bill!"

As Uncle Sam so sharply pointed out, "Bill" is not an uncommon name. For that matter, neither am I an uncommon person. Yet, in all honesty, I can't say that my home environment, my upbringing, and the events of my whole life have been common. When I think back over them, I can hardly convince myself that everything was the way it was and that what happened truly happened to me.

The Cineramic montage of the past includes:

A father whose fortune, while it still belonged to him, ran into multimillions of dollars . . . a mother born an orthodox Jew, educated in a Catholic convent, who unknowingly planted a Christian mustard seed in me . . . myself, a rich youngster who seemed to have everything but couldn't begin to understand, let alone explain, his feelings of emptiness and incompleteness . . . exposure to film and TV stars, celebrities in every social, economic, and artistic sphere . . . a twenty-room New York City apartment on Fifth Avenue . . . a private railroad car equipped by Paramount Pictures to outlavish that of Diamond Jim Brady . . . coast-to-coast train trips geared to my father's executive film production schedules, but not to the seasons (unlike birds, we would migrate to the warmer California clime for the summer and to New York in the winter) . . . an oceanfront mansion with twenty-seven servants' rooms, a dozen guest rooms, private bedrooms with bath for every family member in this Taj Mahal on the white beaches of Santa Monica . . . celebrated neighbors: M-G-M's, Louis B. Mayer, Myron Selznick, Douglas Fairbanks, Sr., Marion Davies, and Uncle Sam Goldwyn . . . a gigantic, spectacular swimming pool (you could almost see from one end to the other) to compete with the Pacific Ocean . . . five Rolls-Royces and lesser imports that didn't use champagne as radiator fluid . . .

There are great advantages and disadvantages to being the son of a living legend—a person such as my father, Jesse L. Lasky, who produced the first American feature-length motion picture. Previously, only primitive short subjects called "flickers" or "chasers" had been made. The feature-length film was yet to become a new dramatic art form that was to attract millions of people to theaters especially built for films, excite critical acclaim, and realize box-office bonanzas, even to becoming a part of world history, for the motion picture has influenced civilization in a greater way and on a larger scale than has any other art form.

The earliest Bible motion pictures were made under my father's Paramount regime. The miracles within these films hardly exceeded the miracles of their technical achievement and the ability to reach the world-wide masses, many of whom had never owned, read, or seen a Bible.

Yet Dad's on-screen miracles didn't always carry over to life with Mother and the three of us children—Jesse, Jr., me, and my sister Betty, born eighteen months after me.

In the seeking of answers to "Who am I?" "Why am I living on earth?" and "What am I supposed to be doing with my life?" one can discover important clues from the past.

It never fails to amaze me how character traits of my father and mother and events in their lives—even prior to my birth—have led me to finding the answers to these three most important questions.

2

Life with Father Before He Was Father

Few persons who knew my father, Jesse L. Lasky, ever came away from him without his indelible imprint.

Certainly I didn't.

Yet it is paradoxical that his most indelible imprints on me were not made by his major experiences such as cofounding Paramount Pictures, discovering hundreds of famous film stars, and producing more than a thousand motion pictures, dramatic triumphs, and equally dramatic defeats.

They were made by minor experiences and events of his life.

One of the important things I learned about Dad was his own understanding and appreciation of his uniqueness—the uniqueness that we all have and that no other soul can possess.

He was fortunate and perceptive enough to learn his identity and his aptitudes at an early age. His many successes can be related to an expression of God-given individuality in his work. Only on several occasions in his first twenty years did he let financial insecurity and lack of faith stampede him into the compromises that many of us make to earn our daily bread, and each time he paid the price.

Dad was born in San Francisco in 1885. He was a second-generation American who did most of his growing up in the neighboring community of San Jose.

Talk about enthusiasm! He had it as a boy and never lost it as a man. His electrically charged mind crackled with so many new ideas that it could have lit up the whole state of California.

Dad was outstanding with the cornet before he graduated from short pants. He and his cornet were so constantly and noisily together that other residents of Santa Clara Street probably thought the instrument was a permanent part of his anatomy. In those otherwise quiet days of the early 1890s, they had a premature introduction to noise pollution and doubtless often prayed for divine surgery to "separate that Lasky kid from his horn."

But young Jesse continued with his horn, and the neighbors continued with their prayers and supplications. (All prayers are heard, but all aren't answered in the way that we might desire.)

One warm and blue-skied summer afternoon the twelve-year-old Jesse, cornet tightly tucked under his arm, was striding toward the Boston Shoe Bazaar, his father's business on South First Street, when he saw a sign in a shop window that was to help mold and shape his life.

John Philip Sousa, renowned bandmaster, and the United States Marine Corps Band were coming to San Jose auditorium for one day only—to give a matinee and an evening concert. The sign announced that the featured performer would be Herbert Clarke, "The World's Greatest Cornettist."

The more the youthful Jesse stared at the sign, the more his wishful thoughts dominated his eyesight. The name Herbert Clarke faded out; the name of Jesse L. Lasky faded in. He had been saving his dime-a-week allowance for two months to buy fireworks for an explosive Fourth of July. With Sousa about to invade San Jose, Jesse sacrificed the fireworks for a ticket.

One way or another, he was going to meet John Philip Sousa and play the cornet so magnificently that he would be hired on the spot. He convinced his doting mother—my grandmother Sarah—that he just had to have a Marine Band uniform for his audition and that she could easily make one on her sewing machine. She worked until midnight, and he got his uniform.

Young Jesse, in full marine dress, arrived at the auditorium for the matinee. It was the day of days. He arrived even before the ticket takers. Once inside, he went backstage for just a glimpse of the mighty Sousa.

No luck. The stage doorman started to shoo him away, and then advised, "Son, the only way you'll get a look at the great man close up is before the evening concert. Our performers often walk down Santa Clara Street."

Right past his house, Dad calculated.

Sousa's brilliant and stirring renditions of his most famous marches, "Semper Fidelis," "King Cotton," and "The Stars and Stripes Forever," had hardly thundered to conclusion before a still-tingling Jesse was sprinting the six blocks home.

Now, for sure, he could play an audition for the "March King," who would soon be walking right past his house! Jesse set up his music stand on the front porch of the Lasky cottage, just behind the rosebushes that embraced the pillars.

Sousa couldn't fail to hear him and maybe even offer him a lifetime contract! The thought was overwhelming.

For three hours, young Jesse's cornet blasted down the streets of San Jose: "Semper Fidelis," "The Washington Post March," and every other Sousa number until his lungs were ready to burst and his lips were swollen.

No John Philip Sousa.

Again and again, he went through the full repertoire.

Still no Sousa.

Finally he heard authoritative footsteps just beyond the front gate. He had got his second wind, and now he drew upon his last reservoir of energy to play his loudest and best that was certain to depose Herbert Clarke from his throne.

He didn't even dare an upward glance but played on, waiting in suspense for the March King to appear.

The footsteps were on the porch. Only now did he stop the music and look upward toward Sousa.

What he saw was such a shock that he couldn't talk. It was not John Philip Sousa at all, but the angry reddened face of Neighbor Johnson looming up inches from his face.

"My wife is sick," thundered Mr. Johnson. "We've had enough of your infernal racket. Now if you don't cut it out right away, I'll call the police."

Shaking a broad fist, he abruptly turned and left, muttering threats. John Philip Sousa never walked by. Yet instead of ending Jesse's career, the Sousa incident built a determination in him that he would blow the cornet and someday achieve fame and fortune.

Gathering together his most talented school chums, Dad formed the All Boys Brass Band. Well, it *was* all boys until his sister Blanche insisted on joining the brass on her piano during rehearsals at the Lasky cottage.

Young Jesse's greatest hero, aside from John Philip Sousa, was his dad, Ike Lasky. Grandfather Ike, athletically oriented, once owned an interest in the San Jose Baseball Club and headed the Athletic Association and the Bicycle Club. But his greatest acclaim came from being the county's best fly fisher, a title he had earned in numerous competitions.

So when Jesse wasn't behind his cornet, he enjoyed hours behind his fishing rod. His father had carefully instructed him in its use. Always a warm and outgoing person, Ike Lasky developed a kind of glow during evenings on the front porch when he and his son practiced the art of fly casting.

Then he introduced his son to his favorite haunts, usually on Alum Creek, which rushed down the California Coastal Range about seven miles from their home.

What sport it was for them to discover pools that held the biggest trout! There was no stopping Ike and his boy from riding their bikes higher and higher up the range until the underbrush caught in the chains, forcing them to continue upward on foot.

They would pick their way through thick undergrowth to discover some new and unfished trout pool. As their creels filled with fish, Ike Lasky would often say, "If you want the biggest fish, look for the pools at the top of the stream. Always go to the top, Jesse."

And my dad handed down this bit of wisdom to me. It was Ike's practice to fish on the first and last days of the season and on as many in-between days as possible:

"Jesse, you and I will never fail to go on the first day because fishing is best on that day, and on the last day because then the time is shorter until next season."

Years later when my dad and I fished together, he would sometimes reminisce about the last days of fishing with Grandfather Ike.

He was thirteen then.

"As usual we went fishing but there was something unusual about Grandfather Ike.

"He tried to make it seem as if everything were all right, but I had to slow down for him. Now and then he would stop to catch his breath and take hold of a tree. He seemed to be in pain. This time we had planned to go higher than ever before. We never did make it.

"It wasn't a bad fishing day, but Dad was bothered that he had let me down. 'Jesse,' he said, 'I just know there are deeper pools with bigger fish up and around the next bend. Next time we'll start earlier and get them!'

"It didn't work out that way," my Dad continued. "On the last fishing day of the season, your grandfather had to stay in bed. I didn't want to go without him, and I couldn't go with him. I pretended I'd forgotten about it.

"*He* hadn't, and he knew I hadn't.

"'Jesse, a first-rate fisherman would never miss the chance on the last day of the season.'

"Then, for the first time ever, your Grandpa Ike offered me his rod and some very special flies he had got from old man Muller. Imagine? *His rod!* 'Jesse,' he said, and there was a mock stern expression on his face. 'If you break the tip or snag the line, just forget about ever coming back home.'

"Next day early, I was on my bike pedaling up the road to Alum Creek, finally leaving the bike where the brush was impenetrable and the cottonwoods were thick. Through dense patches of snake-grass and over and around boulders, I made my way, got near the top of the hill, and my heart began to pound in anticipation.

"At that altitude, the creek rampages, and there *were* deep pools. The first trout I caught was a whopper, wriggling proof of your Grandpa Ike's wisdom.

"Then, suddenly, the trout began ignoring my casting techniques and old man Muller's sure-fire flies. The frustration was bad enough, but the idea of letting Dad down was even worse.

"So I stayed with it until the sun disappeared and the chill of evening was on its way and, finally, I had a creel bulging with big beauties.

"It was dark when I got home, and Mother and Dad were concerned, but when I brought my catch to Dad's bedside, he beamed with excitement and pride.

"'Jesse, you did it! What a catch! It's just as I said. The best are always at the top.'

"I nodded, squeezed his arm gently, and said, 'Sure, Dad. That's what you told me.'

"That was the last fishing day that I ever had the opportunity to see such a special light in my father's eyes. His lingering illness kept him bedfast for a number of years."

The physical condition of Grandfather Ike Lasky had absented him from his Boston Shoe Bazaar for protracted periods, and eventually led to the business going bankrupt and the family uprooting itself for new and greater opportunities in San Francisco.

But rough times and reverses had harassed the Lasky family before. My dad's grandparents had fled czarist persecution in their Polish village of Laski, a setting similar to that of the musical *Fiddler on the Roof*, and escaped to a new land. Grandpa and Grandma had endured the seemingly endless, bone-crushing cross-country covered-wagon trip amid Indian attacks to make their home in California.

Now, Ike, Sarah, my dad, and Aunt Blanche found themselves in a rented apartment in San Francisco with a willing but untried Jesse suddenly promoted to family breadwinner. In San Jose he had earned more than ninety dollars that went into the family teapot by playing in Witherell's Brass Band, which distinguished itself with blood-stirring music for park concerts, parades, fiestas, political rallies, and picnics.

In the family financial council, Dad's Uncle Mark, who lived in San Francisco, was free with advice to young Jesse.

"Forget about finishing high school. If you don't have the training to make an *honest* living, you might as well use your cornet."

Though he was large for his age, Dad was not old enough to join the musicians' union. A friend of Uncle Mark's knew a union official, so political influence and the addition of several years to Dad's age on the application blank led to his acquiring a union card.

He first played for Dr. Silas Crabtree's Medicine Show and then for a succession of events and groups: picnics for the German-American Turnverein, in bands at Golden Gate Park, as substitute cornettist in the Tivoli Opera House pit orchestra for performances of *The Mikado*, as well as at the Bella Union, a glorified burlesque theater on Kearny Street, featuring Little Egypt "straight from her triumph at the Chicago World's Fair."

During this period, Grandfather Ike died, but after burial expenses, his insurance left a few thousand dollars.

Jesse and his mother began to seek a proper investment, but learned that get-rich-quick schemes are usually the slowest and most detouring vehicles toward a fortune.

First, there was a rare opportunity to invest five hundred dollars in a machine and secret ingredients to make maple syrup at home. The owners and inventors of the device, which was transportable in a standard-size suitcase, arrived at the Lasky apartment impeccably dressed, with dazzlingly shined shoes and diamond stickpins (obvious indications of prosperity, my dad remembered).

Their demonstration, featuring proprietary concoctions and powders and water, turned out a thick syrup that tasted as if it had come directly from sturdy Vermont maple trees. It never occurred to the Laskys that one of the main ingredients could have been maple sugar.

My dad and Grandmother Sarah put up a green bundle of cash. Their machinery and supplies, as well as the secret formula, were to be delivered within a week.

That was the last they saw of the maple-syrup-making machinery, the demonstrators, and their five hundred dollars.

To the end of his life, Dad preferred honey to maple syrup on his waffles.

Next Sarah Lasky found an alluring ad for a newspaper route, and decided that a *Bulletin* newspaper route was a substantial business if she had ever seen one. "Everybody reads newspapers every day" was her succinct market analysis. So what more could a young man want than a part-time career in newspaper distribution?

The newspaper route was for real. However, the description of its merits by the owner who wanted to sell immediately took on more than a little poetic license.

Grandmother Sarah and my dad were told that the route had a thousand customers paying twenty cents each a week and that one of the customers just happened to be Jack London, seaman, tramp, gold-seeker in the Klondike, and, most important, a famous author.

Jack London! The name reverberated through my dad's fertile mind. What an opportunity to meet with the great author right on his doorstep! Who could tell what would develop? There might even be the possibility of becoming his protégé!

Both Grandmother Sarah and Dad finally persuaded each other that $1,000 wouldn't be too much of an outlay, especially since the route could be paid for in easy installments out of collections. Best of all, it would not interfere with cornet engagements on two or three nights a week.

Shortly after they had made the down payment, they realized that some things about the newspaper route just didn't add up. Jack London, like John Philip Sousa and the maple syrup promoters, never seemed to materialize. The first month's collection shattered their dreams. There were one thousand subscribers all right, but due to many move-outs, the number was sharply reduced. Only three hundred subscribers paid for their newspapers.

Meeting payments for the route out of profits wouldn't work because there were no profits—which was why the original owner had agreed to sell. But Dad's playing engagements had stepped up, and on many nights he would get home when even the alley cats were asleep, change clothes, and deliver his papers. It was these engagements that made the payments and kept the family afloat. Finally he and Grandmother Sarah decided to sell at a loss.

A born adventurer, my dad, while delivering his newspapers, became excited by headlines about new gold discoveries in Alaska.

Finally, he confided his gold fever (125°) to his mother, who shared the stories and a stimulating new gold rush book which he had found. While she idolized her son and was often infected with his contagious enthusiasm, she listened to his reading with some misapprehension.

Nevertheless, during his daylight hours away from the cornet, Dad spent more time on the San Francisco wharves than a longshoreman, watching mining equipment being loaded on vessels, seeing Alaska-bound ships hoist anchor, and savoring rumors about new strikes in the Alaska territory until he became inflamed with the desire to go to Alaska.

The latest talk had it that gold found on the beaches of Nome, a seaport on the Bering Sea, was finer than flour, which made it hard to recover from the sand. Existing sluices couldn't process it. Nome, touted as a tremendous new source of gold, was said to be "bigger than the Klondike and the Yukon had ever been."

Now, there just had to be a way of making the sand relinquish its treasures, and the mind of young Jesse Lasky wrestled with the problems and possible solutions. Then he discovered that an inventor in San Francisco had already done the job for him.

Enchantment with the Aurn Electrum Depositor was instantaneous. Dad marveled at its gigantic proportions: sixty silver-coated copper plates, a vigorous four-cylinder engine, a dynamo, generous-size boiler, and water pump.

Came the demonstration. A hush fell over the Lasky family and others present. The symphony of sight and sound was about to begin. W. H. Orr, president of the Triumverate Mining Company and controller of the manufacturing rights, set the mechanical marvel into motion.

Ten rockers shivered and shook. W. H. Orr took a handful of sand, hesitated a moment, and then dramatically fed it into the Aurn Electrum Depositor, which went into action.

A short time passed and then Mr. Orr turned off the machine and pointed significantly toward the plates. *Voilà!* The silver-plated copper plates that had gleamed in the sun were now covered with gold powder finer than flour.

It turned out that Mr. Orr and his miner associate, Frederick Vroom, were looking for just one enthusiastic, energetic young partner who had the financial resources to put up "the small amount of $1,200" and who was unencumbered enough to be on a boat to the Bering Sea, along with the Aurn Electrum Depositor, at the first sign that ice was breaking up in the far north.

The game plan was for this "young partner" to set up and work the beach at Nome, while his two partners would temporarily stay at the home base to put their prototype into production, refine their marketing plan, and recruit a sales staff.

My dad's imagination instantly transported him to Alaska, accompanying the Aurn Electrum Depositor, which would shake tons of flour gold from the reluctant beaches of Nome. His body just had to join his imagination there, and a little money remaining from his father's insurance and some of the cornet earnings from the dresser drawer would do it.

When Grandmother Sarah heard the idea, she almost lanced herself with a needle as her sewing fell in a heap on the floor. It was a nudnik idea—nothing, nothing! Hadn't they just had two rotten investments?

But Dad was already developing the quick and persuasive mind which was later to help him to the top.

"Sure, Ma," he said. "But we know that the gold is there. That's proved. And those who reach Nome first with the best equipment will get the most gold. Who else is going to make the kind of money we need for you and Blanche? Doesn't that make sense? I'm almost better with the horn than Herbert Clarke now, but playing dates are still not plentiful for a fellow without a big reputation. *This is* the opportunity of a lifetime."

Grandmother Sarah, always practical, studied Dad's face and then asked, "How much will it cost?"

When a Jewish mother asks, "How much," you know the battle is over.

A family council, including Uncle Mark, gave grudging consent, but Dad said the idea wouldn't seem so ridiculous when he came back wealthy with enough money to send Blanche to the Boston Conservatory of Music and enough to buy Ma a horseless carriage.

Uncle Mark was still shoulder deep in skepticism, but Grandmother Sarah declared herself:

"If my Jesse says it's a good deal, it's a good deal. My Jesse is going to be on that first boat to go."

Stuffed into Dad's huge canvas bag along with woolen socks, long johns, toilet articles, and other necessities was his cornet—a last-minute dockside insertion by his insistent mother. "It might come in handy, Jesse. Between finding gold, you might want to eat."

The horn had seemed like the one item in the world that he could most do without, but now, amid the icy indifference of Alaska and its people in frozen and forbidding Nome, it was his sole contact with his warm and loving home.

A nightmare of sights, sounds, and happenings had assailed him: rude shacks, unpaved, frozen, rutted roads, saloons and honky-tonk pianos, a drunk staggering toward him, pack-laden mules heading toward Anvil Creek, miners yelling, cursing, and fist-fighting, an occasional revolver shot, no sign of a lawman . . . everywhere the air of naked greed and the ferment and movement of treasure seekers like himself . . . bearded, quick-triggered characters unlike any he had met anywhere but in the safety of books or stage plays.

My dad needed a claim along Nome Bay for setting up the Aurn Electrum Depositor. An old sourdough advised him that the best claims were farther north and that he happened to have a good one north of the Snake River that he would consider selling.

So, armed with a small shovel, miner's pan, and a pail, Dad accompanied the old man along the desolate beach through Arctic gusts that knifed to the skin. Punctuating the shore line were grumbling and disheartened prospectors trying to mine the waters with primitive sluice boxes and rockers. Their hopelessness began to dampen Dad's usual optimism.

After a three-hour hike, they came to the claim. The sourdough seemed to study the area carefully—probably making sure he was within bounds of his claim, thought Dad—then chose a spot, and said casually, "Take your shovel and try here. Go deep enough, until you hit the black sand."

Dad's excitement, curiosity, and enthusiasm made the shovel work fast. A few feet down, the black sand began to show. The sourdough picked up a shovelful, emptied it into the miner's pan, swishing it around the edge. Then he washed away the white sand. As he hunkered down swishing the black sand around, gold particles appeared on the pan's bottom. It was like a sunrise to Dad.

"Must be about five dollars' worth of flour gold," said the sourdough offhandedly.

Dad could hardly contain his joy.

"Reckon a fair price for the claim would be two hundred and fifty dollars in advance and twenty-five per cent of the gold take," continued the old man.

Numbers rotated in Dad's mind like the sand that had whirled around the miner's pan. Let's see. Within minutes, one pan of the black sand had given up around five dollars. With ten rockers of the Aurn Electrum Depositor working continuously, it would be easy to get ten thousand pans of gold in a month. Not bad—$50,000 a month . . . $600,000 a year!

Dad signed the lease and agreement and pulled twelve twenty-dollar gold pieces and a ten-dollar gold piece from the money belt around his waist.

Next he acquired a ton of coal, a tent, supplies, food, and a dory to transport the Aurn Electrum Depositor, supplies, and equipment to his claim. Jim Douglas, a shipboard acquaintance with mechanical experience, hired on at twenty-five dollars a day and part of the take to assemble, activate, and run the apparatus. Two disillusioned prospectors were added to work with Dad and Jim to shovel the black sand into the depositor and to keep seaweed out of the intake pipe.

The first twelve-hour day was a king-size disaster—only a few ounces of gold to show for all their work. So were the second and third days, and the endless frustrating days that followed.

Dad had a hard time telling Jim Douglas that his funds were dwindling. He also mentioned that within minutes of his first attempt with the sourdough, he had panned more gold than the present team plus the Aurn equipment was able to produce.

Douglas let Dad have it straight, "This area was salted. You know what that means, don't you, Jesse?"

Dad had heard about such practices aboard the ship. Everybody had talked about planting gold in the sand and directing a prospective claim buyer to the precise spot so that he could dig and make the discovery.

"The shine of gold dims common sense," said Douglas.

"Yes, but there *is* gold here," Dad insisted.

"Sure is, kid," Douglas responded softly, "but you'd better quit now and use what money's left to go back home. At what it's costing you to mine gold, you can buy it cheaper in San Francisco."

Everybody deserted. Then the things that he hadn't had the eyes to see before became starkly visible—rusted and abandoned machinery on various parts of the beach, symbols of other failures.

Dad's remaining $150 was just enough to buy ten or twelve meals in Nome. It had been a discouraging day, so he went into his tent, getting ready for bed early. He would feel better in the morning and have time to think his way out. He had gone too far to quit easily.

Somewhere around dawn, he was wakened by a sound he had never heard before. As he opened his eyes, he saw the flash of a long hunting knife slitting the back portion of his tent. He was frozen with horror and the sudden memory of Alaskan tales of flat-broke prospectors making desperation killings for money.

A hand slipped through the slit and quickly pulled out Dad's trousers and money belt. Then it was gone. Dad fumbled for his revolver, and rushing outside, saw a fleeting figure about twenty paces away. He pointed the revolver, but recoiling at his impulse to shoot another human being, he returned to the tent.

As he put on his spare trousers, blasting winds arose and high waves began to move up the beach closer to him. A sudden gust flattened the tent, and the next gust blew it away. Foam-crested waves began to splash over the Aurn Electrum Depositor and soon submerged it completely. Salt water and rust would make it unusable ever again.

When Dad's belongings started to blow away, he grabbed everything in sight and stuffed it into his bulky canvas bag.

Then suddenly, without knowing why, he started laughing aloud. How crazy! Here he was in a frozen nowhere, thousands of miles from home, in a land of total indifference, without a friend, without money, and only the clothes on his back and the contents of his bag, and he was laughing.

This mess had to be telling him something important. He had already been launched in show business, making gains, and in two of the three cases, he had tried something he knew nothing about to get rich quick. And what did he have to show for the efforts? Three out of three failures.

Each time he had been taken, but even now he had no hard

feelings toward the "takers." If a fellow is honest, he sees honesty in others, he thought. Yet he would have to be wiser in the future, and don't we all have to pay something for knowledge?

As he pulled tight the drawstrings of the canvas bag, his hand collided with a hard metallic object inside—the cornet.

There was a deep sense of security even in touching the cornet—his old friend from the Sousa days. Instantly he knew something that hadn't occurred to him before. Even his three efforts to make a living in lines that he knew nothing about had not been wasted. They had served to show him he should stay with work that he liked and knew best.

With affection, he patted the canvas bag in the area of the cornet. Funny, he had thought the cornet was a big *nothing* to have in Alaska. Suddenly it had become a big *something.* Dance hall jobs would give him eating money, room, and, finally, transportation back home. He could have kissed his practical and insistent mother for having pushed the horn into the canvas bag.

From that moment on, Dad knew something for sure. There would be no more side excursions from his horn and show business, no matter how exciting the prospects appeared to be.

3

On to Broadway

A few short weeks after the hero's welcome home from Alaska by his mother and sister Blanche, my dad was again aboard ship—this time en route to the Hawaiian Paradise of Honolulu.

One of the stories he liked to tell us many years later dealt with his adventures of playing in the Royal Hawaiian Band, something that amused him a great deal because he was neither royal nor Hawaiian. This band was present at all dockings and departures of luxury tourist steamers.

Actually, Dad had come to Hawaii to play in the Orpheum Theater for twenty-five dollars a week. His engagement had suddenly terminated, and he found himself out of funds. It was at this point that he met Herr Berger, leader of the Royal Hawaiian Band. Now, one of Dad's plans for replenishing his dwindling finances was to create a Polynesian Conservatory of Music. Along with this idea, he created a professorship for himself and dubbed his brain child, "Professor Jesse L. Lasky's Polynesian Conservatory of Music." Dad approached his new friend Herr Berger with the idea of his becoming a co-faculty member.

Herr Berger declined the proposition but admired my dad's ingenuity in his project and made a counteroffer.

"Professor Lasky, we need a first-rate cornettist with our band, and having heard you at the Orpheum, I know you would be right for us. Would you like to become a Royal Hawaiian?"

Dad grinned. The idea appealed to him.

"A Jewish Royal Hawaiian?" he asked Herr Berger. "That's fine, but my complexion is very light compared with the dark skins of your band members, and how about my blond hair and blue eyes?"

Dad paused and added reflectively, "But my mother has always told me that I do not have a typically Jewish nose."

Herr Berger's smile expanded roguishly. His thought of having my dad join his band appealed to him even more.

"Professor Lasky"—he bowed formally—"I am not prejudiced against your skin, your hair, your eyes, or your nose. You will be my first bleach-skinned Royal Hawaiian."

Often there were audible remarks about my father as he played in the band:

"He has got to be white," someone would comment.

Another person would counter:

"How can he be? This is an all-native band."

Still another person would offer his opinion:

"Either he's an albino or he's gone through some horrible tropical illness."

One specific observation about my dad amused him most of all. A small girl was about to board ship with her mother when she stopped to stare at the Royal Hawaiians who were playing "Aloha," the farewell song. Her mother tried to drag her away, but she insisted on staring at my father.

Just then the orchestra stopped for a moment. And in the silence, the mother's dialogue came through with crystal clarity.

"Why are you staring at the band, Martha?"

The little girl pointed her finger at my dad.

"It's that one man, Mommy. He doesn't look like a Hawaiian at all. He looks Jewish."

I have always been amused by the story that Dad was the world's first Jewish Royal Hawaiian, particularly so because—in the Lasky Polynesian tradition—I became the world's first completed Jewish Royal Samoan. It happened in western Samoa, where I had participated in a Charismatic Revival Conference and was accorded the honor of being made a Samoan High Chief with the name Falemaa, which translates into "house with a cornerstone of rock."

While my dad was working at being an authentic Royal Hawaiian, he was dutifully sending home much of his weekly earnings to his family. Equally dutifully, Blanche and Grandmother Sarah were working on a surprise for him.

The surprise really belonged to Blanche, who had decided that she, too, was going to master the cornet while her brother was away. Band leader Witherell, who had been my father's conductor and was now transplanted to San Francisco, gave her an audition. She showed such amazing aptitude that he offered her free lessons.

Blanche's brilliant playing in so short a period of instruction not only dumbfounded Dad when he returned to the United States; it later actually launched the Lasky family totally and irrevocably into show business.

Grandmother Sarah urged them to play duets, and soon they were asked to appear as an act in a concert hall charity performance.

"What have we got to lose?" asked Dad. "It might lead to something."

It did.

He and Blanche played, and they both acknowledged that the applause was sweeter than their duets. As they hurried to the dressing room, they were not alone. On their heels was a talent agent named Maurice Levy, who offered to get them a fifty-dollar-per-week booking at Shoot-the-Chutes Park, an amusement center.

Now, Blanche had no visions of trumpeting her way through life and trouping to all parts of the nation, so she was a reluctant half of the duo. It was one thing to learn the cornet to surprise her brother. It was quite another to be trapped in show business. But she was a good sport, and besides, the Laskys needed the money.

Dad began to be concerned about the act. He and Blanche were no longer in the semi-pro leagues. They were sharing the bill with professionals and needed professional material.

Never at a loss for ideas, he thought they would best open with a well-known popular tune. Broadway's smash musical was *Floradora*, so he chose its most catchy number, "Tell Me Pretty Maiden, Are There Any More at Home Like You?"

The audience loved the cornet act and the handsome young couple. After their act was over, Blanche and Dad joined Sarah, and all three Laskys watched the rest of the show in the darkened theater: acrobats bouncing around on the stage and dropping funny lines from crazy postures; two men flailing away at punching bags in rhythm with the music; and oversentimental and sorghum sweet songs by Clinton Montgomery, backgrounded by color lantern slides—lovers romantically paddling a birch bark canoe into a gigantic yellow-faced moon or whispering sweet somethings to each other over a white picket gate entwined with pink roses and a nest of white doves in the leafy tree above.

A significant event happened to Dad that night, but how significant, he didn't realize until more than a dozen years later.

Instead of using exit music to clear out the audience, the theater ended the program with a newly invented novelty of that period—a five-minute moving picture. These films were so bad that my dad mused, "A good way to chase people out of the theater." Intermittent inky black spots of varying sizes dotted the poorly lighted film, appropriately called "flickers" or "chasers," jerky and unnatural action projected on the lantern-slide screen: a dog pursuing a man, who kept looking back apprehensively; a portly woman in a polka-dot dress flourishing a large bandanna to get help from the police; and a cowboy on horseback, silently firing a pistol from each hand.

One of San Francisco's daily newspapers reviewed the program, mentioning the Lasky duo as "clever musicians," but didn't devote a single line to the novelty of the flickering screen short subject, a forerunner of a new international industry.

Their booking agent got the Laskys a week at Fisher's Music Hall and then two weeks at Baker's Theater in Portland at seventy-five dollars per week, but the contract called for a complete change of act for the second week. This meant becoming more professional, more versatile, and developing another act and an entirely new set of costumes. Thanks to designs by Grandmother Sarah and her tailoring ability, the Lasky duo got a variety of changes.

Originally my grandmother had run up military costumes for Blanche and Dad, capitalizing on the excitement over the Spanish-American War. They rehearsed a vast range of army bugle calls and made certain of applause in those days of overt patriotism by lowering an American flag before themselves as they stood statue-still in a salute to the flag. They dramatized their military routine by multiple costumes, and my grandmother devised costumes that could be worn in layers. The act opened with my dad and Blanche in Russian Hussar uniforms, giving an appropriately Russian bulkiness.

A split second in the wings, and they shed the Russian outer garments and became British tommies. Next, as they rapidly peeled the tommies garb, they appeared as two of Teddy Roosevelt's Rough Riders straight from San Juan Hill, their cornets blasting out in perfect harmony the period's most sung and whistled marching-off-to-war songs.

Through Bothwell Browne, a female inpersonator on the Baker's Theater vaudeville bill with them, Dad was introduced to the world of crinolines and dramatic powdered wigs, leading him and Blanche to become the "Colonial Duet" for the second week.

On went Grandmother Lasky's costume creations, and up went the performers' salaries to ninety a week, excellent for those days of the super-solid dollar. Each engagement led to elaborations and growth for their act and on-stage wardrobe, and now my grandmother conceived the plan for a promotion to make the waiting world of vaudeville aware of the trumpeting Laskys.

She found a list of the nation's prominent theaters, with addresses and names of their managers, in the New York *Clipper*, that era's *Daily Variety*. Next she designed a letterhead and a pamphlet displaying characteristic poses of her son and daughter in various costume changes. Then she wrote to sixty major theaters. The adjectives were applied thickly and richly as a good Jewish mother trowels sour cream on cheese blintzes.

Her barrage of mail-outs brought back only one offer—from the Boston Music Hall. My dad's inquiries at the musicians' union revealed that this was not "some kind of a dive," as Grandmother Sarah had prematurely surmised. It was one of the nation's uppercrust theaters.

In later years, my dad confessed to me:

"The Boston Music Hall was one of the worst disasters I ever experienced, but it was also one of the best things that ever happened in my life."

The Laskys had relatives in Boston, the Cobes, who invited them to stay during their engagement. The Cobes even bought tickets for socialite friends to accompany them to the duo's initial performance.

No soooner did my dad see the glitter and elegance of the Boston Music Hall and the attire and jewelry of the audience than he began to feel uncomfortable. The feeling grew as he and Blanche, watching from the wings, witnessed one of the most superb acts they had ever seen: the Phenomenal Rauschle, a genius of mimicry, imitating and characterizing the great personalities of history—President William McKinley, President Theodore Roosevelt, Chancellor Bismarck, Napoleon III, and Admiral Dewey.

Once he and Blanche were on stage, my dad's fears were confirmed from the first cornet notes. Even though they extended themselves beyond their usual capacities, there was a chill in the air which he hadn't experienced since Nome.

"One of the worst things for a performer is knowing he isn't making it with the audience," he once admitted to me.

In the devastating silence of that vast theater, just the lonely handclapping of the Cobes and their party could be heard. Later the Lasky duo learned that only the nation's greatest acts appeared at the Boston Music Hall and that more was required than playing instruments in harmony, patriotic routines, and rapid costume-changing.

What the audience was in no position to put into words, the irate theater manager did—and bluntly:

"Why did I ever engage such rank amateurs? I should fire you tonight."

He didn't, but he made them work three shows a day—rather than the traditional two in vaudeville—and scheduled them for off-hours, "when you can do the least harm." The Laskys, who had come to conquer, played to nearly empty houses—when the theater first opened after lunch, during the dinner-hour lull, and at midnight to close the show.

In all honesty, Dad and Blanche had bombed in Boston, but the compassionate Cobes attributed the cold reception to "standoffish Bostonians." To compensate, they arranged an audition for Dad and Blanche at the Boston Conservatory of Music, where they were offered scholarships.

It was a temptation to stay, but Grandmother Lasky would have had to get a job to support them—as if she weren't already working full-time as their manager, counsel, booker, and costumer.

They were at the crossroads. They had suffered a devastating and humiliating defeat. A family summit conference was called. Always practical, Blanche made the wisest evaluation of their situation.

"Look," she said. "Who needs to study music? Are we musicians or entertainers? We're entertainers—not good, but entertainers. So we got what we deserved! We can either quit like beaten dogs or improve ourselves and the material, and we can go to the top."

Dad beamed approvingly at his sister. "Said like a Lasky." No longer did he consider her a junior partner. She had matured in the process, as had he.

Next day Dad went to Tremont Row and was offered a booking to play the Flynn Circuit of summer parks for three months at forty dollars a week.

What a comedown—a hundred a week to forty! He had occasionally made more than forty dollars as a single performer. When he learned more about the engagement, he was less than eager to accept it. Summer parks throughout New England were run by the streetcar companies that wanted to encourage use of their transportation services. The bait at the end of the line was a program of free shows on a miniature outdoor stage.

Vaudeville has-beens and has-beens-who-never-were, broken-down or aged entertainers, played to audiences who sat on green benches and munched on salami sandwiches and giant soft pretzels and drank beer.

About to turn down the proposition, Dad had second thoughts. So he and Blanche weren't good enough for the Boston Music Hall. Maybe, he reasoned, there was justification in their having been knocked down to forty dollars a week. He accepted the defeat and, always an optimist, thought something good could come out of what seemed so bad.

And he was right. Their new audiences were appreciative and enthusiastic, and the confidence of the young Laskys again began to sprout. Dad shared his disappointment and shattered pride about the Boston Music Hall incident with his fellow performers and found them to be friendly and sympathetic. These seasoned performers spent hours showing the two novices the traditions of vaudeville, tricks they had learned, how to milk applause from an indifferent audience. They suggested new bits of business, novel routines, and rehearsed the two until they had mastered new techniques and perfect timing.

Dad was often thankful that he hadn't let pride build a mountain between himself and learning from these fine and concerned human beings.

After the long season was over, the head of the troupe, Mr. Flynn, came up to congratulate the young Laskys.

"I was at the Boston Music Hall when you put on your act for the first time," he said. "Believe me, you really needed work and experience. You were amateurs then. You're top professionals now."

He handed the duo a letter of recommendation to the William Morris Agency in New York City. It was like a diploma. Soon they were playing at Keith's Union Square Theater, where a booking meant that a vaudevillian had arrived. They were held over for a second week and then, on February 23, 1903, went to the prestigious Tony Pastor's, another mecca for the theater performer. Dad was only eighteen at the time.

On the bill with them was a bulbous-nosed juggler whose dryly humorous dialogue, amid continuously circulating fruit and other flying objects, brought cheers and generous applause.

Breathless after their first performance, Dad and Blanche had just dashed backstage when a small, soft-spoken man in a black silk top hat and evening dress approached them, complimented them on their performance, and suddenly disappeared. Then the juggler came up and said:

"Nice work. Tony Pastor likes your act, too."

"Did *he* tell you that?" my dad wanted to know.

"No, he didn't," smiled the juggler.

Now Dad was confused.

"He told you himself. The guy wearing that black silk top hat was Tony Pastor," laughed the juggler, a star vaudevillian named W. C. Fields.

Tony Pastor's was a real showcase, and Hermann the Great saw the Laskys there. In the early years of the twentieth century, Hermann's company and exhibitions of magic were epic in proportion and unparalleled in show business.

Hermann the Great, whose physical stature was not so great, couldn't do without the three inches of height that lift heels gave him. Accompanied by his ever-present aide, Boomsky, a little black boy in a powder blue page's uniform, Hermann approached Dad and Blanche to join the company at ninety dollars a week for a forty-week season. They were to fill in between his illusions and sleight-of-hand tricks. What a night for celebrations since it was the young Laskys' first steady and dependable show-business employment, and it included paid transportation even for Sarah.

Joyfully the trio joined Hermann the Great's extensive company which included the magician's charming wife, who was never without her canine security blanket, a white and frizzled miniature poodle named Tou Tou that had to be smuggled aboard Pullman railroad cars.

The warmth, charm, generosity, and wit of the Hermanns—plus their engaging French accent—made the Laskys feel as if they had known them for a lifetime.

Despite his Napoleonic stature, Hermann was a towering figure in the vaudeville world. He was a showman without peer. One of his experiences that Dad loved to tell at our dinner table was of the time when Hermann's showmanship almost led to the company being shot.

It happened in Coffeyville, Kansas, a wide-open rip-snorting town, especially on Saturday nights when saloons and theaters were riotously alive with spur-jingling cowboys.

Hermann knew how to say "eet" all right. He had been saying alleled prestidigitation was an audience-involvement trick.

He would dramatize his French pronunciation with exaggerated nasality.

"La*deez* and Zhentlemen, for a grand finale we weel now make ze magic wis somebody's chapeau—how you say eet?—somebody's hat."

Hermann knew how to say "eet" all right. He had been saying "eet" for years and had at least four trunks full of every conceivable kind of hat.

From a peephole review of the audience, he knew the type of hat he would select, and with his sleight-of-hand skill, he would take the borrowed hat, divert the audience's attention, and replace it with one from his inventory. Then, as the audience gasped in horror, he would tear the duplicate hat into shreds and stuff its remains into the mouth of a small cannon.

While all eyes were upon Hermann and the cannon, the stage manager would raise the borrowed hat on an invisible black thread to the ceiling. Then Hermann would aim the cannon at the ceiling above the front edge of the stage and fire it amid clouds of smoke.

Dramatically, he would point upward—toward the hat, now mysteriously reassembled, on the theater roof—and all eyes would focus on the hat. Taking his pistol, he would fire toward the ceiling, at which precise moment the stage manager would snap the thread, and the hat would fall down as good as new.

But that night in Coffeyville, the plan backfired. First the crowd was unruly and packed with drunken cowboys in ten-gallon hats. Many of them had gun belts and Colts loaded with live ammunition.

Whatever Hermann had on his mind, he should never have separated a drunken cowboy from his prized Stetson. He was usually sensitive to his audience and careful to select the right person. But that night he chose wrong, and the cowboy was ready to explode when he saw Hermann take and tear into shreds what appeared to him to be *his* dress Stetson. Then when Hermann stuffed the shredded pieces into the mouth of the cannon, the bleary-eyed victim staggered toward the stage.

Meanwhile, of course, the cowboy's hat had been safely hoisted by the invisible thread to the theater ceiling. When Hermann fired the cannon upward, the cowboy let out a yell of rage that could have been heard all the way to the Rio Grande, drew his six-shooter, and tipsily demanded his hat back "pronto."

Hermann, who had thought he had seen everything in his stage career, hadn't seen anything—yet. His complete composure turned into total panic. Pistol in hand, he pointed shakily toward the ceiling, where the cowboy's suspended Stetson was visible. Then he fired toward the hat—which refused to fall down as expected. Sensing imminent personal danger, the stage manager had pulled the black thread too hard, snapping it off in the wrong place. Now nothing would dislodge the Stetson.

There was no time for rational explanations. To save Hermann and the company, the stage manager dropped the curtain. The furious cowboy's shots perforated the lowered curtain as his curses and threats rang out above the audience's uproar.

"Get out of here," yelled the stage manager. "Run for your lives!"

Other cowboys started firing at the curtain, and the entire vaudeville company took off through the stage door for the hotel, with Hermann heading the group—as all good leaders should.

Soon irate cowboys, shooting slugs into the air, converged upon the hotel. In a matter of minutes the Hermanns, Tou Tou, Dad, Blanche, Grandma, and Boomsky were smuggled out through the kitchen door with shirts and dresses hanging out of hastily closed luggage and rushed off to Hermann's private train waiting at the railroad station.

Noted for his magic, Hermann had performed more artistic disappearing acts on stage but never one that gave him greater satisfaction than when he made his whole company disappear from Coffeyville, Kansas!

Although appreciative of the steady ninety dollars a week, Dad often wondered what Hermann the Great was grossing in relation to his and Blanche's salary. He had heard that earnings were based on a percentage of the box office, and since the business manager was frequently not sober enough to keep an eye on box-office receipts and to count the house as a double check, Dad began to pinch-hit for him, learning that Hermann's box-office take often reached seven hundred dollars a night.

This information suggested to Dad that the cornet was not the best road to riches. There really was a nice musical ring to the cash coming in at the box office.

Finally Hermann, exasperated with his business manager, fired him, and Dad volunteered to manage the show and to continue the act with Blanche.

Hermann accepted.

Dad found that his new responsibilities gave him many new problems which seemed to dissolve when he took them one at a time.

This lesson was to support him throughout his life and served as a foundation for me to grow on.

His new job included booking the company for a whole season, creating publicity brochures and lithographs, functioning as an advance man, and planting publicity. His busy life now also involved arrangements for moving the company from city to city for playing dates, checking on box-office receipts and counting the house, disbursing salaries, and still performing on the cornet with his sister.

But another change of status was waiting for him near the end of his second season with Hermann. One evening at the Majestic Theater in Utica, New York, Dad and Blanche made their onstage entrance to "The Gladiator March," played by the pit orchestra. They were attracted by the outstanding talent of the orchestra's young first cornettist, for they readily recognized his pure tones and technical perfection.

An idea came to Dad during the performance that was to mold his future career, and at the first intermission he hurried out of the dressing room to meet the cornet virtuoso, who was in an even greater hurry to meet him. Dad and Blanche were tired of performing, and maybe the orchestra cornettist would be a solution.

Yes, Ben Rolfe was interested, and—surprise—his wife, Nellie, played the cornet expertly as well.

That was the first of hundreds of talented people whose gifts Dad instantly recognized and whom he promoted to stardom. The Rolfes were the answer to Dad and Blanche's prayer for getting completely into the production end of vaudeville.

Dad got the Rolfes a forty-week booking at a hundred dollars per week. He talked Hermann into deserting his colossal show format—to streamlining the show into a thirty-minute headline performance to reach audiences that were entirely new—and booked him for nine hundred a week in New York's top theaters.

With two acts going and not a lot of effort involved, Dad was taking in a hundred dollars a week. What if . . . ? and his mind caressed the thought of finding or developing three, four, or five Hermann the Greats and a dozen Ben Rolfes. He multiplied these potentials by weekly bookings and became dizzy with the possibilities.

He conceived the plan of booking Hermann in Europe at even fatter figures. Besides, Dad had never been on the Continent with a chance to see what the Europeans were doing in vaudeville.

He was sent abroad, where he engaged Hermann to play the dazzling Palace Theater in London and the Alhambra in Paris. He attended every major theater in most of the European capitals, often skipping meals to eat, drink, and breathe the new and stimulating acts and stage sets.

How far ahead of the United States were the British and European theaters! He could hardly wait to get back, for he realized he was no longer only a business manager and agent. He was going to adapt some of the acts he had seen and develop others from what he and Blanche had done.

Even more was awaiting him. At the tender age of twenty, he was about to become one of the biggest producers of fresh and original vaudeville acts on any continent.

4

Higher and Higher

One thing that Dad learned from European vaudeville was the "More Principle." You had more originality in themes, more costly acts that brought in more money, more people on the stage doing more things, and more artistic and mood-creating sets.

Immediately Dad applied the "More Principle" to some of his and Blanche's original acts, refining and polishing them and adding the continental flavor.

He reached into the past to the "Colonial Duo," adding more instrumentalists and calling the act the "Colonial Septette"—four girls and three boys, the Rolfes included.

Male trombonists were always around, but where could they find three female trumpeters to team with Nellie Rolfe? The Boston Conservatory of Music, thought Dad. His inspiration proved right. And three lovely, cultivated, and outstanding cornettists with zero professional experience became vaudevillians overnight.

Blanche, in charge of wardrobe and sets, came up with rough designs for costumes and stage scenery and supervised their making. Grandmother Lasky was omnipresent, always ready with a generous salting of suggestions—even lending her seamstress talents to the costumes.

While it is true that producers make a far larger cut of the action than agents or business managers, Dad got an early taste of the producer's responsibility for bill paying. Theater managers were not going to book a new act sight unseen.

Where was he going to get $3,000 for the costumes and sets? He was able to arrange for them with a 20 per cent deposit, with the balance to come later.

Even before dress rehearsal, the treasury was empty. He had already managed to use the Bon Ton Theater in Jersey City, New Jersey, for a one-night showcasing. Now he couldn't pay costs of shipping scenery, props, and costumes across the river.

He and Blanche went back to their rooms in Simmons' Theatrical Boarding House with an empty feeling. They had everything ready to show and couldn't show it.

Marvel of marvels! When they entered their rooms, they found Grandmother Lasky with Uncle Mark, fresh from San Francisco. He was infused with enthusiasm for their big audition and he volunteered to pay delivery charges. The Laskys spent all day traveling to and from Jersey City with sets, props, costumes, and instruments.

Mark found it exciting, commenting, "I've always wondered what it would feel like to walk through a stage door unobstructed by a tough watchman. So what happened today? I entered the stage door and even got to carry scenery!"

Response to the Colonial Septette was encouraging. Theater managers applauded enthusiastically. Even more appreciated was the fact that they booked the act at $700 a week, netting Dad a clear profit of $300 over all expenses.

Next came the "Military Octette," which had quicker-than-magic costume changes that Dad and Blanche had developed and used—from Russian Hussars to British tommies to American Rough Riders. Dad added a new flair—a lovely girl in the rear of the theater with baton in one hand and a spectacular long silver trumpet in the other. She played an arresting bugle call and then, in the center of a moving white spotlight, she marched up front to conduct the pit orchestra.

Success was instantaneous at $1,000 per week.

Out of Dad's fertile brain came a parade of imaginative acts and stage settings until he had fourteen acts on the road, many of them drawing standing-room-only crowds in major American and foreign cities.

Some of his lavish ideas exceeded his bankroll, so, in hopes of borrowing capital, he arranged an introduction to Henry Harris, a leading personality among American play producers and manager of the Hudson Theater.

My dad reasoned that Mr. Harris, with his well-documented astuteness, would certainly appreciate and respond positively to fantastic new ideas.

In the offices of the Hudson Theater, Harris listened impassively. Dad began to wonder whether his ideas were really that novel, after all.

"Maybe you've seen some of my acts?" Dad inquired tentatively.

Henry Harris nodded. My father had expected complimentary comment and began to become visibly anxious.

Noting his growing concern, Harris softened, and his face creased with a sudden smile.

"I have seen your acts, Mr. Lasky, and I liked them very much. Now, exactly what can I do for you and how much is it going to cost me?"

Dad, from past experience with his mother, knew he had a deal.

"Mr. Harris, I haven't figured that out quite yet. I don't know what the cost will be. I want to create sets of a quality that has never before been seen."

Harris shook his head from side to side.

"You came to the wrong place for a loan."

Dad squirmed in his chair.

"Look, Mr. Lasky, I like your ideas. They're fresh and have the quality that will make them box-office, but I can't and won't lend you one cent.

"Mr. Lasky, I have a better idea. I'm going to be your silent partner. You can count on my share of the financial backing. You can set up your offices in my theater and rehearse your acts here."

This was one of the few times when Dad was speechless.

One of Dad's brain storms was a new kind of set. This was going to be a giant replica of a phonograph, the likes of which had never been seen before. It was to be big enough to contain a twelve-piece brass band and a drummer. Music was going to be orchestrated and played with the tinny and squeaky sound of the first mechanical phonograph of that day.

Henry Harris wanted to know how he planned to build it. Rarely at a loss for solutions, Dad said he was going to Elkhart, Indiana, to the Conn Musical Instruments plant for technical assistance.

From Dad's crude plans, this firm found a way to build a fully-authentic-appearing phonograph in small sections for easy assembly, breakdown, and shipping.

Instrumentalists were so closely packed in the mammoth phonograph that they called the stage setting "The Sardinophone."

My father's imaginative name for it—"The Immensaphone"—soon caught the nation's fancy. For four weeks people lined up at the box office of Hammerstein's Victoria Theater to see this Jesse Lasky spectacular. Then the act set box-office records throughout the United States.

Now Dad was becoming an idea factory. One new thought would breed another, and the factory was going during all his waking hours and sometimes during sleep.

Once he became so puffed up about his ability to innovate that he bet Blanche that he could create a vaudeville act around any object anywhere.

Blanche obligingly indicated a yellow and green stuffed bird in a glass enclosure and a leather-bound copy of the book *Robinson Crusoe.*

Immediately he came up with an act which he named "Robinson Crusoe's Isle" and still another called "Birdland," and both were top money-makers.

Between 1906 and 1910, he originated and booked forty different vaudeville acts. Once they had run through years on the United Booking Offices circuit, he upgraded them, added a few new instrumentalists, changed some of the dialogue, renamed his brain children and sent them out again through an opposition booking company, Loew's Circuit. Thus the new and the renewed acts often played for four years or more, bringing in tidy revenues. All the while Blanche acted as assistant producer and secretary, Grandmother Sarah hovered over the scene to marvel at the new acts and beam approvingly as she spoke to stagehands, indicating that all these wonders had come to pass "because of *my son Jesse.*"

My dad's enlarging ego was manifest mostly in the importance which he gave to his periods of concentration and creation. Periodically, he would become Mr. Uninterruptable. During such a time, Ruth St. Denis, a pale and lithe young woman whose willowy movement suggested that she was a dancer, met him in the Hudson Theater and requested an audition.

He had a headful of ideas for developing a vaudeville extravaganza called "A Night on a Houseboat" and didn't favor interruption.

"I'm a dancer, Mr. Lasky."

"Where have you danced?" he asked.

"Just about everywhere and all of my life—everywhere but on the professional stage," she replied.

"Sorry," he said, "but, as you can see, I'm a very busy person, and I can't use amateurs. All of our acts are based on original concepts and our talent has to match the quality of the acts, which means *no amateurs!*"

"Mr. Lasky, I have my act all ready, my own sets, everything. All I need is some of your time."

"I'm too busy now. Come back on Sunday, and I'll give you an audition."

"Sunday?" inquired Miss St. Denis. "I'm very sorry, but I make a practice never to dance on Sunday."

At this point, he shunted her off to Blanche to arrange another appointment time, and started into his office, when Blanche called out, "The appointment is to be in one-half hour, Jesse, as soon as the stage is set up."

He could find no way to wriggle out. Within a few minutes, Henry Harris came into his office to learn more complete details on the "Houseboat" act.

Dad asked him to wait until later, saying there was going to be an audition of "some amateur dancer from New Jersey, whose act I just couldn't get out of seeing."

Harris shot a quick glance at my dad.

"It's good that you couldn't, Jesse. Producers should never take a chance of not seeing everyone. The person whose act you don't have the time to see could be a new star. You could lose millions."

"Well, all right, Henry, but if you're so strong in that belief, you had better join me for the audition."

It turned out that Ruth St. Denis was the type of prospect that Harris had been talking about. Her act was not just any act of a solo dancer on a bare stage with a piano accompanist. Ruth St. Denis was an instant sensation.

The curtain rose on a set covering the entire stage so imaginatively and realistically that Dad found himself wishing he had come up with the theme. He and Harris were enchanted. The scenery included natives of India peddling spices from graceful urns before a Hindu temple. To add another dimension of realism, incense burned, wafting its fragrance toward the two men.

Dad and Henry Harris sat spellbound as Ruth St. Denis offered her interpretation of the Hindu goddess Radha, which was so unique, eye-arresting, and completely absorbing that the two showmen lost themselves completely in the dancer's sensitive interpretation.

What they had seen was the preview of a dance classic that was soon to be hailed by audiences throughout the world, including crowned heads. Ruth St. Denis' career spanned many decades. She achieved success that few, if any, have ever equaled.

The dancer whom Dad had almost avoided auditioning brought him recognition as Broadway's newest star-maker.

One day Dad was called to the offices of the William Morris Agency for an interview with William Morris himself. This summons was indeed an indication of how far he had gone in show business.

Morris got right to the point. Certainly everyone was aware that his agency and United Booking were fighting for supremacy in vaudeville booking. United handled booking for the chain of Keith theaters and the Orpheum Circuit. Morris specialized in the opposition theaters, mostly independents.

Morris invited Dad to go to Chicago, the heart of United's strength, establish a branch office, locate and sign new talent, and get publicity, lots of publicity. He promised to keep Dad's acts solidly booked in the interim.

It was a considerable challenge for Dad, and he accepted.

He set up offices with as much fanfare as possible and then began combing the Middle West for talent. He attended mostly medium-size and small theaters where as-yet-undiscovered stars might be found.

Just when his search for talent nuggets began to look like another Alaskan gold misadventure, he heard a new performer in a small, out-of-the-way theater.

The man was a singer and yet he wasn't. The throbbing voice entered my dad's ears and stirred him deep inside. It came from a slender young fellow in black-face make-up who appeared to be about twenty years old. There was a compelling quality in his romanticized Dixie song.

This guy would never make it at the Boston Conservatory of Music, mused my dad, but what command, what presence, what individuality! Here was an original singing style. Nobody else did it that way!

The ringing applause confirmed my father's approval. Before the fellow had sung and whistled his last encore, Dad was waiting for him in a cramped, dimly lighted dressing room.

"I like the way you handle songs," my dad said.

The performer grinned, showing a double row of white teeth that sharply contrasted with his black-face make-up.

"By the way," said Dad, "what's your name?"

"Al Jolson," replied the performer.

Dad pondered this for a short while.

"Good name," he said. "I guess I won't have to change it."

Jolson nodded approvingly. Dad invited him to the William Morris offices next day to sign a contract.

"I'll be there," replied Jolson.

Shortly before the appointment time, Dad received delivery of a checkered suit made for him by his tailor. The fabric's pattern was the kind that would have jarred the eyes of someone sitting in the last row of a large theater's second balcony. Although he was now a formal executive, Dad loved flashy show-business attire.

The suit was still in its open box when Jolson arrived. Immediately he commented on its attractiveness. He seemed interested only in the suit and in the fact that my dad and he were about the same height and weight and had a similar build.

"I like that suit," he said to Dad. "How about selling it to me, Mr. Lasky? Can't you have your tailor make up another for you?"

It was impossible to transact business while the singer's eyes and mind were fastened on the suit, and Dad knew he would never get the Jolson signature until he conceded. So he replied, "Sure, I guess my tailor can duplicate it."

Jolson picked up the suit and ecstatically fondled the fabric.

"Okay," said Dad. "It set me back sixty dollars, but sign the contract first."

Holding the checkered suit in one hand, Jolson signed without reading details of the contract.

"I'm a little short of cash," he explained. "Why don't I send you the money out of my first week's pay?"

Dad eyed Jolson warily, then the suit, and finally the contract. He sighed with resignation.

"Make sure you do that."

But somehow things didn't work out that way.

Al Jolson was immediately booked for an appearance in New York City, and from that point on, his career rocketed upward, and, later, he became a headliner. Still later he starred in Warner Brothers' *The Jazz Singer,* the film industry's first all-talking picture.

At the height of his success Jolson ran into my father at Los Angeles' Hillcrest Country Club, where Dad laughingly reminded him that he had never paid the sixty dollars for the suit.

"My gosh," responded Jolson. "I remember that suit, but I clean forgot to pay you. How about playing a match for it?"

Eighteen holes later, Dad had lost his suit for the second time.

Though he didn't recover his sixty dollars from Jolson, he received a great deal more. While he was producing *Rhapsody in Blue,* the biography of composer George Gershwin, at Warner Brothers in 1944, he needed Al Jolson to sing the song "Swanee." ("Swanee," composer Gershwin's first hit song, was the number that Jolson had actually introduced at the Winter Garden.) Dad had contacted Jolson's agent and offered $25,000 for him to do just the one song.

When Jolson finished recording the number, studio head Jack Warner mentioned that a check for $25,000 would be sent to Jolson's agent.

Al Jolson burst into laughter.

"What check? I don't want a check from Jesse. Just tell him for me that I finally paid for the checkered suit!"

Aside from the triumph of discovery and signing Jolson, Dad's Chicago effort for the William Morris office failed. So after six months he was back in New York City and producing more acts that built his name and reputation in show business.

He created an act called "The Love Waltz," which was such a phenomenon that when he tried to top himself, he suddenly felt inadequate and decided to go somewhere to recharge himself and restore his powers of imagination.

Rarely did he do things solo. So he, Blanche, and Grandmother Lasky checked into the Sagamore Hotel on Long Lake in the Adirondack Mountains.

In this serene and next-to-nature setting, Dad got what he called "the best idea of my life," but it was one he could never use on the stage.

He met the girl he had been waiting for—the girl who was soon to become his wife and, eventually, my mother.

5

Life with Mother Before She Was Mother

My father's first love affair and probably the greatest of his lifetime was his love affair with his career. And it also belonged to Grandmother Sarah and to Blanche, who shared everything with him.

So far as girls were concerned, Dad lived in the glamorous world of show business. As a handsome and successful young producer, he was a prime target for every beautiful, young, career-minded show girl. There were some close relationships with girls, but they were brief, as Dad once reluctantly admitted to me, "with their brevity encouraged in subtle and not so subtle ways by mother and/or Blanche."

The situation could be summed up by a typical Grandmother Sarah remark:

"There are girls, there are girls, and there are girls, but where are you going to find one good enough for *my boy Jesse?*"

Dad would embarrassedly shrug off such a comment as due to the pride of a Jewish mother, but considerably more than that was involved. In truth, the pride was a thin icing over an all-encompassing possessiveness of both his mother and his sister.

So what happened at Long Lake that summer had a tremendous impact on the life of my dad, my grandmother, Blanche, my mother-to-be, and even on me.

Dad had come to Long Lake to recharge himself and his imagination and to get away from it all. This was the first time since he had been a kid in San Jose that he had had enough money and the luxury of time when he could afford to do nothing without suffering a guilty conscience.

At first it appeared he had finally got away from Broadway and show business, but he found that even at Long Lake, his mind was full of plans, ideas, and thoughts about enlarging and improving his numerous vaudeville acts.

Most men do not pursue their vacation with enthusiastic desperation, but Father did all things just that way. Reducing his motor to an idling position was an impossibility.

As soon as he arrived, he was off to the lake shore, where he rented a canoe and paddled as rapidly as he could over the waters reflecting the blue skies. Always health-minded, he stripped to the waist for some sun, took numerous deep breaths, and pounded his chest à la Tarzan. Then he saw a mountain which he immediately resolved to climb.

Having allowed himself sufficient inactivity and relaxation, he paddled rapidly to shore. Back at the boathouse, he checked and found that the fishing was only fair. So as an alternative to possible fruitless fishing, he jogged on the hotel grounds, continually taking deep breaths among the lofty green pines.

In jogging, as in everything else, he was before his time. Finally, in total desperation, he admitted to himself that he could never remember when he had been more bored.

Within hours of "doing nothing," he wanted to be "doing something" and was ready to pack and return to the city. It was now the dinner hour. At least eating would give him something to do.

He donned a dapper blue dinner jacket and white flannel trousers, picking the loudest tie from among the many on his tie-holder.

As the Lasky trio made their grand entrance into the dining room, the orchestra leader, having been tipped off as to my dad's identity, raised his baton and, with a fanfare and drum roll, launched into "The Love Waltz" from Dad's current smash musical.

This was more like it!

Among all the staring diners in the room, a beautiful young

woman at a table near the Laskys' immediately caught and held my dad's gaze. She was with an older woman and a young man, and there was a haunting quality in her large, brown, lustrous eyes that was unlike anything he had seen in many years of assessing feminine beauty. In striking contrast with a clear and flawless skin, without make-up, was a radiant crown of auburn curls. An aura of innocence, sweetness, and spirituality illumined her. She could have been a subject for one of the master painters.

My father couldn't keep his mind or his eyes on his food. To him it was as if they were alone in the room. As he kept looking toward her again and again, their eyes would occasionally meet and hold. What had seemed to him minutes before to be an intolerably long vacation was now going to be an intolerably short one.

Even before completing his meal, he asked the hotel manager the young lady's name.

"Funny. They're mother and daughter registered as Ginzberg, but the girl introduced herself to me as Miss Bessie Gaines," was the manager's reply. "The young man with them is a Mr. Harry Lewis, who's from Gloversville. . . ."

Excellent host that he was, the hotel manager introduced my dad and Bessie Gaines just as the orchestra began to play and couples moved to the dance floor. There was no time to be lost. No sooner was he introduced than he took the obvious step of asking Miss Gaines to dance.

The moment my dad's arm encircled her wasp waist, he knew that this was the girl for him. Impulsively he blurted out, "Could you be true to one man?"

Surprised by the question, she answered, "I don't know."

Meanwhile, Mr. Harry Lewis, in self-defense, had asked Blanche to dance and was openly watching the other couple.

Miss Gaines, my dad soon learned, was studying at the Boston Conservatory of Music to become a concert pianist. She had informally changed her name from Ginzberg to Gaines, because "I feel more gentile than Jewish."

Suddenly that very night, following the first dance, Dad just had to climb to the top of a mountain he had spotted from the center of the lake that afternoon—but not alone. He invited Bessie to go with him. Bessie demurred. Her mother didn't like her to be alone and unescorted, and besides, Harry Lewis might become upset.

These problems didn't seem insurmountable to Dad, however. No problem ever did. He knew Mrs. Ginzberg would give him permission if he got to meet her and she knew him better, and he was also sure that Mr. Harry Lewis would vacate the scene once and for all if Bessie accepted his invitation.

As usual, he was right on both accounts.

In the "wallflower" seats along the edge of the dance floor, the two Jewish mothers were in competition. Grandmother Sarah was overwhelming Mrs. Ginzberg with the many accomplishments of her famous son Jesse. Poor Mrs. Ginzberg never had a chance to talk about her young and beautiful daughter Bessie.

Dad lost no time in pursuing his campaign. Mrs. Ginzberg had to be impressed—and as soon as possible. Using their mutual love of music, he calculatingly asked his lovely dancing partner, "What is your mother's favorite song?"

Unhesitatingly, Bessie responded.

"My mother has one favorite song. I love it, too. Ethelbert Nevin's 'The Rosary.' "

Here was the opportunity he had been hoping for, and he volunteered to sing "The Rosary" for Mrs. Ginzberg and Bessie with Blanche's accompaniment.

The lodge had a piano-equipped recreation room. Why not go there and do it right away? Dad could carry a tune and had a certain flair for the dramatic, but, as he once laughingly told me, "My voice was distinguished by its mediocrity."

I cannot help but feel that although Mrs. Ginzberg was flattered that my famous father wanted to sing her favorite song, she may have wished, long before its conclusion, that there had been fewer beads on "The Rosary."

The song finally finished and having scored some points, he hurriedly asked Mrs. Ginzberg for consent to take Bessie for a hike to the top of the mountain.

Mrs. Ginzberg audibly rationalized, "Anybody so devoted to religious music can probably be trusted with my daughter—kind of like a rabbi, so, maybe yes."

The next morning Dad was up before the birds, raring to fly. Having paced the hotel lobby for an endless half hour before the appointed time, he was rather surprised when Bessie appeared carrying a picnic basket loaded with goodies and a parasol, but wearing high heels.

Obviously, Miss Gaines knew very little about proper attire for mountain hiking. Miss Gaines observed that Dad had noticed her high heels. Very good! She had actually worn them to make herself appear more worldly and adult. After all, she was dating a famous Broadway producer.

Her high heels didn't really bother Dad. They gave him an excuse to steady her frequently by holding her arm.

As they climbed upward, resting periodically under spreading trees, they talked of everything—themselves, their families, religion (and she learned that the Laskys, too, were and weren't Jewish), music, vaudeville, legitimate theater, and even Dad's endurance performance to impress a John Philip Sousa who never showed up.

He had typically done most of the talking, even through lunch, and now he wanted to know everything about her. Her shyness seemed to dissolve with his warmth and interested questions. So she started from the beginning. . . .

* * *

Bessie Gaines recalled events of the distant past in Boston, where she had been born: her unhappiness at the age of five, as she sat on a high, three-legged stool and the barber cut away her long curls, which her Viennese grandmother had referred to as "a cloud of copper" . . . the warmth and security of the family's modest, three-story wood-frame home, with attic and cellar filled with all sorts of interesting clothing, books, mementos to examine and wonder about on rainy days . . . papered walls with a Yankee Clipper pattern, lace curtains, crude wooden rocking chairs, a dark, round, mahogany table in the dining room where the family gathered for birthdays and holidays, and cut glass on the sideboards filled with nuts, raisins, and fruit.

Now she was ice skating in the back yard, which had been flooded to freeze over for her pleasure and that of her younger sister, Louise, her older brothers, Edward and Arthur, and neighborhood kids . . . Then she was on the big hill on Montrose Street in Roxbury, Massachusetts. Oh, what coasting in the early evening, sometimes during a snowfall, when flakes like small feathers or tiny diamonds through the moonlight mist would freeze on her curls or melt on her cheeks . . . And spring. How her lovely red rose garden would bless the neighborhood with its perfume! . . .

Two frightening experiences came next. When she was still a little girl, a large dog had chased and bitten her, fortunately hardly breaking the skin of her leg. There were no medical complications, but she could never master her fear of dogs.

Shortly after this, she had been watching the trains come in at Ocean Spray, Massachusetts, when a tall, lean man offered her a stick of candy and asked her to walk with him to the edge of town. Trustingly, she did. He invited her into a vacant dairy barn where the hay was piled high. She remembered a sickening feeling as the man came toward her. She screamed. One of her brothers, who had seen her from a distance, had sprinted after her, rushed in, and saved her from harm. From that day forward, her father, a self-made man and an orthodox Jew who lived by the Talmud, became overprotective of his family favorite.

How he loved to tell her of the Ten Commandments as they related to mankind. She remembered how he repeatedly said that a person could only live next to God if he never broke a commandment and if he were entirely free of sin.

Of all places for a Jewish girl to go to school—Notre Dame Academy on Berkeley Street, a short trolley car trip from Roxbury! A Catholic convent school was the place Father Ginzberg thought ideal for his innocent young daughter. He wanted the best for her. Why shouldn't at least one of his children benefit from the nuns' quality teaching and develop a refinement so especially becoming to a young lady?

She recalled her first visit to the convent: Sister Superior with large rimmed glasses, a black hood and thickly woven habit which covered her body and arms, a crucifix on her skirt at the end of a rosary.

She remembered the scantily furnished formal room, the bare but highly polished floor, whitewashed walls with a few religious paintings, and plain wooden tables and chairs—the latter with upright and rigid backs exactly like the nuns who came past the open door in "a silent floating movement."

"She's timid and shy and not accustomed to being alone," her father told the Reverend Mother, who made notations, as she accepted Bessie Ginzberg as a day pupil, majoring in music and sewing.

Seemingly thousands of pink roses were in bloom against a high gray stone wall in the convent garden, and Bessie was enchanted. These blooms and her love for them made her feel at home.

Amid this indescribable beauty was "a shrine with a small statue of the Virgin Mary, all in blue and white. It was so lifelike that you expected to see her come to you."

Never before had Bessie had the understanding that a mother could be a godlike woman. In the world of men, the realization gave her hope for spiritual growth and set a pattern for her lifelong search for Truth.

"I began to love all the objects of the nunnery," she said, "crosses, rosaries, religious cloths, and figures of the Madonna and saints."

She felt sheltered and safe. No one forced her to mix with the other girls. And most of the time, she chose to be alone to embroider, practice the piano, and even try her hand at water color painting.

She recalled the attention, the warmth and kindness, of the sisters. Sometimes they remarked that it might be worthwhile for her to consider becoming a nun because of her quietness, gentleness, sensitivity to others, and her life within. One of them mentioned that the only meaningful time on earth is that which is spent with God. She frequently daydreamed herself into a black habit and veil, almost gliding or "tiptoeing noiselessly through life."

Bessie continued to pour out her heart and confided that the overprotectiveness of the convent and her home had limited her worldliness.

An occasional Harvard student would trudge through snowdrifts to spend an evening with her in the family parlor, but by eight-thirty or nine o'clock, her bathrobed father would clump down the uncovered wooden stairs. Pulling aside the parlor curtains and as if in surprise, he would exclaim, "Oh, Bessie. Excuse me. I thought you were in bed sleeping."

Then he would put the big heavy chain on the front door, bolt it noisily, and clump, clump, clump back upstairs. Five minutes later, he would drop his heavy shoes, one at a time, on the floor directly over the parlor ceiling.

Such protective acts unfailingly discouraged the return visits of Harvard beaus.

She recalled attending a matinee performance of Sarah Bernhardt in *La Dame aux Camellias*. Her mother had planned to accompany her, and she had gone to her father's jewelry store to borrow a pair of pearl earrings to make herself "seem more grown up." But her mother, suddenly taken ill, was unable to attend, and she had decided to go alone. She told her father of this decision. It was the first time she had ever done anything like this, and looking back over her shoulder on the way to the theater, she saw her father shadowing her at a distance.

Then she became aware that her father had a justifiable fear that neither the convent nor he could much longer serve as a castle and moat to protect his "little girl," who was well into young womanhood.

And then had come the vacation at Long Lake. . . .

* * *

That was the abbreviated story. And, in a flicker of an instant, Dad and Bessie were back in the reality of their present.

As the young couple sat under the tree, Bessie Gaines had temporarily run out of words. A mood of contentment settled on the two. She knew instinctively that Jesse Lasky wanted to ask her the same question he had asked on the previous night, but for some reason he was holding back. It was quite evident he admired and looked up to her. He had complimented her on her hair, her eyes, and her skin. He had told her she was beautiful. He had further commented that she was immaculate in every way and different from the show girls that were in his past.

"The convent is still all around you," he said. There was no mistaking the love that he silently expressed. Yet in the clear blue eyes behind the scholarly rimless glasses, there was a question mark. And, again, he asked it.

"Could you be true to just one man?"

She looked directly into those blue eyes and replied without guile, "If it's *you*, Jesse, I really think I could."

My dad was aglow. He drew her reverently to him and kissed her gently on the cheek.

"I guess we're engaged now," he said and, losing no time, "we must tell our families."

It had been quite a day!

As he reminisced about it years later, he remarked, "Neither family received the news with jubilation. My mother still felt that there was nobody on earth who could measure up to my standards."

Her comment had been, "After all, she's a nobody," and Blanche chimed in with, "And her father is just a jeweler."

"Mrs. Ginzberg was happy about it at first," said Dad. "And then she began to warn Bessie about the dangers of marrying a theatrical man from Broadway and show business. A good conservative, Jewish businessman from Boston, yes—even a Harvard man—but a man from show business? She raised her hands, beseeching heaven for deliverance, commenting,—'Bessie, I'd better send a telegram for your father to come right away'!"

Mr. Ginzberg immediately answered the summons, and Mrs. Ginzberg and Bessie met him at the railroad station. Mrs. Ginzberg was upset, but he was more upset.

Bessie confessed the problem to my dad after her return to the lodge, and immediately Dad came up with a theatrical plan.

The scene: a picnic amid the pines! That would do it.

They plotted so that the representatives of both families would get acquainted. And that is how it was.

The glorious blue sky, the mountain air, and the serene lake setting—plus fried chicken, pickles, hard-boiled eggs, and even bagels. Bagels were one of Father Ginzberg's favorite food and were calculated to help the situation. Dad had made a special trip to a kosher delicatessen for them.

But nothing seemed to ease their nervous tension, especially Father Ginzberg's. "Who needs eating?" he questioned his wife. He raised his hands skyward. "It's help I'm needing, not food."

Under the trees, he paced up and down, then suddenly began firing questions at no one in particular:

"Is this young man, this Jesse, in love, or is this a poet's dream? What does he do for a living? Why does he want to marry my daughter?"

Then to my dad:

"Do you have money to support a wife? You are an actor? No? Yes? I do not like actors. God does not like actors."

Through the torrent of questions and comments, my dad was able to edge in a few words:

"No, sir, I'm not an actor . . . I have acts, vaudeville acts. I am a manager, a producer—the boss. I hire actors."

"Ah," said Mr. Ginzberg. "A manager, a producer. You hire the actors. That's different. You produce vaudeville acts? You rich, maybe?"

Now it all began to appear more legitimate. Bernard Ginzberg was beginning to see the picture. And besides, Dad had worn a diamond stickpin just for the occasion. Mr. Ginzberg spotted the large diamond flashing in the sun. Then he sighed, and looked into the eyes of the manager-producer for a long moment. He gazed at the diamond stickpin briefly and then studied the sensitive face of his daughter.

Mr. Ginzberg's expression became less stern and relaxed to the hint of a smile. "Jesse. A good name from the Good Book. Right away I like you better. A good man you got to be. From your eyes, I see goodness shining. My consent I give."

My dad and his bride-to-be embraced without kissing and held each other for just an instant as Father Ginzberg said, "If you will both be patient with one another, you will have a happy life together."

The wedding was set for December, and my mother told me many years later that preparations for the wedding and the wedding itself were the highlights of her life.

"As I look back on it, my trousseau was plain. Yet, to me, it was incredibly luxurious: a dozen of a number of types of towels, pure white with hand-embroidered white monograms; feather-ornamented hats; numerous long dresses with floor-sweeping trains; white gloves, glazed and long to my elbows; silken-soft underthings; long-sleeved white nightdresses, puffed at the shoulders, trimmed in hamburg lace and with innumerable white ribbons and bows everywhere.

"It was a wonderful wedding, and we loved each other so

dearly. I could never possibly visualize anything but the heavenly bliss of marriages that I had always read about. And, still, I never realized that the euphoria that encompassed us both would be completely shattered and show us a stark and cold glimpse of the fact that no two persons were further apart in all major areas of life and experience than we two.

"How does the Bible say it? As far apart as East is from the West?"

The marriage took place, not as might be expected in a synagogue, but in a Boston hotel, the Somerset House on Commonwealth Avenue. The newlyweds entrained for a honeymoon in Atlantic City. Two and a half days later, a telegram arrived. "Hurry back home. Much to do here. Blanche and Mother."

Just like that, the honeymoon was over—and so was the chance for Mrs. Jesse L. Lasky to wear all of her carefully selected finery for leisurely dinners by candlelight, for walks along the beach, for intimate talks long into the night.

My mother realized in an instant that her husband's principal preoccupation was his work, and she already felt a passionate rivalry with her husband's sister and mother.

Soon she and Dad were back in New York City, in the vastness of Grand Central Station, which, to the wide-eyed bride, seemed large enough to swallow all of Boston.

"It was as if I weren't there at all," she confessed to me. "Blanche chattered nonstop about acts, sets, costumes. There were rehearsals, schedules, and more rehearsals, and, before she could finish, Mother Sarah was updating him on people who had been waiting to see him. They were crowding him back into his Broadway routine. The honeymoon was definitely over."

The Jesse Laskys didn't try to find their own apartment. After all, Grandma forcefully rationalized, "Why not move right back in? The place is plenty big."

So, against my mother's weak protests, she and her new husband settled into the Pasadena Apartments just off Broadway on Sixty-first Street.

Many years later, my mother wrote a beautiful book, *Candle in the Sun,* in which she said:

"I began to sense dimly the brightness and flare of this new world into which I was coming and, more than ever, I was a small candle. And just as the taper begins at the wick to shine out its last flicker into the room, I withdrew myself and my littleness, as there was no inspiration to touch a flame to my thoughts."

She was *in* the world of Jesse Lasky but not *of* it. My father admitted to me that the spotlights of show business had dimmed his eyes somewhat to human sensitivity and that he was hardly even aware that, while he was giving his wife everything he thought she could want, he had overlooked something much more important. He was giving her only what *he* thought she should have—but too little of himself.

"I wanted a home of our own most of all," my mother once told me. "I wanted my own domestic routine and time to be alone with my husband." And she explained why she didn't protest more. "My ingrown tendencies never let me tell your father what I wanted and what I thought he should know that I wanted and then besides, Blanche and Sarah would never have permitted him the time to listen.

"I didn't really marry Jesse Lasky," she said. "I married Jesse, his mother, his sister, and show business. A polygamous marriage like that never works."

Sarah Lasky said that she didn't want her son's wife to bother with the household routines. After all, the house had been running very well before her and without her and would continue now to do so.

My mother once observed:

"Your dad and Blanche were show-business partners. They worked together with the precision of parading West Pointers—everything was harmonized. How I longed for him to share confidences with me about his career and himself. I was like a guest in the house and, like a guest, I was only allowed limited guest privileges.

"At first I would wake up early to draw Jesse's bath, to lay out a new shirt and studs, but never early enough. The bath was already drawn and the shirts and studs were laid out—by his mother.

"If I would start to put on water for his coffee, his mother would always say, 'No, you just stay in bed. You need your rest. I'll do it.'

"With dozens of show-business people flooding in and out of the apartment at all hours, I couldn't possibly keep up with them, know who they were, or even remember their names and, besides, I was shy.

"Even my beloved piano playing seemed to be an unwelcome interruption. I rapidly became so desperate that I phoned my father and begged him to allow me to come back home. I gave as a reason my failure to fit in and be a good wife.

" 'Bessie, dear,' he would say, 'just be patient.' "

Very soon she learned she was to have a child. Her desire for a normal life, a life in which she had roots, a home where there was time to share and to love and be loved, made her phone her father once again.

"Father, please let me come home. I'm so unhappy here."

" 'Dearest, Bessie,' he said, 'patience and more patience you must have. A good man he is. You are going to have a baby. It is too late to come home. Your home is there. Things will change for you with the baby. I'm praying to God for you.' "

Things did change but not for the better.

There were even more demands on Dad's time. My mother did not try to compete. She really couldn't. More and more she stayed in the isolation her own room. For comfort, she began to devote most of her love and attention to water colors and then to oil painting, which did not disturb business as usual at the Pasadena Apartments as the piano playing had.

6

On to Hollywood

The Lasky apartment was like cold and alien country to my mother, accustomed to the warmth and love of her home.

Now, in the final stages of her first pregnancy, she felt a silent terror of isolation. Where to turn for understanding, comfort, and counsel?

Grandmother Sarah had brought in a doctor—an indifferent, squarish man who reeked of strong cigars, had dirt under his nails, and never washed his hands.

After her last physical examination before my brother Jesse came into the world, the doctor dispassionately discussed my mother's condition in her presence, and she was frightened. She remembered that the doctor unequivocally stated, "Yes, definitely, it will be a dry birth—very painful—one that will take many, many hours."

No medical aid was given to ease the pain. She lay pulling violently on a bed sheet tied to the end of the bed. As pain came with increasing intensity through her spine, she wrenched at the sheet, trying to help herself endure the agony. In the midst of excruciating torture, she made out a blurred object, the blocky little doctor looking at her matter-of-factly. She pleaded with him to do something.

"Be patient," he replied. "By tonight or tomorrow morning it will be over."

Dad, Sarah, and Blanche were in briefly and then out for long periods, cowed by her suffering, and seeming to avoid her as if childbirth were a highly contagious disease.

"It was our utter helplessness to do anything," my father once explained. But that was not the way my mother interpreted it.

Twenty long hours later my brother was born. Many times in that period, Mother had yearned for home and her parents' kindness and compassion. Then came her son, crumpled, red, and strong. He let out a healthy cry, and she was suddenly bathed in joy with him—until Grandmother Sarah put the baby under the care of a nurse. Decisively, she hushed my mother's protests with the cold hard facts that she would handle everything for her because, after all, hadn't she had the experience of bringing up two perfectly wonderful children herself?

Mother did win one battle with Grandmother Sarah, though. She, Blanche, and my father all agreed that the baby's name which Mother had selected—Jesse Lenard Lasky, Jr.—was perfect for the boy.

Mother knew that by choosing that name she would at least be able to have one Jesse around the house.

Excitement applied a thin veneer over the differences, the misunderstandings—plus Grandmother Sarah and Blanche—which separated my parents.

Dad had just leased ground opposite the Globe Theater on Forty-sixth Street off Broadway where he and Henry Harris were planning to build an entirely new kind of theater, the Folies Bergère, whose slogan was "More Parisian than Paris." It was to be the first legitimate theater in the United States where the audience would be able to dine superbly at small tables an hour before curtain time. It was called by a name then new to the American public, the nation's first cabaret, even spelled out "C-A-B-A-R-A-Y" so that the public would know how to pronounce the name of the place to which they were about to go.

My mother once told me, "Your father was around the apartment just long enough to make sure that Jesse, Jr., was born and all right, and then he and Blanche sailed for Europe to sign exotic foreign talent for the Folies, leaving Sarah in charge of me and the baby."

My dad's plainly stated objective for his production was to offer revues comparable to Ziegfeld's Follies and a cuisine better than

Delmonico's. So he and Blanche combed Europe. They discovered Muriel Harding, a fantastic London mimic, renamed her and remodeled her into a Russian import called Olga Petrova.

He signed the exquisite Martha Lenclud, billed as "The Most Beautiful Woman in Europe," Jeanette Denarber, the most toasted French soubrette, an English ballet from the Alhambra Theater (London), and the famous Tiller Troupe, a company of eight who could perform more acrobatics on tall stilts than most people can on their feet.

Among the Tillers was a ten-year-old English boy whose stilts were so far into the atmosphere that he had to mount them with a ladder. Young Archie Leach would have to bend down to show his head under the proscenium.

This particular import of my dad started his climb to stardom in "The Folies" and eventually became one of the best-known stars of the American films under the name of Cary Grant.

The Dolly Sisters, famous for fabulous gowns and feathered fans, wore such a dazzling array of jewels that they seemed to be a mobile display from Cartier's. Selected for the starring role and heading the cast of two hundred was Ethel Levy, former wife of George M. Cohan.

My dad had a great eye for the dramatic and aesthetic aspects of the colossal productions but, sometimes, lost sight of a project's logistics and financial feasibility.

There was hardly room enough for his huge company. Stars, ballet groups, chorus, soloists, acrobats, and others simultaneously went through rehearsals in every square inch of the theater—on stage, in the aisles, lobbies, on stairways—and, when things got really tough, even in the rest rooms.

The Folies' admission price was $2.50—$.50 more than Ziegfeld charged. Opening-night seats were auctioned off at the Lambs' Club. Orchestra seats went for $25 to $30 each. Balcony box seats sold for between $450 and $700, and these were hard-money days!

Celebrities and the socially elite, heavy with jewels, were there. Multimillionaire Diamond Jim Brady bought two front seats which were joined together to accommodate his tremendous size and bulk.

Response was overwhelmingly enthusiastic. The Folies Bergère looked like a real winner, but Manhattan's foremost theater critic's review described the lavishness and spoke of the astronomical first-night seat prices as if they would always prevail and only a millionaire could pick up the tab. Dad immediately started a publicity campaign to counter his erroneous impression, but it was too late. Slowly attendance dwindled, and, with the heat of summer and the usual exodus from the sweltering city in those pre-air-conditioning days, the cost of sustaining the expensive cast began to be more of a burden than my dad and Henry Harris could stand. They were forced to close the show.

Dad was wiped out of everything he owned—more than $100,000. Henry Harris lost more than that and, a little later, his life. He was a passenger on the maiden and last voyage of the "unsinkable" *Titanic.*

These successive staggering blows nearly leveled my father. Soon, however, his love of life, his enthusiasm for doing something new and unprecedented, started his rise again.

One day as he was walking up Broadway toward the Pasadena Apartments, the name "Pasadena" struck a chord within him—California, his native state, the land of sunshine. Just then he looked up and saw a billboard: a colorful advertisement for Mission coffee—an ancient mission, Spanish padres, and copper-colored Indians.

That was it!

A vaudeville operetta about California—a production unlike anything that had ever been done! This was going to be his biggest and best!

To accomplish exactly that, he would need the greatest writer and director on Broadway. Who but William DeMille, whose plays, *The Warrens of Virginia, Strongheart,* and *The Woman,* had built his name into the most illustrious in the theater? Dad once said to me, "Billy, I wanted William DeMille, because I always believe in going to the top."

William DeMille was the most wanted writer-director in the business and commanded unheard-of salaries for those times. He was managed by his mother, Mrs. H. C. DeMille, also a play broker, who had offices near my dad's in the Hudson Theater Building.

Now, Mrs. DeMille was a tough bargainer. Dad went to her and said, "I want to secure the services of your son William to write and direct a new kind of operetta for the vaudeville stage."

Mrs. DeMille froze at the suggestion and then became indignant.

"Mr. Lasky, you must be out of your mind. My son is too big a man for that! Did you think for one minute that *my* son, whose name is the foremost in the *legitimate* theater, would stoop so low as *vaudeville?* It would ruin his career on Broadway."

My father was taken aback, but managed to say, "Well, could you at least arrange a meeting for me with him?"

"A meeting? Sure, I'll arrange a meeting, but it won't do you any good. I'm instructing him not to accept."

The meeting was arranged by Mrs. DeMille, who insisted on being present, and it didn't do any good. William DeMille was equally adamant, as his mother glowered at my dad during the short conversation.

"Absolutely not, Mr. Lasky," said William DeMille. "You don't have, nor could you raise, enough money to lure me away from the legitimate stage."

But Dad didn't give up easily. Soon after, he went back to Mrs. DeMille again. She turned him off, but, then, her eyes shone in a sudden inspiration.

"Mr. Lasky, I have an idea for you. It so happens that I have a younger son, Cecil . . ."

"I know, I've heard, Mrs. DeMille," replied my dad, and the disappointment must have sounded in his voice. He knew that Cecil B. DeMille had played minor roles on Broadway and had written and directed unsuccessful plays, and he objected.

"Wait, Mr. Lasky," Mrs. DeMille began.

"No, you wait, Mrs. DeMille. Let's put the cards on the table. Your son Cecil is a nudnik, and I don't hire nudniks for my acts."

Now, "nudnik" is Yiddish for a good-for-nothing, and Mrs. DeMille was visibly irritated.

"Mr. Lasky, nudnik or not, he *is* a DeMille. He has real talent that will show someday. Anyhow, the DeMille name is worth everything. Cecil is breaking my heart. He wants to go to Mexico to fight in a revolution, and he will probably get killed. He's out of work right now, so why not take my younger son?"

"Mrs. DeMille, do you think I'm crazy? I want to produce the finest operetta that has ever been made, and I want the best writer-director. You want me to take a less than the best?"

"Mr. Lasky, do yourself and me a favor. Meet him. That's all I ask."

"Okay," replied Dad.

It has become an unrecorded legend that their first meeting was a catastrophe. Dad came away, and I remember the references he made to it.

"I just didn't like him. There wasn't anything about him that I liked. He seemed like a nudnik, and I just didn't want any part of him. So I went back to Mrs. DeMille and pleaded with her to get me William DeMille.

"Not a chance, Mr. Lasky. I told you he's too big a man for vaudeville." Then she turned to my father and looked him straight in the eye. "Mr. Lasky, what is your hobby?"

Dad was taken aback at the abrupt change of subject.

"Mrs. DeMille, I have only one hobby—fishing!"

"Oh, *you're* a *fisherman?*"

"Yes," Dad replied. "That's the most important hobby of my life—fishing."

"Mr. Lasky, my son Cecil is a fisherman," said the cunning and ambitious mother.

Cecil had probably never even been in a rowboat in Central Park, but she repeated, "My son Cecil is a fisherman."

Dad had heard her the first time.

"I want to meet him, Mrs. DeMille."

"You just met him, and you didn't like him."

"Well, I want to meet him again. I could have been wrong."

The second meeting was arranged. Cecil B. DeMille told me the rest of the story decades later while I was working on the sound version of *The Ten Commandments.*

"All I did was dramatize to your father about how big a trout I had once caught, and you know what, Bill? I caught him."

My father returned joyously to Mrs. DeMille and thanked her extravagantly.

"It was love at first sight," he said, referring to the second meeting, just like Damon and Pythias. "We're going to be friends for the rest of our lives."

And they were.

Cecil B. DeMille was happy, and my dad had a fishing buddy who had never been fishing and, the bonus, a highly talented director for two of his operettas, and later for his films.

My mother filled me in on some of the fascinating facts about what happened at this point. Dad had gone about as far as he could with vaudeville—two overwhelming hit operettas which he had done with Cecil B. DeMille: *California* and *In the Barracks*—and he needed new worlds to conquer.

Meanwhile, who should come on the scene but Samuel Goldfish, an energetic and able glove salesman from, of all places, Gloversville, New York.

Inflation had hit the nation and, especially, the glove business. The cost of hides and suede leather was so high that the profit had fallen out of gloves. Sam Goldfish, a friend of my mother's family and a frequent visitor to the Lasky home, got together with Dad.

Goldfish strongly urged Dad to capitalize on his unusually fine reputation and his depth of experience in show business and consider starting a film studio for making entertainment rather than "flickers" and "chasers." It was his plan to turn out quality full-length films to lure people into theaters instead of chasing them out, as had been the purpose of the original short subjects.

They each had $10,000, and on this minimum capital they founded the Jesse L. Lasky Feature Play Company. Now Samuel Goldfish, who later became my Uncle Sam, married my dad's sister, Blanche. He also changed his name to Goldwyn.

When Samuel Goldwyn lost his bachelor status, he married more than a wife. He married the Lasky family, and, according to the past pattern, moved into the Pasadena Apartments. Grandmother Sarah had remarked to Blanche, "And vy not shouldn't Sam move in? Bessie did. Your room is big enough for two."

The marriage made sense from three standpoints—one emotional and two practical. One, Sam loved Blanche. Two, he could learn a lot from Blanche, his built-in encyclopedia of show-business information. Three, marriage would ensure a solid position in my father's company.

Cecil B. DeMille was the company's third principal. He had been on the verge, once again, of going to Mexico to fight in a war when Dad convinced him that he would find plenty of excitement in directing action moving pictures. At first he was hesitant, but Dad came up with the solution. Well aware of DeMille's frustrated military carreer ambition, he said, "Cecil, I have a title for you within the Jesse L. Lasky Feature Play Company. You are to have the highly strategic position of director-general."

DeMille accepted. After all, it was a generous military promotion.

The prime requirement in motion picture making in 1913 was similar to that of today: you had to secure a good story.

In 1913 the most successful stage play on Broadway was *The Squaw Man*, and Sam Goldwyn, in his new role of negotiator, secured the film rights to it for $15,000.

The next requirement was obtaining a top show-business star.

Francis X. Bushman wouldn't tolerate the thought of leaving Broadway. He was too big a man to demean himself in "flickers." So Dad went to another top star—Dustin Farnum. As enticement, he offered Farnum a 25 per cent interest in the company for playing the film's lead. This would have put him on an equal basis with Dad, Goldwyn, and DeMille. The offer was generous because, after paying $15,000 for the film rights, there was only $5,000 left in the treasury.

The first thought was to film the picture across the Hudson River in the Indian country of Fort Lee, New Jersey. But the very prospect of a two-mile trip made DeMille balk and speak of deserting the project for war adventure in Mexico.

To keep DeMille from heading for Pancho Villa land, Dad came up with a master stroke. After all, *The Squaw Man* is an Indian picture, he remarked, so why not shoot it in real Indian country? From his bookings with Hermann the Great, he remembered a place with Indians galore—Flagstaff, Arizona.

DeMille was immediately intrigued and forgot all about Mexico. He was ready to clamber aboard the first stagecoach west. Dustin Farnum, however, was equally dismayed. He wouldn't have minded fording the Hudson River and roughing it in nearby New Jersey in exchange for a one-quarter interest in the company. Then, at least, he would be near his beloved Broadway. But if he had to go west, he would have to have $5,000 cash. Forget the stock! The Jesse L. Lasky Feature Play Company was about to founder when Dad remembered an uncle of my mother's who would occasionally take flyers on wild investments. This uncle took another flyer and bought the stock intended for Farnum, who got his $5,000 in cash. Had Farnum hung onto his stock for several years, it would have been worth more than $2 million!

Neither Dad nor Uncle Sam Goldwyn wanted to scout for a western location to film *The Squaw Man*. They were both too big men for that—also too busy. However, Cecil B. DeMille was all wound up for adventure, and Dad thought he should go. So did DeMille.

When he got to Flagstaff, Arizona, DeMille tried to recruit the local Indians into appearing in the film. Legend has it that they turned him down.

I can only conjecture that they were too big men to appear in the flickers, or maybe they had Jewish mothers, Super Squaws, who were holding out for more wampum. In any event DeMille concluded that Flagstaff wasn't the right location.

Cecil B. DeMille had heard of a place in Southern California called Hollywood. In those days, Hollywood was a little town—mostly citrus groves. Most streets were dirt roads—even Hollywood Boulevard—on which horses and buggies traveled.

At the corner of Selma Avenue and Vine Street there was a big orange grove, in the center of which was a good-sized barn. Already several companies were turning out flickers in Hollywood. These companies used barns as studios for making their short subjects, and DeMille followed suit. He negotiated with the owner of the orange grove for rights to use the barn at $75 per month, but he wanted authorization from his boss to cement the deal, so he wired my dad in New York:

> FLAGSTAFF NO GOOD FOR OUR PURPOSE. HAVE PROCEEDED TO CALIFORNIA. WANT AUTHORITY TO RENT BARN IN PLACE CALLED HOLLYWOOD FOR $75 A MONTH. REGARDS TO SAM. CECIL.

My father shot back the following wire to DeMille:

> AUTHORIZE YOU TO RENT BARN BUT ON A MONTH-TO-MONTH BASIS. DON'T MAKE ANY LONG COMMITMENT. REGARDS. JESSE AND SAM.

That's how the Lasky Studios began.

In the next few years, Dad discovered and developed the largest group of screen actors and actresses ever brought together—and he started the star system, later copied by all major studios. The term "stable of stars" originated from the fact that dressing rooms of actors and actresses were in the stable of this large barn. When you think about it, many stars have come from stables and one, the biggest star of all—the Superstar—nearly two thousand years ago.

The Squaw Man was the first American full-length feature film. Although *The Great Train Robbery* was earlier, it was only about eight minutes long. *The Squaw Man* was so successful that my dad's desk was covered with congratulatory telegrams.

One that impressed him most was from Adolph Zukor, who had owned a penny arcade on Fourteenth Street in New York City. The telegram commended Dad for his foresight, courage, and faith in producing the nation's first full-length dramatic motion picture.

Short of stature, Adolph Zukor was a man of courage and vision who foresaw that the infant film industry was on the way to becoming a giant. A few years earlier, he had imported and distributed a full-length feature made in France, *Queen Elizabeth*, starring Sarah Bernhardt.

Now Adolph Zukor's Famous Players had followed suit and was producing its first full-length feature picture in New York, *The Prisoner of Zenda*.

A friendly rivalry sprang up between Dad and Mr. Zukor with each battling to corral the best screen stories and stars.

Finally, Zukor proposed a merger of Famous Players and the Jesse L. Lasky Feature Play Company. The purpose was to secure better financing for pictures and more advantageous terms from distributors of films.

Although Zukor had some of the greatest stars under contract—Mary Pickford, "America's Sweetheart," among them—he offered Dad a 50-50 stock equity to make the deal too enticing for Dad to resist. Zukor would head the financial end (in the East) and Dad would be in charge of all production, mostly in the West.

Dad couldn't resist. The new company was called Famous

Players-Lasky. This division of authority usually worked quite well, but, on occasion, there was conflict.

Once when my dad sent his quarterly budget to Zukor for review, Zukor invited him East and referred to a decimal point he thought was in the wrong place for the budget of a new picture. He was always formal and never addressed Dad by his first name. "Mr. Lasky, the entry says that the budget for this picture is $500,000." It should be remembered that very good pictures were then being produced for $40,000 to $75,000. Nevertheless, Dad politely corrected Mr. Zukor, saying that the decimal point *was* in the right place, and that this was to be an epic—a new chapter in motion picture history.

Zukor then gave his okay and it was good that he did, for my dad had already spent much of the budget in the filming. The picture was *The Covered Wagon,* the nation's first Western spectacular, complete with a huge cast, and it came in for $782,000. It ended up as one of the greatest box-office attractions and artistic endeavors in the silent film era and so epoch-making that it was eventually made a historical document by the state of California.

Another crisis occurred when Cecil B. DeMille began making the religious extravaganza *The Ten Commandments.* Throughout his career, DeMille was noted for putting the spectacular ahead of budget—with casts numbering thousands.

Mr. Zukor was puzzled by the allocating of funds into a production of this kind. No one had ever done a film of this breadth with a totally spiritual theme. There was no precedent for budgeting such a film at $1 million.

The sales department in the East was of the firm opinion that the public just might prefer to get its religion in churches, not theaters, and the New York office protested in no uncertain terms, but Dad was able to convince them that this film was to be even "bigger and better than *The Covered Wagon.*"

Stressing art, realism, and the colossal, DeMille got halfway through the film's production when he ran out of funds and requested more.

The money men in the East began to see red.

One of the executives there had the sense of humor to phone Dad and "request on bended knee that you bring DeMille down to earth from Mount Sinai." Dad backed DeMille, reminding the executive that DeMille was still the company's director-general and deserved special treatment. Additionally, he said, he had seen some of the footage shot and that "it was truly magnificent."

Despite admiring DeMille's dedication, genius, and creativity, Dad, in candor, had to let him know about the hurricane blowing all around him.

"Cecil, the eastern office is exploding because here you are just halfway through the production and you're already all the way through the budget."

DeMille was furious. His eyes blazed. As he stomped out of Dad's office, he raged, "Do they want me to stop production now and release the film as *The Five Commandments*?"

Despite the financial war between the arty and prodigal West and the pecuniarily conservative East, the picture was finished DeMille's way.

This film not only paid its production costs and millions more, setting box-office records, but set a precedent of filming religious subject matter.

7

Bill Is Born

Near the height of Hollywood's silent film era, I made my debut on earth at the local Good Samaritan Hospital.

That was a big year for the once sleepy citrus town that Dad had helped transform into the film capital of the world, but not because I was born.

No, my birth was big news only to my parents.

So far as Hollywood is concerned, 1921 was the year of the Egyptian—that is, it was the year when the Egyptian theater was born.

On the corner of Hollywood Boulevard and McCadden Place, Sid Grauman, in whose vaudeville theaters Dad and Blanche had performed, unveiled his multimillion-dollar motion picture palace. This was the brain child of the famous Hollywood land developer Charles E. Toberman, who had sold my parents acreage in the Outpost area for their first home by themselves.

Both Dad and Sid Grauman were master showmen whose objectives were always "the biggest and the best." This was Sid's second achievement of creativity in building lavish make-believe theater settings for the film epics of that day. Films had achieved dominance in the entertainment world and deserved better than ordinary settings.

Theater owners and developers from all over the nation came to observe the Egyptian and borrow ideas for their own picture houses in metropolises and even small cities.

Grauman's Egyptian, the "spectacular" before his nearby and even more famous theater-to-be, Grauman's Chinese (famed for star footprints in its lobby), really appeared to have been transported from the banks of the Nile. The heavy block construction and gigantic pillars faithfully resembled the ancient temple of Ramses. A long approach offered bazaars for selling Egyptian souvenirs, candies, scarves, and knickknacks of all sorts. A mammoth sphinx impassively surveyed theatergoers. Wall carvings and specially woven golden-thread curtains and plush, deep carpets contributed to the desert mood. Grauman's most talked-about bit of showmanship was an Egyptian soldier in head cape and full uniform doing guard duty along the roof's ridge pole.

It was fitting that the first motion picture to be shown at the Egyptian should be a romantic adventure classic, *Robin Hood*, starring the dashing Douglas Fairbanks, Sr., and featuring great costumes and settings—castles and the Sherwood Forest.

It is quite natural for a child to take his environment for granted, even though it is the fabulous Hollywood of the twenties. So it was not strange that the most vivid memories of my earliest years were not mainly of Hollywood. Though there much of the time—and despite the fact that my family was pivotal to the film capital—my major interests were in other directions.

But the showmanship of Hollywood was not lost or neglected in my father's second California home at 609 Ocean Front in Santa Monica. In my dad's ample garage, there were five Rolls-Royces, only two short of a weekly supply. Our huge swimming pool boasted salt water continually pumped from the ocean—one of the first of its kind. The guest rooms of the earliest home that I remember ran the gamut of every color of the rainbow. I recall blue, pink, orange, and the green room, but, no, it didn't stop there.

At the rear area of the house and above the garage were twenty-seven servants' rooms that took care of the two chauffeurs, two butlers, two cooks, four maids, two governesses, and a full cast of understudies. In those days, we even had a live-in gardener, whose name was Andrew. Strangely enough, the memories of this wealth are really dulled in my mind by the starkness of the truth that my father and mother had separate living quarters.

My father's suite and balcony, overlooking the ocean, was on the right-front corner of the two-story home, and my mother's on the complete opposite side on the left-front corner.

The downstairs area of our home supported a huge glass-roofed solarium/game room, where regular screenings of my father's latest Paramount films were shown. (Paramount Pictures was the new name of Famous Players-Lasky and its theater chain for distributing company products.) These screenings were attended by stars and many Hollywood luminaries. In the center of the home was an open garden with beautiful tropical flowers in which my mother cared for her collection of carefully selected rosebushes.

My mother's first reaction to me when she first saw me was that the nurse had given her the wrong baby. I looked Oriental with a wisp of black hair and slant eyes.

Memories that flood back of my early years were of numerous cross-country trips in our own private railroad car and a little boy's love of traveling and trains. I further remember that I loved train travel because it physically enabled me to be much closer to Mother and Dad.

Aside from the travel time set aside for Betty's and my French lessons with our imported French governess, Mademoiselle Bernadette Branche, we, as a family, did not spend a great deal of time together.

While at home in California or New York, Dad would always be rushing off in the morning with a brief case bulging with scripts, correspondence, and contracts—most of the time before we were out of bed. Mother would ordinarily be in her own large bedroom suite or in her studio, where she always seemed to be oil painting.

My parents were very busy people—too busy. Sometimes it was as if I had a dad and mother and didn't really.

So many of the kids we knew—even wealthy ones—were impressed by the fact that we had our own private railroad car, as did Diamond Jim Brady and others of the nation's most publicized millionaires and presidents. One of my friends once said, "Your family must have tons of money."

Aside from such remarks, I took all these things for granted. As far as I was concerned, every boy in America had a father with a private railroad car and a home theater for projecting movies.

Yes, it was fun to have a home on wheels, where we kids and

Mademoiselle Branche could sleep. Dad and Mother had compartments adjacent to ours. We had everything we needed to eat and drink. We could watch towns flash by, but the most fun was looking out over the desert countryside of New Mexico and Arizona for cowboys and Indians. Whoever was first in spotting a cowboy on a horse got two points. Whoever saw an Indian on a horse scored three points. That was Betty and my version of cowboys and Indians.

When it was time for us to go to sleep, Dad and Mother would retire to their individual compartments and Mademoiselle Branche would put my sister and me to bed, saying a little prayer, ending like this:

"God bless Mommy and Daddy."

And I would always add, "Mademoiselle Branche," because I loved my dear governess like my mother.

Then I would lie awake, wishing Mother and Dad were there, too. As soon as Mademoiselle Branche had left, I would release the window curtain and look up at the passing stars and wonder about them.

Where did they come from? How did they get up there? Who made them? Everything that's out there and here on earth had to be made by someone or something, I guessed.

When I asked Mademoiselle Branche, she said, "God made them, Beelly." With her French way of speaking English she couldn't pronounce my name "Billy" if she had wanted to. Yet, I always liked her way, because it was loving.

"Who's God?" I wanted to know.

"God is everything, *mon chéri*. God made us and the earth, the sky, the stars—everybody, everything," she explained.

"But where did God come from?"

"God has always been here, Beelly."

I had still more questions, but she said, "Go to sleep, Beelly dear. We will talk more tomorrow."

And we did talk, but I never got enough answers because although Mademoiselle knew all the answers about teaching French, somehow she could never satisfy all of my questions.

Many years later, Mademoiselle Branche reminded me of the time I had asked where babies come from. One of the maids had told me babies were found under cabbages, but somehow I could never quite believe it.

Mademoiselle Branche said that God made them, but that was not enough for me. God had to have a little help from someone, I felt.

Later, when I asked Mother, she referred me elsewhere—to Miss Helen Lunt, my nature teacher at Ethical Culture School in New York City.

Miss Lunt wisely answered my questions and hoped her answer would satisfy my curiosity. She simply told me that people are like birds and that babies came from eggs.

One of my lifelong characteristics is that I always have to know more on a subject. So I persisted. "Miss Lunt, does this mean that I have eggs inside of me?"

"No, dear," she answered. "Only little girls have eggs."

I went home and promptly reported my newly acquired knowledge to Mademoiselle Branche and to sister Betty.

"I know where babies come from," I blurted. "Miss Lunt told me, and I know all about them. Babies come from eggs, just like birds. But I don't have eggs. Only girls do."

I had no idea how my sister would react to this newly acquired partial truth. Visualizing birds' eggs which we had seen in nests, she exploded in a manner reminiscent of Grandmother Sarah. "It's a lie. I'm a girl, and *I* don't have eggs."

Whenever we returned to California from New York and I saw our Santa Monica home, I was reminded of a castle in fairy tales.

Often angry waves would come thundering far up on shore, invading our back yard at extreme high tides. Though I loved the ocean, I was frightened of it at times—its tremendous power. There had been several occasions when I had had to be rescued because I wandered too far into the surf. Many times I wondered where the ocean came from and asked Mademoiselle Branche. She always had the same answer.

"Beelly," she replied, "I have told you many times. Everything comes from God."

This was an era of fabulous Hollywood parties, and it was nothing for my parents to host fifteen hundred to two thousand people at one time.

At such times, the Santa Monica castle would be transformed into a make-believe fairyland of hanging colored lights, Japanese lanterns over dance floors erected on the sand. The swimming pool was often filled with floating artificial water lilies and candles. Orchestras and small combinations of musicians seemed to be everywhere. Minstrels wandered among the guests with accordions, guitars, and violins.

It was always important to have a large full moon to set the mood for these affairs. When Mother Nature didn't co-operate, one telephone call to the Paramount Studios property department would guarantee a first-quality moon complete with control wires attached.

Parties were going on all the time. Some would last for a week, and people never seemed to go home.

Once Mother remarked, "This is a house of parties. We are either having a party, getting the house in shape after a party, or preparing to have another party."

With dance floors highly polished and torches flickering yellow light to match colors with the Hollywood-style moon, it was all like a DeMille-staged scene from an Arabian Nights fairy tale, complete with a star-studded cast.

Under a plastic moon or a real moon—sometimes two when the real moon finally showed up—Mother never liked parties or large numbers of people. Perhaps her early convent training enforced her natural shyness. Even in later years, her one desire in a crowd was to escape, but in those days she would reluctantly but graciously receive my father's guests—most of whom she didn't know.

Then, as soon as possible, she would disappear to her bedroom to read or go to her studio to paint. My mother never indulged in drinking or smoking and had an aversion for both. Though my father did drink and smoke cigars, I can never once remember seeing him intoxicated. When I was very young, he told me, "If you are going to drink, you have to be responsible for how you act and what you do." When I was very young, my father did insist on my taking puffs of his strong cigar, and the combination of strangulation and nausea that came over me killed any desire I might ever have had to smoke.

So far as the parties were concerned, we children were not invited. This was an era when children of the wealthy did not ordinarily eat with their parents. There were two distinct worlds within our home—our parents' and ours.

Mademoiselle Branche would get us all dressed in our best, and, on occasion, we would be invited down to be displayed to guests by our proud parents. Then we were quickly dismissed into the charge of our governess, who would take us hand in hand back to the children's wing.

As we did not actually see the parties, my memories of them were mostly of watching the servants, caterers, and trucks serving and delivering food and beverages to make these affairs run smoothly.

Many times Betty and I were actually removed from the house to the Miramar Hotel in Santa Monica, where we shared a guest bungalow for a night or a week with Mademoiselle Branche. I remember feeling unwanted during these times. However, on most occasions, we did remain at home in the isolation of the children's wing.

One specific night comes back into my mind. In the darkness of my bedroom, I recall the sounds of the party. Music from the series of bands and minstrels entered my room along with the laughter and the tinkle of cocktail glasses. Everyone was having a good time, but I was all alone in my room. I lay in bed looking at the dimly lit ceiling. Both Dad and Mother had been so busy that I hadn't seen them for a long time. How I wished they had tucked me in! Mademoiselle Branche had substituted earlier in the evening, but how I longed for a mother and father. I guess I was just lonely. This loneliness, which to me is an expression of insufficient love, was a missing key to many doors throughout my life. Until I could find this key, these doors would remain locked.

The party, I remember, was like something out of a motion picture such as Dad used to show at home in our solarium almost every week. There were rows of brightly colored silk tents set on the sandy beach, and cabanas fronted the giant swimming pool. Caterers and additional servants for the party kept the food and liquor flowing. No sooner had one musical group stopped when another started. And talk about vaudeville acts! There was a constant stream of entertainment—tumblers, jugglers, singers, and famous actors and actresses of the day giving impromptu performances under the yellow plastic moon. Everybody seemed to be having such a good time—and I wanted to be there, too, but not to laugh with them. I just wanted to get a glimpse of my parents.

Many times people would stay over from the parties, and the multicolored guest rooms were always ready for them. I remember Mother telling an amusing story. After certain parties, she would see the same familiar faces day in and day out at breakfast. As she didn't know most of the people, one day she whispered to Dad, "That little semi-bald fellow with the pink cheeks down at the end of the table—he looks important. Is he a friend of yours?"

"No," Dad answered. "I thought he was a friend of yours."

"No," she responded. "I never saw him before in my life."

There were similarities between the Santa Monica beach home and the New York apartment. Both were large and both were decorated with rare antiques which Mother had purchased while traveling throughout Europe. In addition, throughout both places and particularly in Mother's bedroom, which always represented a retreat from the outside world, there were many Madonnas, religious pantings, and crosses. Wherever my mother went, she was unable to turn down an ivory figure of Christ on the cross or other sacred objects of art. On the pianos were antique altar cloths, and large church candelabra and sconces decorated the walls. My mother was selective in her religious objets d'art, so selective that I cannot remember ever seeing a Jewish Menorah. However, strings of rosaries with crosses were wrapped around my mother's bedposts.

Dad once said to Mother, "Bessie, with all your Madonnas and crucifixes around, your bedroom is more like a nunnery than a bedroom. I'm never comfortable with you there."

Another similarity of our two major residences was not a physical characteristic, but one that bothered both Betty and me, but especially me. This was loneliness. As I look back, I cannot blame my parents for this loneliness because they anticipated and attempted to fill this need with governesses, servants, closets full of toys, and frequent trips and entertainments and diversions.

Even at that early age, though I didn't realize it, the loneliness I felt stemmed from within. I did not know it couldn't be satisfied from without. I sometimes thought my brother, Jesse, Jr., could supply what was missing, but he was ten years older than I, had his own circle of friends, and there were basic differences in us.

Though I loved Jesse dearly and have always admired his skill in writing screenplays, novels, and poetry, for which he is well known, I found him to be a very emotional child, who fluctuated from flights of fancy to fits of temper.

While I was a youngster, my brother and his childhood buddy, Bill Buckland, the son of the famous motion picture director, Wilfred Buckland, decided they would set up a fright room in the hopes they could catch the gardener or little brother Billy unawares. Their most imaginative plan was to take a skull of a Rocky Mountain sheep—the souvenir of a High Sierra camping trip—and paint the skull red and the eye sockets and teeth a luminous gold. They placed this atrocity in a dark basement tool shed, where there was no artificial light. My brother told me that on the way up the stairs, they had to look back just once to see the frightful product of their imaginative minds. The glowing skull so horrified them that nothing would lure them back into the room, even the promised reward of scaring brother Billy. I never did see it.

Another incident that left a mark on me and caused me to fear heights took place while I was a toddler. Jesse, Jr., and Bill Buckland had set out a battlefield of the invading armies of Europe. These were lead soldiers set on the nursery floor. The battle was in full progress when I toddled through the battlefield, decimating both armies as effectively as Hannibal, Caesar, or Napoleon Bonaparte. In a fit of temper, my brother grabbed me by the legs, carried me to the open window on the second floor, and dangled me, screaming, out of the window. When my mother and the governess rushed in to see what was the matter, they found only me, sobbing in fright on the nursery floor and unable to tell what had happened, because, as yet, I had not learned to talk well enough to explain.

From the time that Betty and I first discovered that babies, like birds, came from eggs, we shared a close relationship. As a little boy, I loved to collect butterflies and snakes, and, up until the time that she discovered that little girls—according to society's expectations—were not supposed to do these things, Betty shared these deep interests with me. While most small children would fight over a favorite toy, Betty and I, while sharing a bath in one of our huge tubs, would battle over my favorite gopher snake. My mother reluctantly had to intercede in the snake's behalf when Betty decided she wanted all three feet of him for herself!

While in New York, Betty and I shared nature walks, but in California, one of our greatest pastimes was being with Mother on those rare occasions when she would invite us into her studio while she was painting.

Mother would give us brushes, canvas, and paints and allow us to express ourselves. Even though we shared her all-encompassing passion for painting, this did not allow us to share her, because, although she was with us, she lived in a world apart.

Shortly after this period, I began having a recurring dream that persisted for many years. I didn't understand it, but there seemed to be more to it than just what happened in the dream.

Its hidden meaning was to take fifty years to be revealed.

I would be traveling in a long dark tunnel, moving steadily forward and deeper inside. There was no escape. There seemed to be no end to the tunnel. Would it ever end? I could feel the weight of the weightless dark. My body seemed to be at once crushed and smothered by it. Fear grew into terror, and terror turned to stark hopelessness. Then when I thought there was no hope—no escape—I would see a tiny pinpoint of light way off in the distance. It seemed far away, as if I would never get to it. Slowly the pinpoint began to grow. I seemed to be traveling toward it. As I came closer, it became larger, and then, as I neared the end of the tunnel, the light seemed to spread all around me. This light was purer and brighter than any I had ever experienced. Then, suddenly, my attention was drawn to what appeared to be the center of the light—a small white flower that I recognized as a daisy. There was something beautiful about this flower, unlike anything that I had ever seen. As my attention was focused on the flower, it seemed as if my whole being was at once bathed in white light and a part of its quality of brightness. In this pure light there was warmth, love, and a feeling of peaceful contentment—the total opposite of the fully engulfing lonely despair of the tunnel.

Now that I was in the light, I received everything that I had been lacking. Then I would wake up, and the light would be gone, but some of the feeling of happiness would remain for a while.

Sometimes I would talk to Mademoiselle Branche about the dream and ask her to explain it to me.

"Beelly, do not think so much about these things," she once said. "Your dream may mean nothing, or it may mean something you will not understand until you have lived more life. *Le bon Dieux* will have the answer for you when you are older and wiser."

It was at such times that my wonderful and understanding French governess would hug me to her and bring Betty over to tell or read us stories—*Alice in Wonderland,* which we loved, *The Arabian Nights,* another great favorite, or, best of all, animal tales. I couldn't get enough of them.

Mademoiselle Branche never failed to finish with stories about *l'enfant Jesus,* the baby Jesus.

There was no way of my knowing then that this was to be a small mustard seed in my life.

8

No Dogs Allowed

Every boy wants a dog of his own, and, in this respect, I was no different, but I had a problem. My mother, when still a very young girl, had been bitten by a dog, and from this experience, she had developed a fear of dogs that remained with her all of her life. So when I repeatedly asked her for a dog of my very own, I was just as repeatedly turned down. It seemed to me that I had an ideal solution when I suggested a puppy, but she countered me firmly.

"Billy, puppies do grow into full-size dogs, and dogs do bite."

Little boys are often insistent, and I tried again, but she was adamant, finally refusing my request with a statement that I subconsciously held her to for the rest of the years that I lived at home.

"Billy, for the very last time, I don't want a dog in my house. *Anything* but a dog!"

Well, that is what Mother got—*anything* and *everything* but a dog: the widest range of creatures in fur, feathers, and scales that anybody outside of Noah himself had ever assembled in one place.

This wasn't done to get even. I respected my mother's point of view. Yet something inside of me cried for something outside of me to love and something to love me back. Still there was even more to it than that.

Today I understand that all of God's creations were a mystery to me. I wanted to learn as much as I could about everything that lived on the face of the earth. Beyond a search for knowledge, this was a search for truth.

My love of birds may have started when I was six—from the first time I began to look out of our New York apartment windows that faced Central Park. Strutting up and down on the stone window ledges were motley-colored pigeons that I was delighted to discover. They nested each spring and laid eggs along these same ledges many stories above noisy Fifth Avenue.

Betty and I were Rolls-Royce-delivered to the then-progressive Ethical Culture School, opposite the Museum of Natural History in Central Park. It was in this school's nature room that I first met many of the creatures that I learned to love.

The nature room was like a complete little world of enchantment that awaited my discovery. No Alice through the looking glass ever explored her world and its creatures with more enthusiasm. Nature class was a fleeting hour long, and I couldn't get there fast enough or stay there long enough.

The nature-study room was a miniature zoo-museum. Its cages, terrariums, and jars held mysteries that my searching mind craved to solve. I was happiest when given assignments of caring for orphan baby rabbits, a squirrel rescued from the park, a porcupine, opossums, raccoons, mice, rats, toads, frogs, turtles, salamanders, and snakes.

I experienced one of my first love affairs with two fat toads, who lived in a ten-gallon terrarium half-filled with humus and moss. I can still remember the pungent smell of the rich soil as I daily dug out the sleepy toads.

I loved to feed Billy and Betty, as I named them. Their sleepy eyes would pop wide open at the sight of big, fat, wriggly earthworms that we children were assigned to bring in from the park. It was funny how they appeared to me at first—ugly, warty, and bug-eyed. After watching and feeding them for a while, observing their habits—even tugs of war with worms—I grew to love them as I would gently brush lumps of moist earth from their heads.

Snakes and I always seemed to have a kinship, and this kinship was strengthened by my studying the beautiful specimens living in the long row of glass-fronted cages.

I have never understood why people think that snakes are slimy and disgusting. If they would observe closely and handle them, they would learn that they are dry and among God's cleanest creatures.

Each snake became an individual personality to me, each with unique feeding tastes, requirements, and living conditions—much like people. I learned early to understand all creatures of the earth and, because of this understanding, have never regarded any of them as repulsive—merely as creatures to become better acquainted with. From this closer understanding grew a wondrous fascination and respect.

What an assortment that row of cages held: garter snakes, water snakes, green grass snakes, black snakes, and milk snakes, as well as the tiny DeKay's snakes that we discovered on trips to the park. Their individuality was much like that of snowflakes that collected on our New York apartment windows. On first observation, they all looked alike, but when I saw blown-up photos of snowflakes in a science book, I was fascinated that there were no two alike. I would watch the snowflakes collect and eventually blur out the view of the park. I remember how cold the glass felt on my nose as I pressed close to get a better look. No two snowflakes alike, no two creatures and no two people alike.

I'll never forget my nature teachers—Miss Boice, who was there when Betty and I first enrolled, and Miss Helen Lunt, who came later.

What patience they had with me!

I was a continuously bubbling fountain of questions that needed instant answers. Never once did either of them try to shut off that fountain. I admired them, too, for their honesty. When they didn't know something, they said so, and we went to the many heavy books, or more often, to the animals themselves for answers.

So far as that nature room was concerned, I guess I had more than a little of my dad's desire to improve on existing things and conditions. Sure, the snakes behind the glass were great, but we needed something bigger and different, and I talked Dad into making me a special Christmas gift—a wonderful three-foot bull snake, purchased from a Texas snake farm. The perfect name for this reptilian tiger-colored treasure seemed to be Tigro, and Tigro he became.

I could never understand why people were bothered by seeing a small boy in a Little Lord Fauntleroy suit and fur-trimmed hat and coat exiting from a long, black Rolls-Royce and carrying a three-foot snake. Tigro was a sensation on Fifth Avenue and an even greater sensation in the nature room. He was the only snake to date who traveled in his own private railroad car across the United States to California when school was finished.

I'll never forget the "ohs" and "ahs" of the kids at Ethical Culture School when I let Miss Boice borrow Tigro for all the school classes to see. It was here that I learned to share.

Tigro seemed to like school all right, but eventually he was expelled for conduct unbecoming of a good Texas bull snake.

One day Miss Boice came to me very concerned. She had discovered that Tigro was missing from his cage. It seemed that someone had accidentally left his cage door ajar.

I was put in charge of the posse to track down Tigro, the much "wanted" snake. We combed the whole school and the grounds, but the fugitive had found a hide-out that none of us could discover. All we could do was post notices on bulletin boards about him: "Wanted! Texas Bull Snake, Escaped From Nature Room. REWARD!"

A week went by, and still no Tigro. We had decided that he had managed to slip out a door, probably when the janitor was sweeping at night, and had gone back to nature, if Fifth Avenue can be called nature.

And, then, one day we heard screams coming out of the nature room. Miss Boice, who had been in the hall, came running, as did many of us children. What we saw wasn't quite believable. Our tall, slender, and bespectacled principal, Miss Bratton, was cowering on top of a desk. Eye to eye with her was Tigro, the fugitive, staring at her from the upper ledge of a case of stuffed birds.

Miss Boice attempted to calm the nearly hysterical Miss Bratton, dramatically directed a few sharp words at Tigro, and turning to me, said, with the suggestion of a smile, and covertly winking, "Billy Lasky, this is the very end. As of this exact moment, Tigro is expelled from school!"

Not long after the Tigro incident, Miss Boice called me into the nature room and introduced me to her new assistant, Miss Helen Lunt.

"Billy," she said, "I want you to help Miss Lunt get acquainted around school." Instantly I felt proud to have been chosen. "Please introduce her to all of our children," and, with a grin, added, "human *and* animal."

Miss Lunt was a middle-aged woman with graying, straw-colored hair tied up in a bun at the back of her head and held together by a tortoise-shell comb. She had a ruddy, outdoor complexion and long, sensitive fingers. Most of all, I remember her kindly smile and warm eyes. I loved her right away. It was as if we had known each other all our lives. Here was the perfect companion for nature walks and sharing my love of animals.

Miss Lunt was a Cornell University-trained ornithologist—a zoologist who specializes in birds.

On the first day in her new class, she told us that every bird, animal, fish, reptile, and insect was an individual and had first and last names, just as we did. Because she loved birds, she wanted each of us to borrow a particular bird's name for our own, and we would play a game in which we were to refer to one another only by our bird names. When it came my turn to decide on a name, I didn't hesitate a moment.

The greatest treasure in the world to me was in a small box on a shelf of stuffed birds. Nestled on cotton was a tiny iridescent-colored, stuffed South American hummingbird. This minute, feathered jewel I passionately desired to own more than anything else I had ever seen. What a wondrous thrill when Miss Boice had permitted me to hold this little creature in my hands and examine it closely! I had never been close to anything so beautiful and had never dared to think I could possess such a priceless treasure, but here was the treasure I wanted. I imagined it feeding among giant, tropical blooms in the faraway wonderland of South America.

Someday, I decided, I would own one or more hummingbirds, and many years later this dream came true. My love and desire for hummingbirds was to direct me into collecting these living jewels and maintaining four hundred of them in a large greenhouse annex that supported a waterfall, running stream, giant fuchsias, bromiliads, and other flowers that these creatures enjoyed as supplemental diet.

Now in the classroom, I jumped to my feet and said, "Miss

Lunt, I want to be called 'Rubythroat,' after the rubythroat hummingbird."

Betty, who was as shy and retiring as a beautiful little hermit thrush, chose the name "Hermit Thrush," and when we children insisted, Miss Lunt chose a name for herself, based on her favorite bird, the veery thrush, and from then on we referred to her as "Veery."

Thanks to Veery, my love of walking, hopping, crawling, and swimming things expanded even more rapidly to include flying things. On Saturdays, she led nature excursions to enable us to see all forms of life in their natural environments. I was always happiest when Betty and I were the only ones who showed up for the field trips because then we had Veery all to ourselves.

We would take notes and make lists of the different kinds of birds and animals we saw in the most secluded areas of Central Park, the Botanical Gardens, Van Courtland Park, Staten Island, and Inwood Park on Manhattan Island.

It was fun to put on our hiking boots and explore with Veery. Sometimes we would stray off by ourselves. Veery used to say that there were things you could best enjoy discovering by yourself.

One early spring day, we were out to study wild flowers in Van Courtland Park. I wandered off by myself, and a strange and beautiful thing happened to me. Out of the frozen mud along the edges of the marsh, I saw brown-and-yellow-spotted jack-in-the-pulpits (similar to lilies with hoodlike coverings arched over flower spikes); bright, yellow marsh marigolds; pink and white dogwoods, bloodroots, cup-shaped white and purple anemones; violets of many kinds that I had never before seen—purple, yellow, blue, and even brown dog-toothed varieties (more a lily than a violet)—and magnificent, mysterious pitcher plants.

Never before had I seen so many beautiful flowers in one place. I don't know how long I stood there. I was almost hypnotized. It was as if a river of love flowed out of me toward these beautiful flowers and as if it were flowing back to me from them. Soon I no longer felt as if the flowers were over there, and I was here. I was part of them, and they were a part of me. It was as if my roots were growing in the marsh, too.

Then I heard Veery's voice, and it came as a shock, "Rubythroat, where are you?"

She saw the look on my face.

"Rubythroat, are you all right?"

It was like the shattering of a beautiful dream.

"Yes, Veery. I'm all right," I replied. "I was just growing in the marsh with the flowers."

To tell the truth, I had never been more all right.

I couldn't share my feeling—not with anyone. Who could really understand what had happened? I was afraid even Veery couldn't. I had experienced a oneness with living things as simple as flowers.

The experience seemed to bring me even closer to all of life, and each field trip excited me more. I remember saying to Veery, "I wish every day was Saturday."

Veery smiled at me and said, "Rubythroat, every day will always be Saturday in your heart."

Such wonderful birds were everywhere, waiting for us to discover them. Tiny and rare, migratory, multicolored warblers that Veery told us had traveled thousands of miles from South America, the West Indies, and the southernmost part of the North American mainland flitted from tree to tree.

It was fun feeding the wild ducks swimming in the ponds. I was thrilled at seeing my first belted kingfisher and hearing his rattly, croaking call that I would remember and recognize in distant places all my life. The memory of my childhood would flood back with the kingfisher's rattle along the swampy bayous of San Blas, Mexico, or the lagoons of Malibu, California.

I recall holding peanuts on my hand for little chickadees and nuthatches, luring them from the safety of the budding trees for a delicacy. It was thrilling to see the trust these feathered mites had for a little boy, and this trust translated to me in love.

During one of these excursions I came face to face with my namesake, the rubythroat. It hovered with wing beats so rapid that its wings were indistinguishable. For a fleeting second, he visited a nectar-laden blossom, his throat flashing iridescent scarlet in the sun. I cried out to Veery, "I've seen him. I've seen me."

Veery, Betty, and I teamed up on many expeditions to penetrate the forests and marshes of Van Courtland Park.

Constantly lured on by the promised treasures of nature, we discovered the carefully hidden nests of red-winged blackbirds and marsh wrens. Sometimes our discovered treasures were the caterpillar of a butterfly, the cocoon of a glorious, green luna moth, or the mysterious seventeen-year emerging of loudly singing cicadas. But discovery had its dangers, and curiosity led to surprises. Once I slipped my hand gently into the nest of a tiny marsh wren and pulled it right out, yelling in pain. The nest had been appropriated by a homeless group of hornets, whose fiery stings were insistent protection of their appropriated home.

No bird, animal, fish, or snake in God's kingdom was off limits to me.

Every boy has a hero, and mine, even to this day, is the late Dr. Raymond L. Ditmars, author of animal adventure books and curator of the Bronx Zoo.

Imagine my thrill when I met my hero, Dr. Ditmars, face to face. Some little boys would feel the same on meeting with King Arthur or Sir Lancelot, but my hero was the lead character in all his books that invited and led me on literary expeditions to collect the rarest poisonous snake on earth—the giant, tropical bushmaster—or to collect and exhibit in the zoo the first living vampire bats. I solved with Dr. Ditmars the problems of feeding these rarely captured, blood-drinking bats. We learned together that bottled blood was an accepted substitute to the bats.

It was the thrill of thrills when Dr. Ditmars invited me to ride one of the huge, ancient Galápagos Islands tortoises, which I coaxed into movement by holding a whole banana in front of his eyes.

Dr. Ditmars topped off the wonderful day by permitting me to hold, for the first time ever, a brilliantly colored, yellow-and-black-banded mangrove snake. This four-foot, coldly shiny beauty instilled dreams of tropical snake-collecting trips that were to materialize many years later.

My love for Dr. Ditmars instilled in me a desire to work in a zoo. Anytime anyone asked me in my younger years what job would I like to do most, I would answer unhesitatingly, "Work in a zoo like Dr. Ditmars." Years later my wish came true when I deliberately left film work and took a job as animal keeper in the original Los Angeles Zoo. It didn't matter to me that my job consisted of raking and cleaning all the cages and enclosures of the various antelopes, monkeys, bears, and birds. Oh, yes, I even had to sweep up after the elephants, but these tasks seemed glamorous because I was following in the footsteps of my childhood hero. The only thing that kept me from staying in the zoo field was lack of education and a college degree—basic requirements for progress and promotion.

During my boyhood, my life and my parents' were always separated, but especially so in the realm of my animal collecting.

One day my mother ventured into my bathroom in our Fifth Avenue apartment. It had become a miniature replica of the Ethical Culture School nature room.

Tigro, who had been dismissed from school, was the star boarder among an increasing collection resulting from Veery's and my field trips—DeKay's, black, milk, and green snakes, salamanders, a baby gray squirrel, several frogs, toads, moth cocoons, and chrysalids of a variety of butterflies.

Mother took one horrified look at my menagerie-zoo and cried out in despair, "God, why didn't you cure my fear of dogs?"

I had displaced myself from my own bathtub, now taken over by a baby alligator that Dad had ordered from an alligator farm in Florida, as a special birthday surprise.

There had been considerable delay between time of ordering and time of delivery, but finally a mysterious package arrived at our New York apartment. It was a Havana cigar box, apparently containing Dad's favorite type of cigars. Dad, who was used to receiving gifts from people in all corners of the world, opened the box, dipped his fingers under the cover, and yelled out in surprise and pain when the expected cigars turned out to be the baby alligator which attached itself bulldoggedly to his fingers!

Although Mother feared and avoided most of my pets, she had a special love for butterflies. These could not threaten her in any way. Their unending diversity of color and pattern appealed to her painter's appreciation of beauty.

We had also always shared a tremendous love of flowers. Our

miniature garden in the beach house displayed the most beautiful roses that Mother could buy, and I loved to wander through this garden every morning, searching for the perfect rose to give to the first lady of my life—my mother.

On one particular day, I found a huge red rose, the largest I had ever seen. It was perfect in shape and an intense blood-red color. The perfume from it was so strong it distinguished itself from all of the surrounding flowers. For a moment, I hesitated to pick something so glorious. Then I plucked it and carried it to my mother's studio, where she had been painting for hours. Mother was wearing her favorite painting costume, an old flowered smock, which, when she wore it in the garden, almost caused her to blend in with the symphony of flowers.

As she stood before the easel, studying her latest oil painting, she was not aware of me. Then she noticed me. I presented her with the red rose. No knight of the Middle Ages offered a flower to his lady fair in a more formal manner. Nor was any knight swept up into a warmer embrace and hugged more tenderly than I, amid the odor of paints, linseed oil, cologne, and the rose itself.

"Bill, how do you always manage to find the most glorious rose in my garden for me?" she asked.

I looked at her and then at the rose in her hand and thought that she herself was the most beautiful flower in her garden, but I didn't know how to say what I was thinking.

It was such a fine day and the sky was so blue with not a cloud in sight that Mother decided to move her easel outside under her favorite jacaranda tree that was now in full bloom. We went outside together, and I helped her carry her paints. Just as we were getting up, she saw a lovely butterfly near her small garden pool of water lilies and Egyptian lotus.

"Look, Billy, look!" she cried in excitement.

The butterfly was brownish blue with yellow-margined wings bordered with tiny perfect dots of azure blue. Closer and closer he flew to us.

"Mommy, don't move," I cautioned her.

The butterfly gently brushed her face, fluttered around her time after time, and finally flew away.

"He knows that you like him," I said.

"Yes, Billy, he does. He's showing us how beautiful he is."

Next morning we deliberately returned to search for our butterfly, and, sure enough, he returned. Mother put out one of her graceful, artistic hands.

"Don't be afraid," she said in a soft voice, holding her hand very still. "Here, come rest on my hand."

He fluttered around her and finally eased down into her palm. Then she gently slid her fingers under his threadlike legs, and he held on. Mother walked under the jacaranda with him, talking softly, telling him how much she needed him as a friend.

Day after day he returned at the same time, lighting on my mother's shoulder or forehead. Sometimes he would rest for almost an hour there, never moving his wings. As she walked around the garden, he would often ride on her fingers. I suggested she put a drop of honey and water on her finger for him to taste, and he seemed to enjoy this treat.

He visited her all summer, and then, when it was time for us to travel back to New York, I quietly watched her farewell to her butterfly.

Mother said to him, "Dear butterfly, we have to leave for a while, but do come back and wait for me."

The butterfly flew to her brow. He seemed to speak in a way that neither of us could understand. Suddenly it was as though an electric impulse went through her body, and I saw a startled look on her face. She tried to explain what she had experienced but finally ended up saying that there are many things in nature that we can't fully understand or begin to explain.

Even as our black Rolls-Royce backed out of the long garage onto the pavement, Mother searched for the butterfly and finally said sadly, "Good-by, dear butterfly. Wait until my return."

Many months went by and we were back in California. Dad and I were sitting under the jacaranda tree when, suddenly a butterfly, tattered and faded brown with shortened and worn wings, flew near.

"Mother," I called, "your butterfly is back!"

Mother came running, and the butterfly flew toward her, circling over her head. No longer rhythmic and steady in his movements, he was nervous, jerky, and heavy. It seemed as if an old man butterfly were coming to her for one last good-by.

"Butterfly, you kept your promise," she said softly, her voice full of appreciation and love. "I thank you so much."

Suddenly, the butterfly seemed much younger. He flew with more rhythm, and he apparently knew he had been recognized. He lighted on my mother's head. Then joyfully, he flew around her. Mother closed her eyes, and he came to rest on her right eyelid, just for for a moment, as in times past.

Then, his farewell promise kept, he flew off for the last time. Again his movements were labored and heavy, as if he were sad to go.

I told my mother what I had learned about this type of butterfly.

"The mourning cloak usually lives only for a season, Mother—sometimes to late spring—so I'm sure he is old and tired and ready to go on, but, you know, he lived a little longer than he should have just to see you again."

After the butterfly experience, I tried to share my many animals with Mother—field mice, garter snakes, bats, gophers—but she would shrink away, even though I pointed out their beautiful coloring and design.

And, just like that, we were again in two different worlds.

That night I had again had the strange dream about the endless, dark tunnel and then the beautiful bright light and the daisy. When I awoke, it was hard to fall asleep again because away from the bright light, I felt lonely.

Yet there was more to it than loneliness. I began to feel frightened, as if something terrible was going to happen.

The next day that feeling became a reality.

I was then too young to understand all the reasons for events of the day. Only now am I able to put together the pieces of the story.

Mother's deep sense of loneliness and frustration was a powerful factor in her passionate pursuit of painting. She tried to find there the love that was gone from her marriage. At this time her closest companion was her sister Louise, and when Mother was troubled, she always conferred with Louise.

On this particular day, she had experienced a heartbreaking and traumatic incident that she told me about many years later. She had been tidying up my father's dresser drawers when she discovered an aged packet of letters tied up with a faded blue ribbon, love letters to my dad from a young woman with whom he had been deeply in love early in his marriage to Mother.

It seemed inexcusable to me that a young man, recently married, could have been having an affair with another girl. I had not as yet learned that we are not to judge one another, that that is only God's right to do.

I now realize that my parents' early married life had been maneuvered and encroached upon by Grandmother Sarah and Aunt Blanche. The constant interference by Grandmother and Blanche, as well as by show business and schedules, undoubtedly had posed a separation threat right from the start and had left them with a need for more love than they were receiving from each other. And then there were the religious symbols—rosaries, crosses, and paintings of the saints—from the convent period, to which my dad could never adjust.

Because of exposure to my parents' marital problems, I received many severe trials that, later, turned out to be a blessing. Like my parents, I have never received enough love from anyone or anything.

In any event, my mother's distress upon finding the letters and her realization of her failure as a wife early in marriage caused her now to be aware of an inadequacy as a mother where she had suspected she was failing, too, though money had permitted her to buy a substitute for her own love of her children—specifically, Mademoiselle Branche. So she had told Louise about the letters and also that she was aware that her children loved Mademoiselle Branche more than they loved her. She asked her sister what she could do about it.

"Get rid of Mademoiselle Branche," Louise promptly responded. "Then the children will have to return to you."

"But how can I possibly do that?" Mother asked. "Mademoiselle Branche is a perfect governess. She is flawless in every respect."

You'll have to invent something, Bessie—a reason to fire her," Louise responded. "Suppose you say that she stole something. How about your exquisite pearl necklace from Cartier's? That would be excuse enough."

I can now imagine the terrible dilemma my mother faced, but I also can imagine how desperate she really had become. There were separate bedrooms. There were the discovered letters, added proof of her failure as a wife. Now there was a dawning realization that she was also failing as a mother. Mademoiselle Branche was definite proof—like the letters—of her failure. She would get rid of the letters and also of Mademoiselle Branche.

So she took her sister's advice. I have grown to realize how much each of us needs love and when we feel we are not receiving it, how desperate we become. I will never forget the events that followed.

It seems only yesterday that Mademoiselle Branche was tucking me in and softly crying.

"Beelly, *mon petit chou,*" she was saying, "I have some little presents for you, and there is something I must tell you. Years from now you will understand this better. Your momma has decided that it will be best if I leave you and Betty. I believe she feels that you love me more than you do her. She said something that makes me very sad, and it is not the truth. She has said that I took her pearl necklace. You must understand that your momma loves you so much that she will do even this to get you to love her."

Before I could say anything, she continued.

"The little presents that I give you are gifts of love. I give them to you because I love you just as much as if you were my own little boy, but, you see, dear, there is one who loves you even more than your momma or I do."

First she gave me a painted postcard and explained, "This is my patron saint, St. Theresa."

Her tears made her pause. She then opened a little metal box, and in the dim light, I could see a delicately carved ivory statue of a little baby. In his hands, he held a tiny ball.

"This, my dear Beelly, is *l'enfant Jesus*—our precious little Jesus child. Keep him always with you. His love and my love for you are eternal."

"But, Mademoiselle Branche, what are you saying? You are not really going to leave us, are you? I can't believe that Mother would do such a bad thing."

I started to climb out of bed. "I'm going to get Betty, and we're going to tell Mother that she can't let you go. You'll see!"

Over Mademoiselle Branche's protests, I went to my sister's bedroom and, waking her, told her quickly what had happened: how Mother had made up a story that Mademoiselle Branche had stolen her pearl necklace, so that she could get rid of her. Before Betty could say anything, I took her by the hand and led her, sleepy-eyed, down the hallways to Mother's bedroom.

Mother was reading on the chaise longue, and I confronted her about Mademoiselle Branche. Through tears, I added, "Betty and I are going to run away. You'll never see us again. You'll be sorry."

Betty started in, uttering the first words of reaction to this dramatic situation, "Mommy, I don't love you. I hate you! I hate you! I'll always hate you!"

Immediately Mother jumped out of the chaise longue, grabbed Betty by her long brown curls, and shook her violently, shouting, "Don't you *ever* say that to me again!"

I wanted to protect Betty somehow. I wanted to fight off my mother, but I couldn't. My mixed emotions of fear and hatred stopped me, and I ran out of the room, crying, "I hate you, too. I hate you, too!"

Mother did not give in to us. Mademoiselle Branche left the very next morning. The damage that this incident caused in my relations with my mother took many years to heal totally. Yet, somehow, even as a young person. I could understand her motives, even though I didn't approve of her methods, and eventually I forgave her. Yet how do you sponge such memories from your mind?

From that day forward—I was about seven then—up to her very last days, I never again called her "Mother" or "Mommy." I called, and referred to, her by her name, "Bess."

There is a tremendous truth imbedded in the story of our relationship. Something must die so that something else can be born. None of us can be reborn until we totally die to self. And a tremendous love for Bess was later reborn out of the hatred that I experienced for her.

Only a little later that evening did I realize I was still holding Mademoiselle Branche's gifts in my hand. I looked at the loving and radiant face of St. Theresa and it seemed to fade away and Mademoiselle Branche's face appeared there.

I studied the little ivory statue in my hands. I had no idea that it would turn out to be the most important influence in my life.

I thought about the tunnel dream of the night before. It seems strange that an abstract dream, darkness and then light, and a little ivory statue of the Jesus child would one day lead me to the greatest truth, which would fulfill my need for a special kind of love.

I looked at the globe in the hands of the infant Jesus. It was the world, of which I was a part, and, one day, I would realize that I had always been in his hands.

9
On Wings of Eagles

Like many American millionaires, my dad was wiped out by the history-making stock market crash of 1929, the forerunner of the Great Depression of the 1930s. He lost his entire fortune, $25 million, in a single day. Fortunately, although not a particularly spiritual man, he had a deep faith in powers within. One day he could be in the pit of deepest despair, and the next he could be on top of the highest mountain.

Many years later, he admitted to me the emptiness he felt on the day of the crash—the devastating blow to his ego that the empire of Jesse Lasky had been reduced to rubble.

One of the most interesting aspects of his life in this period would never have come to my attention except for a chance meeting with one of his long-time friends and associates.

I had been hired to work on a wardrobe and make-up test unit of one of Hollywood's boldest and most moving religious films, *The Greatest Story Ever Told*, based on Fulton Oursler's still best-selling classic of the life of Jesus. As I began to read the call sheet on the set, I felt a tap on my shoulder and turned around. What a pleasure to see a dear friend of the family, Ed Wynn, now transformed to a beggar's rags of the Bible. Ed had gained fame in the golden days of radio as a comedian, the Texaco Fire Chief. Now he had been cast to play the blind man whose sight is restored through a miracle performed by Jesus.

After we caught up on personal news, he said, "You know, Bill, seeing you today reminded me of something I hadn't thought about in many years. There's a story I want to tell you about your father. It's one that you will never hear from anyone else. I was with your father on the day he lost $25 million in the stock market crash.

"I was living in New York City at the Algonquin Hotel. As I approached the entrance I was surprised to see your dad sitting on the front steps. It seemed strange for a man of his stature to be sitting there.

"He was very depressed, even though he was doing his best to conceal it. I said, 'Jesse, how did it go with you today?'

"Your dad raised his head, saying, 'Ed, I have lost my entire fortune—every penny I have managed to save in my entire life. My attorney tells me it's in the area of twenty-five million. Here I thought I was secure for life.'

"With emotion, he asked me a question for which he knew the answer: 'How can anyone lose twenty-five million dollars in a single day without raising a finger or making a move to cause such a tragedy?'

"Without explaining any of the details to your dad, I said, 'Jesse, come on up to my suite. There's someone I want you to meet. We're having a little party. Come, join us.'

"Your father refused. 'Thank you, Ed, but no. I don't need a party today and I don't want to meet anyone.'

"Come, Jesse. Don't sit here feeling sorry for yourself. I guarantee you'll be cheered up.

"Once in the suite, I introduced your dad to a waiting gentleman and poured him a drink. 'Jesse,' I said. 'I want you to meet a very dear friend of mine. He's had a stock market loss today, too. Mr. Whitney, you, of course must know Jesse Lasky.'

" 'Mr. Lasky,' said the gentleman, 'Ed tells me you and I are kindred souls so far as the stock market goes. Do you mind telling me how much you lost today?'

" 'Every cent I have—more than twenty-five million,' replied your dad, and then your dad returned the question. 'By the way, Mr. Whitney, how much did you lose?'

" 'More than fifty million' was the answer. I noticed the startled look and then the beginning of a smile on the corners of your dad's mouth.

"I had been right. Your dad did feel better!"

Because I was a boy at that time, I was not aware of the nation's financial situation, and my dad was very careful never to show any feelings of despair in front of us children. Bess was the same way in this regard. If anything did start to slip out, she would say immediately, "Jesse, I want to tell you about a new flower that bloomed in my garden today. Let's talk about the other things later."

On our next trip to California, we no longer had the lavish, private railroad car, but that didn't matter to me. I found it much more exciting to travel in the first-class Pullman. Besides there were more people to see and other children around to play games.

While we were oblivious to it all, blows coincident with his financial loss were falling heavily on Dad. His ego suffered an even greater trauma.

In a matter of a few days, he learned that through his stock market losses and a realignment of principal shareholders, he no longer held an equal controlling interest in Paramount Pictures. Upon coming to his offices, he received notice from the board of directors that his services as first vice-president in charge of production were already terminated. For the first time in many years, he didn't even have a job.

Never one to wallow in regrets or slights, Dad immediately began to put out feelers for a new opportunity. Every day in his life was a new challenge, and shortly after the crash, he was in Darryl Zanuck's office, telling his good friend, then executive head of 20th Century-Fox, ideas for future motion pictures.

At that time 20th Century-Fox was only a few years away from its tremendous growth surge led by child star Shirley Temple, whose charms, curls, dimples, songs, and dancing captivated the world of talking pictures as Famous Players–Lasky's Mary Pickford, America's Sweetheart, had captivated silent films.

Dad's enthusiasm must have been contagious because he landed a ten-year contract to produce independent motion pictures financed and released by 20th Century-Fox. In this capacity, he started a new trend—the independent motion picture producer.

His rise from the rubble of the 1929 stock market crash has always seemed to me a lesson of hope. More than once in my life when I experienced personal and financial defeats, I learned from Dad that I, too, can rise from the rubble.

Appreciative of his precedent-setting career and his milestones of movie industry accomplishment, Darryl Zanuck had a production office designed and built to Dad's specifications—the Lasky building, still used at the 20th Century-Fox Studios.

The films Dad produced during this period showed the beginning of spiritual growth. Among his fine productions were *The Power and the Glory*, the story of a priest that launched Spencer Tracy and Colleen Moore's careers: *Zoo in Budapest*, which helped establish Loretta Young and Gene Raymond. Following this was *Berkeley Square*, with Leslie Howard and Heather Angel, a sensitive, spiritual love story, in which the *crux ansata*, or the ankh, symbolizes the eternity—God's love. This film was ahead of its time and its spiritual messages were missed by much of its reviewing public.

But I was as oblivious to Dad's importance in the motion picture industry as I had been to his stock market disaster.

I knew he had produced *The Squaw Man*, the first American, full-length, feature film, but there were many other achievements that underscored his leadership in the rapidly growing film industry, aside from founding the star system in Hollywood. He established the first writing department, produced the first all-Technicolor film, *Wanderers of the Wasteland*, a Zane Grey Western, and initiated many additional industry innovations that have been lost by Hollywood historians.

A small thing impressed me most—that our family tradition about going to the top was symbolized in the Paramount Pictures logo—a snow-covered mountain against a royal blue field, encircled by white stars.

I was proud of my dad and loved him, but I lived in my world and he lived in his. I accepted without question the Hollywood atmosphere into which I had been born. On the other hand, my love of all living creatures had been born into me. So, on one side was the Hollywood influence, the imitation trying to look like the real, and, on the other, the real that needed no pretensions.

Early in my teens, my dad, when finances were lowest, made a down payment for me on an old Ford station wagon. This prehistoric bus, as Dad liked to refer to it, gave me wheels for traveling to the nearby mountainous areas where many of Southern California's now vanishing hawks and eagles still existed. Max Silvernail, a grade school teacher, had caught and trained a baby peregrine falcon, the classic hunting bird of the courts of Middle Ages. He led me on excursions to Chatsworth, where these falcons still lived, to secret nesting spots of red-tailed hawks and Cooper's hawks in the Santa Monica Mountains, and to the Sespe Mountains, the last stronghold in the world of the endangered giant California condors.

Sometimes I would drive to these places alone and lie with my back on the warm ground watching for countless hours the spectacular birds as they climbed, glided, courted, and dived, defying the law of gravity. Then I was no longer earthbound, for I was soaring on the wings of eagles.

More than that, I wanted my deep love of these birds to be reciprocal. I wanted a bird of my own, one that I could love that would love and trust me.

Someday . . .

There was always the underlying spirituality of the birds—really, of all living things—and I never failed to admire and love whatever power it was that made and sustained the smallest to the largest creatures: hummingbirds to eagles.

I couldn't believe that all these wondrous things had just happened accidentally, and many times I thought back to my beloved Mademoiselle Branche and her simple but deep understanding of nature.

A certain fascination continuously grew in me. This fascination spanned the miracle of metamorphosis from caterpillar to butterfly to the wonder of babies of every kind—rabbits, chipmunks, raccoons, and, of course, tiny human beings.

Each one was a living miracle—all of their many parts in miniature. How marvelous to know that their small parts would gradually grow through the sustenance of the same force that created them.

Despite the underlying spiritual elements, I enjoyed many worldly aspects of my numerous pets. Their maintenance and care provided many funny experiences that went back as far as I can remember.

While still in our New York apartment, Bess and Dad were having a swank soiree in honor of playwright-actor Noel Coward.

Present were many of the elite effete of the international theater set.

Just before dinner was to be served—as per Bess's custom—she sent one of the maids to bring little Billy and Betty to say good night to their guests.

It just happened to be dinner hour for my special small tree frog, Hoppy, as well as for the guests. Only Hoppy was to have a meal worm, while the guests were prepared to dine on frog legs.

No one noticed me holding Hoppy tightly in my left hand as Betty and I were led into the living room. Bess went over to Noel Coward and said, "Noel, these are our children, Billy and Betty."

He was holding a full brandy glass in his hand, and just managed to comment, "Chahming." The wriggling Hoppy must have noticed the fluid in the glass. In any event, in a split second, he leaped from my hand landing squarely in the center of the brandy snifter.

No doubt the burning sensation of the firewater caused him immediately to leap against Mr. Coward, but, by now, Noel Coward had leaped to higher ground—the top of the sofa.

I understand that Mr. Coward, whose appetite had been lost, didn't stay to dine on frog legs that night.

On another occasion Bess was about to take a shower. Just as she had disrobed and reached in to turn on the water, she saw a six-foot boa constrictor hanging full-length from the shower rod. She ran out in panic, too frightened to try *any* of the bathroom showers for days.

Bess prided herself on her interior design artistry—the selection of paints, wallpapers, draperies, objects of art, and antiques. Somehow she was never quite appreciative of my additions to her interiors: pet bats hanging head down from her imported silk draperies, snakes basking in the sun on the floor, and unsightly jars of tarantulas and black widow spiders.

A pair of unhousebreakable hunting hawks which had the freedom of my sitting room never did head her popularity poll.

Bess never did like my menagerie, but she liked it even less on the day she was dressing for a tea to be given in honor of writer-historian H. G. Wells and saw my family of seven pack rats scurrying across the floor of her room. First she was paralyzed with

The author and his mother, Bessie Lasky. COURTESY OF WILLIAM R. LASKY.

Ike Lasky, grandfather of William R. Lasky, who discovered early in life that you always go to the top of the stream for the big fish. KORYEA BROS. SOUVENIR PHOTOGRAPHIC STUDIO.

Four of the five members of the Jesse L. Lasky family photographed on the terrace of their mansion at 609 Ocean Front on the Pacific in Santa Monica, California. Left to right: Jesse L. Lasky, his daughter Betty, and sons William R. Lasky and Jesse L. Lasky, Jr. PHOTO BY BESSIE LASKY.

The mansion (below) had twenty-seven servant's rooms, a huge swimming pool with salt water pumped in from the nearby Pacific, and a garage housing five Rolls-Royces and numerous lesser imports. PHOTO BY JESSE L. LASKY.

A few minutes after William Lasky's birth, his father proudly burst into the office of his brother-in-law Samuel Goldwyn to announce the arrival of his second baby, to be named Bill. "Goldwyn screwed up his face in obvious distaste: 'Vyfore you call him Bill? Every Tom, Dick, and Harry is named Bill!'" COURTESY OF SAMUEL GOLDWYN, JR. PRODUCTIONS.

Some years later Bill Lasky began his lifelong love affair with animals in the Nature Room of the Ethical Culture School, Central Park, New York City. Billy Lasky (center) is shown with one of his favorite teachers, Miss Boice, fellow students, and his pet bull snake Tigro (held by second girl from left). PHOTO BY BESSIE LASKY.

William R. Lasky (left) with trained peregrine fal- con and star Gary Coope on location for *Sergean York*. Lasky served as ap prentice assistant director Cooper won the Academy Award for playing Sergean York in the film of th same name. COURTESY O UNITED ARTISTS TELEVISION

On the set of *The Ten Commandments:* Director of colossal films Cecil B. DeMille (left), Bessie and Jesse Lasky, parents of William R. Lasky, standing. Young Lasky trained birds for use in this film, whose screenplay was written by his older brother, Jesse Lasky, Jr. COURTESY OF PARAMOUNT PICTURES.

fright and then she became furious as the pack rats began dining on the bottom of her rose taffeta drapes.

These pack rats had become a part of the Lasky menagerie quite by accident. I had been camping in the Mojave Desert for several days, collecting snakes and butterflies. The friend I was with observed that there were quite a few large pack rat nests close to where we had put our sleeping bags.

Just before we left home, I had noticed that my wrist watch was not working and I had asked Dad to lend me a watch. About the only one that was not among the extras stored in a safe-deposit box was a Cartier gold, diamond-studded watch that actor Edward G. Robinson had given him. This, he had let me borrow with great reluctance, cautioning me to guard it with my life, due to its personal and intrinsic value to him. When he gave the watch to me, he had turned it over and showed me an inscription on the back. "Bill," he said, "it's one of a kind—irreplaceable."

I had noticed the nest mounds of the pack rats built of sagebrush, sticks of all sizes, and cholla cactus. Deep in the center of these nests, where the baby rats are raised, is a soft, grass-padded, cuplike depression where the parent rats deposit their young.

I had decided the safest place for Dad's watch was in my hiking shoes, which I had carefully placed near my head before going to sleep.

When I woke up the next morning, I first thought of the watch. I shook out the shoe carefully. Alas, what fell out was not my dad's watch, but an old rusty nail.

At first I suspected my friend of chicanery, but when I woke him up to ask about it, he was so irritated he said he wished he had thought of the idea of hiding it on me.

Then the truth dawned on me. The only other place it could have gone was with one of the pack rats. They have a habit of collecting and packing off to their nests shiny objects that catch their fancy. Pack rats are not thieves, though. They are traders. When they leave their nests, they frequently carry some objet d'art from their collection of nest goodies and hold onto it until they locate something that appeals to them more. Then they trade.

It became apparent to me that some pack rat had found the

Cartier diamond-studded watch more appealing than his rusty nail and had made a trade.

As I explored the first pack rat's nest, I could see the large guilty eyes of a tremendous female, and I captured her with my butterfly net to take home to study. Then removing the last pieces of the nest's wood, I discovered what I had been searching for—Dad's watch, back side up, with the inscription, "To My Friend, Jesse Lasky—Edward G. Robinson." Not to be outtraded by the rat, I left the rusty nail in its place.

I thought the transaction was over, but when I got home, I received the final payment. The female rat I had captured presented me with a nestful of pink naked baby traders, who eventually grew up and worked on Bess's rose taffeta drapes.

After retrieving and caging my pack rats and assuring Bess that all was well, I went outside to gather termites to feed my bats. A shrill outcry from Bess interrupted my K.P. duties, and I went inside on the run.

Bess had decided to rest for a few minutes on her couch to recover from the pack rat army invasion when she glanced toward one of her picture windows and there, lounging on the window ledge, sunning itself, was a four-foot diamondback rattlesnake.

Once I had taken my pet back to his cage, Bess managed to get up enough strength to go to the tea, ominously promising that she would never again return to her own house.

My fascination for snakes, stemming from the nature room at Ethical Culture School, had evolved into my studying and capturing rattlesnakes as pets. These highly specialized creations never ceased to amaze me as to color, pattern, and behavior.

When we moved from Beverly Hills to our new Brentwood home on North Saltair, I built up a collection of rattlesnakes, copperheads, and water moccasins that I housed in a homemade wood-sided snake pit at the end of our property.

Across the street from our home lived actor Gary Cooper, whom my dad had developed from a bit player in his World War I epic, *Wings*. When Gary heard of my snake collection, he came over to see my pets. Since he was as much of an animal lover as I, we became friends right away.

During one of our conversations, he invited me to his den to see a beautiful new hickory bow-and-arrow set which he had just had custom-made for hunting. He was as proud of his bow as I was of my snakes.

"This little beauty cost me over a thousand dollars, Billy," he said. "It's the finest bow that money can buy."

He let me feel the smoothness of the hickory bow, and the first thing I knew, I asked if I could try it out in his back yard.

"Yup," he said with typical Cooper verbosity.

He strung the bow for me and handed it over. Without asking for instructions, I decided to test the bow without using an arrow. There was a sickening cracking of wood and the tip of the bow snapped off.

My heart missed a beat, as Gary commented, "You shouldn't have done it that-a-way!"

I began to visualize the endless number of weekly allowances that would have to be accumulated to pay back my famous friend.

Gary got a peculiar look on his face, then grinned that slow, infectious grin of his.

"Don't worry about it, Bill. Ain't your fault. Forget it. If it weren't able to take ordinary use, 'twern't much good in the first place."

He put a consoling arm around my shoulder.

Suddenly I understood why millions throughout the world loved Gary Cooper. He came across so genuinely and warmly on film because he was that kind of a guy.

Gary was fascinated with my snakes and once asked, "Ain't you feared of 'em, Bill?"

Kidding him, I answered, "Nope. With gentleness and love, they quickly learn that they have nothing to fear, but you have to learn how to handle them safely."

I will never forget my mother's Day of the Snakes. A friend phoned me one evening to borrow my trio of three- and four-foot rattlesnakes for a few days.

"Sure. I'll bag them for you and leave them in my room for you to pick up."

I told Bess that when the fellow rang the doorbell, all she had to do was let him in and he would pick up something in my bedroom. Then I went off to my classes at Beverly Hills High School and forgot all about the snakes, but somehow the drawstring worked loose.

Bess had been taking a rest after a long painting session, when out of the corner of her eye, she detected movement on the floor and glanced sharply in that direction. She was horrified to see three diamondback rattlesnakes moving toward her bed.

Scrambling onto the bed, she grabbed the phone and nervously dialed the studios for my dad, who was in the midst of a production meeting with the director and stars of one of his motion pictures.

"Jesse," she exclaimed, "there are three live rattlesnakes in my bedroom. I'm standing on top of my bed. Come home at once and save me!"

"Bessie," he said in a low voice, "I'm in a very important production meeting. And what do I know about snakes? I'll phone you later."

Bess gasped, and Dad knew that that was the end of his business conference. He was about to get into his car and race home when he came up with a better solution. He phoned Beverly Hills High and got me out of a Latin class. I welcomed leaving school early, and it was no major problem to capture my delinquent pets and rescue Bess from on top of her bed.

That night Dad and I had a father and son conference, and I promised to move all of my snakes to the University of California, Los Angeles, Zoological Department.

Aside from his experience with the baby alligator, my father's exposures to my pets had been pretty mild compared with those of Bess.

And, yet, a member of my menagerie turned out to be one of the most unforgettable characters of his life.

While our Brentwood home was being built, I stayed with Dad at the Miramar Hotel with a third guest who hadn't bothered to be registered, my adopted crippled barn owl, Bubo. As a matter of fact, he and I entered the hotel through a rear door and made it to the proper floor by the service stairs.

Bubo had taken over one of the suite's bathrooms as his roosting place. I'll never forget the maid's shrieks when she had her first surprise encounter with him. Occasionally during the night, Dad, sleepy-eyed and forgetting about Bubo, would use my bathroom, and he would be startled as he found himself looking into a pair of wide eyes that never blinked. The owl, upon seeing Dad, cried out, "Hoo-hoo," and my dad, after his initial shock, replied, "Everybody knows 'hoo-hoo' but you."

During this period and throughout my youth, my constant companion from grade school days was Fred Gates, who shared my love of butterflies. This was the first time in my life since Ethical Culture School and Veery that I had someone to share my love of nature.

Our first meeting had taken place in the schoolyard on our first day at El Rodeo Grade School. While the other boys were loudly participating in competitive athletic activities—baseball, volleyball, and football—I had deliberately retired to the vacant swings that bordered one end of the playgrounds. Here I became involved in a dream world of butterflies and birds.

Suddenly interrupting my fantasies was a skinny, shy young boy who climbed on the swing next to me and started to talk. Instead of asking a question, he made a statement. "You don't like athletics, either, do you?"

"Right," I replied. "I wish I could go butterfly hunting. That's what I like to do."

Instantly, Fred's shyness vanished and he said, "My name's Fred Gates and I like to collect butterflies, too. Let's go!"

We disappeared around the flower hedges in a joint search, the first of many that were to continue throughout the years—through grade school and high school until the time we entered military service.

In those days, I had very little spending money—not only because of Dad's shifting fortunes, but because of his philosophy about allowances. Not one of us received more than twenty-five cents a week until we enrolled in high school. That was the amount Dad had received early in his life and, unaware of changing times, he said that was enough for us.

It was not easy to keep up with other Beverly Hills High School students whose families were wealthy and whose allowances reflected this. Yet I can't blame Dad's frugality on the fact that because of my every-weekend excursions to collect and study all creatures, I seldom dated. At this point in my life, girls were more of an inconvenience than anything else. Dating required time and interfered with my other pursuits.

I loved dancing, though, and during my senior year of high school I did neglect collecting trips to attend enjoyable school dances. I didn't have a steady girl friend but dated several who were good sports and fun to be with.

Even though Dad didn't provide a great deal of spending money, he furnished me with a car and credit cards for gasoline. Further, Fred and I were free to raid the refrigerators and cupboards loaded with canned goods. There was always more than enough food to sustain us for two- or three-day camping trips.

Not only was I grateful for Fred's sharing of my deepest interests, but also for his being a buffer against the first anti-Semitism that I ever encountered.

I was completely bewildered at some of the names certain students called me. After all, we Laskys were Jews and we were not Jews. I had never been in a synagogue, so nothing surprised me more than occasions when I was pushed around by a group of youths and called "a rich, fat Jew boy" and a "Christ killer." Actually, I was so un-Jewish that I didn't even have the vaguest idea what they were talking about. I'll never forget, and will always be thankful for, Fred's loyalty to me in those times.

When "people" problems were most pressing, I always turned with even greater interest to my animals. Although I had had a couple of pet-shop-purchased hawks, I had never learned how to acquire them and train them as falcons. This fascinated me so I read everything I could find in the public library to prepare myself for the day when I would be able to capture my own bird.

An article in an old *National Geographic* magazine inspired me by explaining step by step how to take a wild hawk or eagle, tame it, and train it to return when you turn it loose. More than that, though, I wanted to train one as a hunting companion and to take game with it.

Shortly after this period, I heard about a man named Minard Stevens in the northern California community of Livermore who, because of tuberculosis and inability to work at a nine-to-five job, spent his entire time training falcons.

After corresponding with him for a while, I had the thrill of being invited to visit him and his wife in Livermore and persuaded him to trap me a wild falcon. I had worked after high school classes and had also saved money from allowances, so I had enough to pay around two hundred dollars for his efforts.

A great thrill of my life was receiving a telegram from him that he had trapped for me a magnificent peregrine falcon which he had named Shahinah.

Shahinah was the female of the shahin, a North African falcon. Minard had started her tedious training, which began by carrying her, hooded or blindfolded, on his fist day and night without resting. It was four or five weeks before he had her flying free again and he allowed me to pick her up and take her home to our Saltair house. How thrilled Gary Cooper was when I showed her to him! When I asked Gary if he knew that falcons could fly almost as fast as one of his arrows, he responded with a classical "Yup!"

I could hardly wait to let Shahinah fly free and to exercise her. I attached a small pair of Indian silver bells to her legs for indentification purposes and to speed her recovery if she became lost. These bells help locate a bird if it is in a tree or on the ground in heavy brush. Then I put a brightly plumed, Dutch hood over her head and drove her to Mines Field, which eventually became the site for Los Angeles International Airport.

I thought it would be simple to remove her leather leash and swivel, strike her hood, and throw her up into the air, but when the time came to perform this, I found my heart pounding so hard that my shaking hands could scarcely do their job. What if she failed to return?

Once free, Shahinah climbed straight up into the sky and then terror struck within me. It seemed incredible that she would ever again become earthbound. Out of my falconer's sack, I pulled my feather-decorated, leather-padded lure, swinging it around my head by the leather leash attached to it. I whistled in falconer's fashion for Shahinah to return. My mouth was so dry it was nearly impossible to make a sound, but Shahinah, well trained by Minard, turned in her flight and then came downward. In her enthusiasm to capture the meat-garnished lure, she misjudged her flight and, instead of striking the lure with her feet, crashed into the hard ground with her breast.

To my horror, she collapsed in a feathered heap and lay unconscious near my feet. At first I thought she was dead, and my heart was in my throat as I picked her up in my arms and cradling her in an unfalconer manner, carried her to the car. Hurriedly I drove home and for several weeks gently cared for her. While recovering, she rested each day on a block of wood beneath a large walnut tree in our garden, until finally she again seemed ready for training.

Hooding her once more, I drove her to Mines Field, and removed her leash, swivel, and hood. I cast her into the air. Immediately she caught an updraft and soared ever higher. For just a second it seemed as if I were riding with her on her wings.

Minard had trained Shahinah to "wait on"—to fly overhead, back and forth, setting her wings while watching me for live or flushed game. This is exactly what she did. Suddenly she saw a flock of pigeons about two miles away, and took off after them. By the time I could run over to where I thought she was, there was no sign of her and I couldn't find her.

It was a heartbreaking experience. First had come her accident, and now I was faced with leaving her out overnight. This was especially upsetting, because I realized how dangerous this separation could be. I struggled through the sleepless night, waiting for daylight, then returned to Mines Field and spent the whole day looking, calling, and searching for Shahinah.

Finally at twilight, I returned home, discouraged. There I found Bess extremely excited.

"Your falcon has been sitting in the walnut tree over her block in the back garden," she exclaimed. "I know it was your bird because she had the Indian silver bells on her legs."

It was dark as I rushed out into the back garden, but there was no Shahinah. She had become tired of waiting for me and had left.

"It's incredible, Bess, that this wild bird was so attached to me that she flew all the way from Mines Field to Brentwood to find me. Do you realize that she had never seen that course of flight because she was hooded the entire trip between here and Mines Field? You know, in her eyes, Bess, it wasn't she who had been lost. It was I. While I was searching for her, she was searching for me. Perhaps that's what she's doing now."

I never saw Shahinah again.

In a sense she was lost and then, again, she wasn't, for she had taught me about the strong bond of love that it is possible to build between men and a so-called wild creature and gave me confidence to face some strange challenges in training more than one hundred birds of prey in years to come.

10

"Shtupid, Shtupid!"

Several weeks after my graduation from Beverly Hills High School, I suddenly realized that the words of our commencement speaker were too true.

Graduation was surely a time of decision.

So far as I was concerned, college was out. High school had made me all too aware of my mediocrity in mathematics, physics, and chemistry—basic requirements for the zoology course of study I would have chosen.

Without a college degree in zoology, how could I move ahead in my favorite field? The line of least resistance would be a career in Hollywood. Yet without experience, just how could I be of value to anyone in film production?

I had gained a certain degree of skill in taking still pictures and movies of my animals and birds, which Dad had said were "very, very good," but to think of following in the footsteps of my dad or my brother did not seem realistic to me.

No one could possibly follow in Dad's footsteps. My brother Jesse's impressive screen credits were unattainable to me: many of Cecil B. DeMille's epics—*Samson and Delilah, Northwest Mounted Police, The Greatest Show on Earth,* and *The Ten Commandments.*

One night Dad, sensing that I was disturbed about the future, cornered me to ask what direction I would like my career to take.

"Well, Dad, my first choice would be a zoologist and, maybe someday, the director of a major zoo, like Dr. Ditmars. Yet, without a college degree I couldn't possibly go to the top."

"Bill, how about motion pictures?"

"I've thought about that, too. What I know about the business, I love, but I've also seen the bad side of it, Dad, how your career has gone up and down. The insecurity of it bothers me. There's something so solid, safe, and quiet about working with facts, with scientific research, microscopes, books, and tangible things. It seems to me, the motion picture business is like a lightning bug, an undependable source of light."

I will always be appreciative of Dad's understanding and sensitivity to my needs and feelings. As a matter of fact, both Bess and Dad had always let us children make our own decisions—for successes or failures. If we fell down and made a mistake, they always reached out a hand and pulled us up. I think that is loving.

"Bill," Dad said. "As far as making a living with your butterflies, snakes, birds, and animals, I don't know how that would work out. I can't be of help to you in zoology, and as a father, I would like to help you. If you go into the motion picture business, you could still keep your interest in Zoology as a hobby. That's great. I have my golf and fishing, and I understand how important it is to have hobbies.

"If you go into the motion picture business—whether I'm there or not—you will always have my name, which I've spent my life building to one that's recognized and respected everywhere. Any door will open to you. All of us have to make our own careers, Bill, but I could get you a start."

After much thought, I decided to take his advice—although not entirely pleased with my decision—and put my love of animals in a secondary position.

"Okay, Bill, you know I always go to the top to get things done," he said. "I'll phone your Uncle Sam Goldwyn and tell him that 'Every Tom, Dick, and Harry is named Bill' wants a job."

He did, and about a week later I was hired at the fabulous salary of eighteen dollars a week in the film cutting department of Samuel Goldwyn Studios. I was to be an office boy to answer phones and to take film to and from the vaults. It was the very bottom rung.

My first day at Goldwyn Studios is still deeply etched in my memory.

For several hours I had watched people running around—not

understanding what they were doing. My boss, Sherm Todd, now Academy Award film editor, said, "Well, it's lunchtime, Bill. Now that we have you to answer the phones, the rest of us are going out to the Farmer's Market."

I became a little nervous. "Yes, but what do I have to do?"

"Not much," said my boss. "Hardly anything happens during lunch period. Just take phone messages and hold down the fort."

Five minutes went by, then suddenly the phone rang. A rich and forceful Russian-Jewish accented voice came over to me—unmistakably that of Sam Goldwyn.

"Hello, hello," the voice said. "Dis is Mr. Goldwyn. Da film, da film! Put da film in the projection room. I come right down to see it. Yah?"

Then he hung up. I never had a chance to say anything. "Oh, boy," I said to myself. "I have just heard from my boss, the head of the studio. Now I get to do my first job for him personally."

I was much impressed with my own importance until it dawned on me that I had no idea what film Mr. Goldwyn wanted.

Obviously it must be marked in some way or have Mr. Goldwyn's name on it.

There were stacks of film cans piled high in all corners of the room, on racks, on desks, and tables—even on the floor—and I began to get panicky. I couldn't find a single film marked in a particular way for Mr. Goldwyn.

One course of action seemed right for me, a recent high school graduate and a reasonably intelligent young man: "I'll phone Mr. Goldwyn and ask him which film he is expecting to see." I found Mr. Goldwyn's extension number in the studio's phone directory and dialed it. I was surprised when he answered himself.

"Yah, yah, vot is it, vot is it?"

He had a habit of repeating himself. He repeated himself once, while mockingbirds repeat themselves twice. I guess that made Mr. Goldwyn a rare bird.

"I'm new here, Mr. Goldwyn, and I can't figure out what film you want delivered to the projection room. Will you please describe it to me."

Instead of a description, I got an explosion.

"Shtupid, shtupid! The film, the film, the film! Put it down in the room, the room! I be right down. Yah? Yah?"

And, boom, he hung up again.

I thought, "I must be 'stupid, stupid!' but I can't figure out which film it is," so I carefully searched the room again.

Now I really became terrified because I was afraid I'd get fired. I dialed the number again, and again Mr. Goldwyn answered. I began: "I know I'm stupid, but this is my first day here. Please tell me what the film is that you're supposed to see."

He didn't speak, he screamed. "Shtupid, shtupid! The film, the film—any film. Put it down in the room, the room. Yah? Yah? come right down," and, boom, he hung up.

I had heard him correctly. He *had* said "*any* film," so I picked up the nearest can of film and took it to the projection room, told the projectionist to put it on, and that Mr. Goldwyn would be right down.

In a few minutes, I saw Mr. Goldwyn leave his offices on the upper floor of the executive building, walk down his private staircase—like descending from heaven—and enter the projection room.

I hid behind the cutting-room door, not knowing what to expect. Perhaps there would be another explosion when he left the projection room, but nothing happened. Only silence.

All he did was walk up his stairs—back to heaven. I never did learn what the real story was.

Our household was a study in contrasts during this period. For months at Goldwyn Studios, I had worked at many different jobs —coding film, breaking down rushes, and splicing film—for *Hurricane, Cowboy and the Lady, Stella Dallas,* and *Wuthering Heights,* pictures still being shown on TV.

Meanwhile Dad had been working at one thing, securing the film rights to the life of World War I hero Sergeant Alvin C. York. He had been trying to tie up these rights for twenty years, and now that he had them, he was in a state of euphoria, threatened by nervous tension. The job of solving numerous story problems seemed insurmountable.

And, speaking of contrasts, I realized for the first time in my life, through Dad's behavior, that we human beings are inconsistent and consistent, by turns, with an assortment of admirable and, sometimes, laughable qualities.

Dad was always the world's greatest enthusiast for any idea or philosophy that he believed in. In sharp contrast within him were his hypochrondria and, at that period, a deep dedication to the positivism in physical and mental realms of Christian Science as blueprinted in Mary Baker Eddy's *Science and Health*.

If someone two or three blocks away from him on the street sneezed, he would immediately develop sniffles. Many times, in his activity-crammed days—especially in the Sergeant York period—he would develop slight headaches from nervous tension. Frequently, then, during odd moments, he would read *Science and Health*.

One unforgettable day while he was deeply absorbed in reading Mary Baker Eddy and had a slight headache, I saw him walk to the medicine cabinet with *Science and Health* under his arm and, with his free hands, pour himself a glass of water and down a couple aspirins.

His biggest headaches, however, were certain dull spots in *Sergeant York*, the film in which Gary Cooper starred and, subsequently, won an Academy Award for best actor. To solve these dilemmas, Dad confided to me that he and screenwriter Harry Chandle were going to meet Sergeant York at his home in the valley of the Three Forks or the Wolf in Fentress County, Tennessee. Would I like to come along?

"If you want to quit at Goldwyn's, we could sure use your help. Bill, I would like you to shoot footage with your sixteen-millimeter camera to help us get local color and ideas to make the story come more alive."

Here was an exciting challenge, a promise of adventure—a chance to work closely with Dad and to learn from him.

Off and on for years, I had heard bits and snatches of the York story, which Dad often referred to at the dinner table as one of the greatest he had ever known.

Sergeant Alvin C. York had been one of the most decorated heroes of World War I, winning the Congressional Medal of Honor, the highest award our country can bestow. York, single-handedly, had wiped out a German machine-gun battalion in

France's Argonne Forest, killing 28 Germans with 28 bullets and capturing 132 soldiers and 15 machine guns.

Before his service in the war, York, a simple Tennessee mountaineer, characterized by a lean towering body and bushy red hair, was noted as the most deadly turkey shooter in the state and a rough character. Then an evangelical country preacher, Pastor Pyle, made him realize there was something missing in his life—a spiritual dimension, a personal relationship with God through his son, Jesus Christ. York told the preacher he wanted to be forgiven of his sins and fulfill his life by inviting Jesus in. Instantly, the transformation was complete. The tough character became gentle and loving—a model citizen.

With the coming of World War I, Pastor Pyle, who had led York in his conversion and had emphasized the commandment "Thou shalt not kill," was head of the local draft board. He informed York that he was about to be drafted into the Army for combat duty overseas. A conscientious objector, York at first refused to be drafted, and when he finally reported to camp, he adhered to his Bible teachings and said he would not use a gun on another human being.

No amount of military persuasion could make York change his attitude. One of his officers tried another method, telling Alvin that there are sometimes mitigating circumstances, in which killing is justified. He gave York a history book to read and a leave of absence to return to his mountain home to read and think.

Alvin York took his Bible and favorite hunting dog to a hilltop, where he thought about the matter and prayed through the night for God to give him the answer to his dilemma. A Bible passage showed the way: "Render therefore unto Caesar the things that are Caesar's and unto God the things that are God's." With new understanding, he reported back to camp for full military duty.

Sergeant York's incredibly accurate turkey shooting with his long rifle made him a deadly infantryman and, as General Pershing put it, "the greatest civilian soldier of the war."

This moving story made a profound impression on me.

Beyond York's personal story of heroism was one of personal unselfishness. Rather than take fifty thousand dollars and a percentage of the gross profits that Dad had contracted to pay him for the screen rights to his story, he gave the full amount to complete a Bible school that he had started in his community of Jamestown (nicknamed "Jimtown"). Having been brought up in Hollywood's materialism, I was most impressed that anyone could be that dedicated and selfless for a cause. Such idealism, such altruism, such dedication to God, made a deeper and wider inroad into my consciousness and my future conduct than I could possibly have realized at the time.

Sergeant Alvin York proved eventually to be the second mustard seed in my life, joining with the first mustard seed—my precious governess, Mademoiselle Bernadette Branche.

Dad didn't have to ask me twice to go to Tennessee.

As soon as we arrived in the Valley of the Three Forks o' the Wolf, I learned why story problems existed.

The major problem stemmed from York himself—from his innate modesty and lack of desire to exalt himself with rich details about his life.

Alvin York knew that all things come from God—as Mademoiselle Branche had told me—and that the works of man amount to little in the magnificent universal scheme. When he invited Jesus into his life, his human ego decreased. It was more important for him to talk about God than about Alvin York.

We interviewed backwoods neighbors who had known Alvin since he was a boy, but their replies were laconic and devoid of the needed color, remarks such as "Alvin, he was always a good boy"—not film material.

Dad induced York to stage a turkey shoot, offering prizes of prime steers to the winners. Mountaineers from the entire area came to town. With my sixteen-millimeter camera, I filmed the shoot. Many story and visual qualities of the finished version of *Sergeant York* were based on characters and bits of business that we captured on film.

One highly individual characteristic of Alvin York emerged on film from the turkey shoot—a much-talked-about act that contributed to the Academy Award winning performance of Gary Cooper. Each time he prepared to shoot his Tennessee long rifle, he would wet his thumb and touch the sight. This was to reduce the sun's reflection on the sight so that he could draw a more accurate bead on his target.

Noted film director Howard Hawks adopted this unique characteristic for Gary Cooper's turkey shooting and later for the climax scene—the battle in which Sergeant York moistened the sights of his army rifle and, using twenty-eight bullets, hit twenty-eight German soldiers and captured the machine-gun nest.

With many story problems solved, we returned to Hollywood and Dad invited me to work on the picture: "Look, Bill," he said, "so far your motion picture experience has been limited to editing —to the finished product. Why not learn about production?"

It was too great an opportunity to miss. I would have a chance to see the filming of a screen story, to which I had made contributions, however minor; I would be working with Dad again, too, and I was excited about the prospect of meeting with Gary Cooper again.

My first day on the set of *Sergeant York*, at Warner Brothers Studios in Burbank, was even more hectic than my first day at Goldwyn's.

I had been hired as an apprentice assistant director—again at the bottom. I reported to my boss, the first assistant director, a hard-drinking Irishman with a flaring temper.

Before I had had a chance to introduce myself, he let me have it straight.

"Look, Lasky, I don't care whose son you are. I'm going to train you my way. Understand?"

I understood.

He would stand in the middle of the sound stage screaming orders at me. I had lived in an environment where I had never been talked to in this way before, so I didn't know how to act or react. All I knew was that I was eager to do everything to the best of my ability to please him. One thing I didn't want was to get fired from my own dad's picture. Whether this would have been possible, I never stopped to consider.

I had no idea what my job was. When you've never done something before, you have no pattern. In these days there was no school of instruction. There was no union or Screen Directors' Guild training program. It was learn as you go.

Every set has a minimum of two assistant directors. The first assistant stands by the director—in this instance, Howard Hawks—oversees the whole set, rolls the camera, and makes sure that the director's needs are always met. It is up to the second assistant director to do everything—to be the runner, the co-ordinator, the supplier, the requisitioner.

The second assistant has probably the roughest job on a motion picture company because if anything goes wrong, he's always the fall guy. He is responsible for all equipment and personnel—and for arranging to have them on the right sound stage or location at the right time. He sees that the cast has the right scene numbers to study and rehearse on the night before shooting, that the extras have the proper wardrobe for the day's shooting. He carries a tremendous responsibility.

An apprentice assistant director is the fall guy for the second assistant director—the place where the buck stops. So if anything is wrong with the second assistant director, he looks to the apprentice and says, "It's all *your* fault."

I never knew what fault was my fault and what fault I was being faulted for. When the second assistant would say, "It's Bill's fault," the first assistant would scream at me and launch a salvo of profanity. Not only did this make me sick in heart and soul, it made me sick in body, too.

More than once that first day, I went to the men's room to throw up. It wasn't a happy experience in one way. Yet, in another way, it was. How wonderful and exciting it was to see a screenplay brought to life on the sound stages—the sets, costumes, the cast (Gary Cooper, Joan Leslie, the lovely young star who played Alvin York's wife "Miss Gracie," and Dickie Moore, the boy star who played York's young brother).

Here was born my desire to write and direct screenplays, activities I would be pursuing for the rest of my life.

The company of *Sergeant York* was a large one with nearly a hundred-man crew, plus actors and actresses. Before shooting they would be chattering loudly, each group in their world. Director Howard Hawks, a lean six-foot-three figure, would sit slumped in his canvas-backed director's chair, looking somber, his heavy graying eyebrows meeting in annoyance over his prominently hooked nose. The effect was one of a fierce bird of prey.

Then the first assistant director would scream in a very loud voice that would disturb everybody, "Mr. Hawks wants quiet on the set."

Immediately the second assistant director would scream, "Mr. Hawks wants quiet on this set."

Then when it came my turn to yell, "Mr. Hawks wants quiet on the set," there was anything but quiet on the set. This routine went on at numerous intervals throughout the day. Mr. Hawks would not work until there was quiet on the set and the three of us had stopped shouting for quiet.

On the set I became aware of a very attractive young lady—a blue-eyed blonde with a lovely trim figure. I learned her name was Margery Lowe and that she was Mr. Hawks's efficient and valued personal assistant, serving as dialogue directress, secretary, special problem solver, and girl Friday for him. If somebody wanted to communicate with Mr. Hawks and make sure he received the message, he always went through Margery.

My excuse for talking to her was to pass on information to Mr. Hawks every day as to what scene or scenes we were planning to shoot on the next day, as well as related information he would need.

She must have sensed my confusion during those first hectic days and weeks and my deep desire to do a good job, because she was patient, kind, helpful, and understanding.

One day I got up enough courage to invite her to lunch. She informed me she had something tentative with the boy script supervisor but said, "Bill, I'd love to go with you."

It was raining hard, and I said, "Margery, I don't want you to get wet. I'll drive my car around to the sound stage entrance to pick you up."

Just as I wheeled up in my new DeSoto coupe—the first car I had ever bought with my own money (a salary of seventy-five a week)—the script supervisor came up to my car. I rolled down the window. He was angry and said, "Well, I know your kind! You're the kind of a person who has champagne and caviar in your refrigerator," and he turned on his heels.

Nothing could have been further from the truth. In my entire nineteen years, I had never tasted either champagne or caviar, but that was apparently his way of putting me down because Margery had chosen to lunch with me.

Margery and I laughed over this remark for many years to come. From then on, we had daily lunches in the Warner Brothers Studio commissary, and as I got to know her better, I sensed she was as lonely a person as I was.

She lived with her mother in a little house in Laurel Canyon. Her mother had been divorced for a number of years. Margery had grown up without a father and had been brought up very strictly. Every time she went out on a high school date, her mother accused her of all sorts of things that had never happened. So she had had a very unhappy and lonely childhood. She had come into the motion picture business right after graduation from high school and had quickly grown into this very responsible position with Howard Hawks.

It soon became apparent to me that I liked her more than just casually, and then a development at the studio led to our becoming even closer. A lady costumer on the picture, Jeanette Storch, owned a cabin in Crestline, a picturesque mountain resort just above the city of San Bernardino. Most of the young people on the set looked forward to the time when they would be invited to spend a weekend at the cabin.

As I became better acquainted on the set, I finally received a much-coveted invitation to be one of her guests. She said, "Bill, if you'd like to bring a date, that's fine with me."

Not only did I bring one girl. I brought two. I had been dating a vivacious and curvaceous brunette daughter of a famous film personality. Evalene was the epitome of what I thought a date should be—mysterious, flashy, witty, and desirable. I was attracted to her in a wild, kicking-up-my-heels, cha-cha-cha sort of way. It happened that I was a better than average dancer, loved Latin music, and Evalene was a fabulous dancer. So far as Marge was concerned, I didn't even know if she could dance, but I was attracted to her in a much more serious way because, though she was less flashy than Evalene, she seemed more mature and dependable. So, as I have often done in my life, I put my foot in my mouth and asked Marge to go, too.

Now that I had a second date, I had to square things with Evalene.

"Evalene," I said, "I hope this won't hurt your feelings, but I have this friend on the set—a quiet, businesslike girl—and I've asked her to go with us. Do you mind?"

She didn't.

We three drove up to the cabin in Evalene's fire-engine-red convertible, and she was bubbling with energy and fun.

Once we got to the cabin, I learned by accident that Evalene's continual effervescence resulted from Benzedrine rather than natural sources. I had never been interested in anything such as pep pills and really didn't even know what Benzedrine was until much later.

When dinner was over and Jeanette and other studio guests were doing the dishes, Evalene and I danced to some of my favorite Xavier Cugat records I had brought. Margery sat quietly on the couch patiently watching. I don't remember how many dances Evalene and I had, but I was enjoying them all when I became aware that Evalene was becoming heavier on her feet, slowing down, subdued. Then when I wanted to continue dancing, she became irritable and wanted to rest.

Evalene curled up on the couch and was soon fast asleep, and it was then that Margery blossomed out. We started to dance, and what a dancer she was! In a minute, we had been transformed into a dance team that threatened the theatrical supremacy of Fred Astaire and Ginger Rogers. Her presence was magic to me, and we seemed to float across the cabin floor. It was ecstasy and, for some reason, I thought of my mother's story of how she and Dad had danced together the first night that they had met at Long Lake.

One of my favorite records came up next, a slow number, "The Girl That I Marry." The mountain cabin, the flickering candlelight, all added to a mood of romance. I have never experienced such tenderness as when I held Margery in my arms.

"Let's take a walk, Marge," I said impulsively.

The moon was almost full and gave a silver sheen to the Douglas firs and the lodgepole pines. Only when Marge stumbled and I quickly caught her did I realize she was in high heels. I had to hold her arm to steady her.

High heels!

Again my mind went back to my mother's story of her and

Dad's walk in the mountains. Mother had also worn the wrong thing for hiking—high heels.

There seemed to be so many similarities between what had happened to Mother and Dad and what was happening to *my* Margie and me.

"*My* Margie," I almost said aloud.

We came upon a large flat rock in a majestic pine setting and sat under the trees to talk—just as Mother and Dad had before their marriage.

We talked for what seemed only minutes but proved to be hours.

"You know, Bill, I must confess to you I've been lonely all of my life," Margie said. "I never really have had a steady boyfriend."

Her loneliness was like an echo of my own, and my arm was around her waist before I realized it. I drew her to me.

"Never until now," I replied, and an overwhelming desire came over me to fill her lonely void with all the love within me.

"Loneliness is something I understand, too, Marge. I've always had it—always until now. I do love you, Marge."

We kissed tenderly, holding each other tightly. I don't know how long we held one another, but suddenly we realized it was getting late and we began to wonder where we were going to sleep. As far as we knew, Evalene was still crashed on the couch.

"Wouldn't it be romantic if we slept in our sleeping bags under the pines and stars?" I asked.

"Oh, Bill, that would be great!" Marge replied.

And so we did, talking, kissing, talking, and finally sleeping until we were awakened by a concert of birds—blue jays, chickadees, and nuthatches.

When we returned to the set Monday, somebody had told Howard Hawks that we had slept in our sleeping bags at Crestline. Howard had a wry sense of humor. He called attention to those on the set. Everybody was listening, and everybody knew that we had spent the weekend at Jeanette's cabin.

"Margery, come over here," Howard said. "I want to talk to you."

"Yes, Mr. Hawks," she replied, poised with her steno pad and pencil ready.

He continued, "Margery, I have accepted a contract to direct a very distinguished motion picture based on a Hemingway novel, *For Whom the Bell Tolls*, and Ingrid Bergman and Gary Cooper play a scene that I think you can help me with. They sleep in sleeping bags, and I understand you had some experience this weekend that could help me write and direct the scene."

Margery turned a violent red and ran off the set. Later we laughed about what Mr. Hawks had said.

At this time I was ecstatically happy in having found this new companionship and love of Margery and next I introduced her to my snakes, falcons, and other pets. She not only accepted them but began to feel a strong affection for them, and her interest in my unusual hobbies brought us even closer. She had a favorite animal of her own—a lovable black long-eared cocker spaniel named Topsy.

For many months, Margery and I worked together on *Sergeant York*. Soon it got so that when we had to be apart on an occasional evening, we would spend a great deal of time wishing we were together—or talking on the phone.

"Marge," I said, "being apart from one another at any time seems kind of ridiculous. Let's get married."

Her warm embrace told me she felt the same as I did.

Both Bess and Dad objected mildly. They agreed that Margery was a lovely girl, but I was only nineteen, this was my first close relationship with any girl, and they had had in mind my marrying a daughter of another prominent Hollywood family.

"I've made up my mind," I told them. "Margery is the girl for me, the *only* girl for me, and she always will be."

My determination settled things, and we were married. Fred Gates was the best man. Margery and I had decided to have our honeymoon at Yosemite National Park, a wonderland of pines and pure white snow in this winter season.

Marge wasn't a ski enthusiast, but I didn't want to miss the skiing opportunities of Yosemite. At this point, I made my first mistake with her. In my boyish enthusiasm and thoughtlessness, I said, "Marge, I think it would be a good idea if Fred came to Yosemite Lodge to ski with me when you and I are not together."

I have never seen a face gather such thunderclouds as Marge's did. Her unspoken look seemed to say, "Am I marrying a boy or a husband?" Then she said in an ominous, controlled manner, "Bill, if *he* goes on our honeymoon, I'm not and that's final."

Fred didn't.

Despite my horrible blunder, our honeymoon in this winter paradise was idyllic. We took hand-in-hand moonlight walks to the Firefall and ski slopes, and we even skied together. One night when gentle snow was falling, we walked until our jackets were white and we looked like animated snow men.

Then we went back into the cheerful warmth of the lodge, shed our coats, and sat before a roaring fireplace. We talked and talked like people in love, because we were people in love. In our minds and in our words, the unlimited future before us unreeled. Our warm and lingering dream was too pleasant to let us think of the war threat that hung over us, our nation, and much of the world.

11

Everything from A to Z— Army to Zoo

From the dazzling heights of the glorious mountain and our honeymoon, we eventually came down to ground level and our new little rented home in West Los Angeles. It was ready and waiting for us, but so was Margery's mother and bad news.

"Guess what?" she asked Margery.

"*What?*"

"Your dog Topsy has been run over and is dead. I took Topsy for a walk on her leash, and she stepped off the curb into the street and a car killed her."

Margery was furious and then overcome with grief. It was a sad homecoming that destroyed the mountain magic.

On top of this, the next morning Marge eagerly offered to prepare breakfast for me, although her mother had never allowed her to cook.

"Wonderful," I said.

She unwrapped a wedding gift, a waffle iron, but she was in such a hurry to make a good breakfast for her new husband she didn't read the directions.

Without oiling the new waffle iron, she turned it on, mixed the batter, and poured it in. The batter cemented the waffle iron shut, and even with hammer and chisel I couldn't open it. Amid Margery's tears, we had to throw the whole thing out.

To cheer my bride up, I decided to get her another dog. Without telling her my intentions, I asked her to take a ride with me. Our destination was Stockdale Kennels, where we reviewed a bevy of beautiful baby cocker spaniels. One black-and-white puppy with long Theda Bara lashes and such long ears that she would step on them and fall over was the star of the group. Marge took one look at this puppy, and it was love at sight. She just had to have Susy.

The rumbles of war in Europe had become louder, and I joined the National Guard, where I received military training and took part in monthly drills and guard duty in the Los Angeles Exposition Park Armory.

Shortly after December 7, the day that Pearl Harbor was bombed by the Japanese, I was drafted into the U. S. Army.

It was then that another negative event took place in our young married life. I was inducted in downtown Los Angeles before being transferred to Fort MacArthur in San Pedro.

Orders were for us to get very short G.I. haircuts. My wavy brown hair ended up on the barbershop floor and my nearly bald head made me look like a convict in one of the numerous Warner Brothers prison films. I will never forget the incident that started Marge's dislike for the service.

I phoned her to ask her to hurry down to the Union Station in Los Angeles if she could. "We can have a few minutes together before our group is sent to Fort MacArthur."

Soon she was at the station where I spotted her among hundreds of soldiers and civilians. She took one look at my shorn head and cried out, "What have they *done* to you?"

The tears flowed down her cheeks.

It was a terrible time. Most young people in uniform lived with a combination of suspense and fear. With Hitler's hordes conquering most of Europe and the Japanese taking island after island in the Pacific, no serviceman knew whether he would ever come back to those he loved.

Even though Marge and I had realized from the beginning that there was a good chance of our being separated by war, we still suffered the agony of parting that is experienced by two people deeply in love.

"Marge, dearest," I said when the train for Fort MacArthur was about to leave, "I've got a problem." I was concerned about my falcon, Danny, from whom I had never been away for more than a few days in the several years I had owned him. "Marge, please take care of Danny as I would."

"Bill, you can count on it. He's a part of you that's still with me."

She had learned the procedure of feeding Danny fresh meat on her fist and other routines—the special way to bathe him and to take him in and out of doors, but we never thought she would have to do it by herself. I loved her even more for taking on this difficult task so willingly.

My parting words to her were, "I'll send for you, Susy, and Danny as soon as I'm permanently based."

We kissed good-by, and as the train pulled out, I felt a wave of loneliness. Here Marge had come into my life to heal my loneliness, and now that ache was deeper than ever.

From the fullness of satisfaction and love from the most beautiful person who had ever come into my world, I was thrown into a mob of men whom I didn't know and didn't care to know. I didn't realize then that many of them were farther away from home than I, just as painfully separated from loved ones and suffering the same inner agonies as I.

That first night I was in the barracks with a conglomerate of men from every possible area of life. I had never been with more than a half dozen persons anywhere but on a sound stage. I felt uncomfortable and unable to adjust. I lay on my cot amid clouds of cigarette smoke, staring at the ceiling and listening to guys loudly playing poker, somebody telling of his conquest of a girl, and everywhere there was swearing and four-letter words. My life had been sheltered. I couldn't be a part of the men and the service, and yet here I was a part of it.

I thought of Marge, our honeymoon and early weeks of marriage, of Susy, Danny, and the studios, of Dad and Bess, and a wave of loneliness engulfed me.

Eventually lights were out, and I lay awake for hours, listening to the snores. I felt I could not endure one more minute of this desperate loneliness.

Suddenly I heard a sound that I recognized: the honking of geese. I was in my sleeping clothes—my shorts and T-shirt—and impulsively ran outside. I looked up, and there was a sight I will never forget—a long V formation of migrating Canada geese flying across the pale moon. Their honking was like a personal message for me. Though I had been separated from all the human beings that were dear to me, I still had contact with some of God's beautiful creatures. It was as if their very being was a reassurance that, really, all was right with the world and I wasn't quite as alone as I had felt. I went back inside the barracks, and it seemed, with this gift, that the Army became a little easier for me to accept.

Upon transfer to Joplin, Missouri, for infantry basic training and rifle range markmanship qualification, I suddenly felt the reality of war impacted upon my mind.

I was going to have to kill people!

The thought was sickening. All my life, I had had a close relationship with animals and had what Dr. Albert Schweitzer called "a reverence for life."

If I ever made a thoughtless remark that hurt someone, I suffered more than he did. How could I point a gun at anyone, let alone shoot to kill? For some reason, I remembered my father's story of his Alaskan gold adventure and how he could not shoot at a man who had stolen all of his money. Also, the influence of the young Sergeant York added weight to this feeling.

At Fort MacArthur, I had read about Captain Poutrey's Pigeoneers, a branch of the Army Signal Corps, which had newly developed two-way pigeons—something that didn't exist in World War I. Pigeons were trained to go to an objective and then return to their lofts.

The idea intrigued me—as did an article I had read about "The Kaiser," a carrier pigeon still alive from World War I action and a mascot of the Pigeoneers.

My Army Form 20 was packed with information about my bird and animal training—along with movie experience—and finally I was able to arrange a transfer to the Pigeoneers, who were based in Joplin.

It would be a joy to handle birds again. Danny, my falcon, was the last one I had been near. After three months of basic Signal Corps training, I finally got into actual Pigeoneer work and found that even "The Kaiser" wasn't all that glamorous. The training of two-way pigeons went to noncoms, and as a private I got a full-time job, day in and day out, of cleaning cage after cage of pigeon droppings. I never before realized how productive pigeons can be.

Word had come through about the need for laboratory technicians at the Army's Fitzsimmons General Hospital in Denver, Colorado, and I talked to my commanding officer about releasing me for a more skilled occupation in keeping with my experience. I was surprised that he was agreeable.

After transfer to Fitzsimmons General, I found I had to go through basic training all over again—this time for the Medical Department. But I had made contact with a career army bacteriologist, Colonel Hugh Mahon, a fine and dedicated man, and, filling him in on my background with animals, told him I wanted to join his outfit as a lab technician.

"Lasky," he said, "I would like very much to have you with us, but first you'll have to pass a rough six-week course."

This crash course showed me that I would have to learn the subject in which I had been weakest in high school—math, chemistry, and physics. I was eager to pass and studied night and day. I had the hope that if I completed the course successfully, Marge could join me.

The day of the final test came, and it was far worse than I had feared. I was almost sure I had failed, but when the test results were announced I had passed—near the bottom of the class. Added to the reward of a promised position with Colonel Mahon's laboratory was the joy that now nothing prevented me from having Margery with me in Denver.

A telephone call was all she needed. She told her shocked boss, Howard Hawks, that he must understand—her husband had to come first. Marge was kidded on the set about giving up a Hawks for a hawk. Packing Susy and Danny in the DeSoto, she drove to Denver, joining me.

Another reward for success was my promotion to corporal, which allowed me living quarters for Marge on the base. It was almost like civilian life with a military job, a vast improvement from barracks life, which I never learned to like.

Following several months of army base living, we bought a little house, and life took on a much brighter luster.

Colonel Mahon noted my lifelong hobby of collecting butterflies and, needing a special research study of the mosquitoes of Denver, gave me the coveted job with the remark, "Lasky, a bug is a bug. If you can collect butterflies, you can collect mosquitoes."

My trapping and tramping turned up several species of mosquitoes that were new to Denver. A highlight of three years of this work was the discovery of malaria-carrying mosquitoes which were not known to be present. This discovery shocked my army supervisors and served to raise my status to a sergeant.

How were the Denver mosquitoes infected with malaria?

Many of the windows of Fitzsimmons General had no screens. We had a malaria ward for treatment of soldiers from jungle war areas. Mosquitoes would bite these men, filling their bodies with blood infected with malaria organisms, and posed a serious threat to other soldiers and to the Denver population.

A combination of my interest in my new-found army career, recognition from the service, and my promotion to sergeant—easing our financial situation—helped Marge adjust to being an army wife. However, she never did adjust to army routine and the fact that the Army came first.

Yet we did have a number of happy times together in Denver, where our son, Ronnie, was born.

At the time of Ronnie's birth, I was working in the hospital on my mosquito survey and as a laboratory technician. Both Marge and I loved our modest Denver home and the old, legend-filled city of Denver, the ever-blue skies, clean invigorating air, and the wide-open prairie around the city—land where rabbits and pheasants were still plentiful—and the friendly neighbors who took the young Laskys into their hearts.

Late one afternoon toward the end of Marge's pregnancy, we were both at home when I heard her in the shower.

"Marge," I said, "why are you taking a shower at this time of day?"

She normally showered in the morning or just before going to bed.

"Bill," she replied, "you'd better get a bag of things ready for me, if you don't mind. We're going to the hospital."

"Why are we going back there?" I naïvely asked. I was thinking more of mosquitoes and hawks.

"My sac is broken, and I want to be clean before I go in to have our baby. I'd like to do my toenails, but the baby's in the way. I can't quite reach them. Will you do them for me?"

"Marge," I replied sharply, "the sac is broken and you want to do your toenails! You'd better finish that shower and get dressed!"

"Bill, everything's going to be all right. Just take it easy."

Marge's very calmness seemed to make me more jittery, so jittery I don't remember what clothing I threw into a small suitcase for her. All I remember was that I clashed the car gears as I backed out of the driveway to pick her up.

I got her checked into the maternity ward and went to Colonel Mahon, my commanding officer.

"Colonel, I would like to have emergency duty tonight, because my baby will be born any time now. It would be convenient for me to sleep right in the emergency room of the hospital. They can call me from the maternity ward, and I can attend my wife if necessary."

That was fine with the colonel. All night long, the hours seemed to creep by. I couldn't sleep for worry about Marge and the baby. Finally, about 6 A.M. I had just decided to have a quick bite of breakfast when the phone rang.

It was a nurse from the maternity ward who said, "Sergeant Lasky, your baby has just been born, and everything is fine. It's a boy."

I was so excited, all I could say was "Oh, boy! Oh, boy!"

My curiosity then began to gnaw at me.

"Tell me quickly," I said. "Does he have blue eyes and red hair?"

"As a matter of fact, he does," replied the nurse, "but how did you know?"

"I didn't. That's what I told my wife I wanted," I responded.

Well, as so frequently happens with babies, both the red hair and the blue eyes changed to brown.

I couldn't wait a second longer. "When can I see him?"

"Just give us a little time to clean him up. Come to the nursery in about an hour."

That hour turned out to be longer than my whole sleepless night. Finally, I ran up to the nursery, where—unknown to me—it was feeding time. Mothers were encouraged to leave their beds and walk down to the nursery, where they would breast-feed their babies. Soldiers were not allowed in the area during feeding times, but my white lab technician's gown was my open-sesame. As I came rushing in to see my baby, there was a rustle and the young mothers attempted to cover up.

Trying to put them at ease, in my excitement I blurted out, "Oh, ladies, please don't mind me. My-my-my baby has just been born, and I'm going to be doing *that* myself soon."

This caused such an uproar in the hospital that the *Army Times* ran a short feature story about the nervous sergeant who blundered into the nursery and predicted that he would soon be nursing a baby himself!

I couldn't wait to see my baby, so I rushed to the window behind which there were several infants. I picked the prettiest baby I could find and signaled to the nurse for confirmation. She shook her head and pointed to one that was all red and shriveled and horrible-looking and nodded that *that* was my baby. I had to adjust my thinking, but in no more than an instant even the red and shriveled one began looking beautiful to me.

That was how our Ronnie came into the world. Because I loved animals and birds so much, I wanted my son to share my love for them, so our house was always like a small zoo.

It was a pleasant coincidence to me that while Ronnie was just learning to toddle in our sunny back yard, we had fledgling prairie falcons just learning to fly. He always did love birds and a gopher snake named Tigro II that I caught for him.

Around the age of two, when most kids had floating bathtub toys, Ronnie had four-foot Tigro as his bathing companion. Marge was somewhat dubious about the whole business, but she was a good sport once she was sure the snake wouldn't hurt Ronnie.

Early in his childhood, I taught him how to make a noose to catch lizards, how to net butterflies, and, at the Gunnison River, how to fish when he was hardly old enough to hold a rod in his tiny hands, and he admired and loved our peregrine falcon, Danny, which Marge had brought to me in Denver.

I was elated that Ronnie seemed to love all creatures of nature as much as I did—and that he was getting an even earlier start at it than I had.

One of the disquieting elements of army life was that Marge never accepted the service, especially my being a part of it.

Even the plaudits that I had received from my mosquito study were only a temporary satisfaction for her. She missed Hollywood, her job, and the creative atmosphere of the studios, although her adjustment to motherhood and domestic life was wonderful. Many times money became a little tight, and Dad would send us a generous check, but our financial limitations and stresses resulted in a few disagreements. But nothing on earth is forever. The war ended and my separation from the service followed.

After being discharged, I took Marjorie and Ronnie back to Los Angeles where Dad, to make our transition to civilian life easier, had given us a free apartment in a large complex he owned in an older part of the city on Coronado Street.

I became depressed with the new environment of the apartment—amid smog and pavement, which were the replacement for clear skies and animal-filled prairies. Instead of the beautiful vista of the Rocky Mountains to begin the day with, I was surrounded with high-rises, dirty, old gray buildings—the vista of the city.

Added to all of this was the shock of learning that my parents were considering a divorce. Each one tried to make me understand his and her individual positions, and I felt torn in half. I was attempting to assume my mature responsibilities as a husband, and they were pulling me back to being a child and an umpire over their differences.

My army work had been absorbing, pleasant, and secure, and I had no such promise in the uncertainty of motion picture work.

"Marge," I said, weighing army career against past civilian life, "I've decided to become a zoologist. To do that I have to go to college."

Her facial expression showed concern.

"What about money?"

"The G.I. Bill will help, and maybe I can work a little, too."

She sighed deeply. "We've just had five long army years—five years of very low income, and now you want four more. When are you going to stop preparing?"

"Marge, I can't succeed in zoology without a college degree."

Again she sighed.

"I don't like the prospect, Bill, but I'll go along with it, if you feel this is really the career you want to pursue."

Immediately I phoned Bob Stapler, a respected falconer with whom I had corresponded for some time. Bob was a professor of zoology at Swarthmore College near Philadelphia. I told him of my decision to earn a zoology degree.

"Great, Bill," he said. "Why don't you come to Swarthmore? We have a fine zoology department. I can guide your progress. We can fly our falcons together, and our wives and children can be friends. We'll help you find a home, too."

I went by myself on an exploratory mission to Philadelphia. I liked the school, Bob Stapler, his wife and their farm, and eastern life. It was all new, attractive, and fascinating.

Within several weeks, Marge, Ronnie, and I were together again. With the money left from the sale of our Denver house, we put a down payment on a comfortable home in Media, near the Philadelphia suburb of Glen Mills.

Everything would have been beautiful, but Marge, California-born, didn't care for Philadelphia, or my role as a student rather than a money-earner, or the nebulous career prospects when I would graduate. She had married an assistant director with an infinite potential for a rise in an industry she knew so well. Underneath all of these objections was her loneliness for her native state, her career job, and the friends from whom she had been separated through the army years.

I began to slip in favor with her. I shall always admire her for the good sport she tried to be, despite her objections to our new life.

Our financial problems started to pile up. We had to go to my father repeatedly for help, and he was always generous.

"Bill, your dad shouldn't have to contribute to our support," Marge would remark, and I sensed the beginning of a coolness and critical attitude that had never before existed between us.

A considerable number of years had passed since my last formal schooling—in high school and for my crash course to qualify for a lab technician—and it wasn't easy for me to adapt to a study routine. Doubt set in from the very start.

I found the academic life difficult, but I couldn't admit to another mistake and quit before a fair trial. The stress and strain of math, chemistry, and physics grew like evil genies, and I was soon far behind my class and daily growing more apprehensive.

Late one afternoon, I returned home from campus, discouraged and depressed. I had just received my test grades: an A in zoology but failing grades in math, chemistry, and physics, the same old bugaboos.

Margery couldn't help noting my low mood and asked what was the problem.

"Math, chemistry, and physics, as usual, Dad and Mother's marital problems, and the constant lack of enough money to pay our bills."

"I could work, Bill, but that would mean paying for a full-time sitter for Ronnie. At your age, you should be able to meet our financial responsibilities and give us the support we need. You're an adult now but still playing the role of a schoolboy. When will you grow up?"

There it was right on the line.

"What do you mean by that, Marge?" I stammered. My mouth was dry.

"Well, first I was married to a young boy with a big future, then a soldier and—just when I thought my husband was going into a substantial career—I find I'm married to a boy again, a college student who isn't bringing in enough money."

It was her lack of anger and her deep sense of disappointment that hurt me most. How I wanted her to be proud of me! How I wished I could be what she wanted me to be!

Obviously she wanted an older and more mature man, somebody she could lean on rather than someone who put heavy burdens on her. Lack of money seemed to be tangible proof that I was not mature and responsible. Then a chill began to prickle the hair on my arms and legs—a horrible thought. A specter from my childhood rose up. I was afraid that the growing differences between us might lead to separate bedrooms as they had with Mother and Dad. Quickly I tried to kill the thought before its implications could overwhelm me.

Problems began to avalanche upon me until soon I began to feel that hundreds of tons of snow were burying me and cutting off my breathing. This sensation of suffocation and hysteria carried over into my classrooms. How could I learn when I couldn't even breathe? The voice of the instructor faded in and out.

One negative thought would build on another, and the accumulation was crushing:

"Where are we going to get this month's house payment? If I ask Mother or Dad, one of them will send a check, but then there will be certain strings attached, certain obligations, involvement in their lives. . . . I wonder if Marge could leave me and take Ronnie? . . . Not that! . . . Wonder how I'll do on the math exam. I can't afford to fail and have to take it again. Oh no, that would mean even more schooling than four years."

I tried private tutors, but that didn't help. In all lecture classes, I was soon listening to my inner thoughts and concerns and missing important information. It was growing impossible. I would sit in the tests and panic, unable to finish.

Only one course of action seemed open for me: to give up college and return to Hollywood and the motion picture business. College had been a failure, but in consolation Marge was obviously delighted to return to Southern California.

The Coronado apartment was no longer available. Dad had sold it to pay off debts, so we moved into a guest room of my mother's Saltair home. Here our problems pyramided, magnified by those of my parents, and a growing separation between Marge and them.

How could I solve my parents' marital problems when I couldn't even solve my own?

Fortunately, this situation was only temporary. We soon moved into a little home that we bought in Santa Monica. Once more, Dad helped us with the down payment, which contributed more to our marital tension and caused Marge to remark, "I feel more married to your father than to you." The Santa Monica house had a beautiful yard, backed by several redwood trees—ideal for Ronnie, the falcons, and Susy.

I returned to work as an assistant director on several motion pictures but was always haunted by the frustrated desire to be a zoologist. Then one day, while visiting the San Diego Zoo, I learned that a keeper of the reptile house was quitting. What a temptation! Perhaps even without college, I could become a Dr. Ditmars. I was accepted for the job and planned to move to San Diego when the opening closed as fast as it had presented itself, but I was left with one shred of hope. If I could work at one zoo, why not another?

So, following a heart-to-heart talk with my old friend Charlie Allen, then director of the Los Angeles Griffith Park Zoo, I was offered a job as an animal keeper. Though it was a lowly job, I was finally working in the field of zoology that I had desired for so long. Dreams of expeditions to collect rare animals filled my troubled nights.

As moderate as the pay was, Marge went along with this job for the three years I was there. Our home was constantly filled with falcons, snakes, lizards—animals of all kinds that Ronnie enjoyed. And I believe that a good part of the force that held our marriage together was Ronnie's sharing of my deepest interests.

Returning to California hadn't helped our marriage. Compounding everything, we made the terrible mistake of letting Marge's mother, who had no means of support, come to share our home.

Then came catastrophes at the zoo.

First, a chimpanzee that was in my care for the day escaped. The lock on the cage had been left unlocked either by me or by another keeper. There was no way to know for sure, but the resulting bad publicity for the city gave me a serious demerit.

A few weeks after this, one of the pythons, for which I was responsible, mysteriously escaped from its cage—a cage that I was sure had been locked. The snake was discovered on a zoo walkway by a reasonably hysterical zoo visitor, who threatened lawsuit. I was called up again and this time was asked to resign.

Completely heartbroken—my world of hopes and dreams shattered—I had no choice but to comply and, besides, although I doubted my own negligence, in my upset frame of mind, I could have been guilty of these oversights.

So, once more, I was without a job or means of supporting my family.

Then something happened that temporarily helped. Dad strongly urged me to return to the motion picture business and give it all I had. The opportunity that presented itself would accomplish just that, but in a unique way would combine my love and knowledge of eagles with the making of a motion picture.

If the plan succeeded, I felt I could even regain Marge's respect.

With a friend, Dan Mannix, who is one of the nation's most renowned animal authors and trainers, I decided that I would make a film about an eagle. The idea was born when I visited with Dan and his wife, Jewel, at their Malibu Beach home and became acquainted with their wonderful trained eagle, Aguilar.

I felt confident that I could produce, direct, write, and even film a picture. It would be a challenge to make a dramatic half-hour film in sixteen millimeter and then sell it to a major motion picture company which would blow it up to thirty-five millimeter, score it, dub it, and release it in theaters as a featurette.

The Boy and the Eagle was born, and the story went like this: A boy who is crippled from polio finds a crippled eagle in the Malibu hills of Southern California.

During the boy's slow recovery from polio, he has lost confidence that he will ever walk without a leg brace. Doctors have told him he can walk if he will only try.

His hobby is watching birds, whose grace and movement in flight he admires—especially because of his restricted ability to move. One day he sees a tremendous bald eagle, wounded by a gunshot, floundering on the ground. He rescues the bird and nurses her back to health, feeding and training her. Once the eagle is well, she is ready to return to her life in the wild. While contemplating whether to let the eagle go, the boy is walking up a hill carrying the eagle on his fist. He stumbles, and the eagle flies to a nearby rock. The boy slides down a dirt embankment landing within striking distance of a coiled rattlesnake.

The eagle sizes up the situation and flies to attack the snake. Blows from her talons distract the snake long enough to save the boy's life. Realizing that the snake is still a potential danger to the eagle, the boy takes his crutch to help his friend. He forgets that he can't walk and does so, using the crutch as a weapon to do away with the rattlesnake and return his friend's favor by saving her life.

As he throws the snake over the embankment, he looks at the crutch and—for the first time—realizes he no longer needs it to walk.

I had met and become a close friend of Dickie Moore on the set of *Sergeant York*. When I told him about my planned picture, he offered to play the crippled boy for an equal share of the profits, and I agreed. We used Dan Mannix's Aguilar to play Aguilar.

Many funny things happened around the making of the picture. For one, I needed a rattlesnake to play the rattlesnake, and it was a year when there just weren't any rattlesnakes available. I tried all of the animal dealers and looked in every conceivable place but couldn't find one. Then, to my amazement while in the Malibu hills scouting for a location to shoot the eagle and the snake sequence, I saw a beautiful, large black rattlesnake sunning itself on the road in front of my car.

There he was, ready, just as if he knew I needed him—as if he had wanted to be cast for the film. So I caught him and decided to try out the eagle around the snake to see how they would work together. The eagle was too valuable a bird to risk. For this reason, I had to take extreme precautions with the snake to protect Aguilar from a possible fatal accident. I actually stitched the snake's mouth shut. (This didn't hurt it any, for these reptiles do not have any feeling in their lips, but now it couldn't open its mouth to bite the eagle. Of course, as soon as I finished shooting with the snake, I removed the stitching and returned him to the hills.)

What happened when we tested the snake and Aguilar together? Not what we expected. The eagle went into hysterics. She wouldn't behave at all like a normal eagle, and I had to experiment to see if she would act properly with a stuffed snake. I had a rope and an old snakeskin and fixed up a dummy snake. Again Aguilar went into a tizzy. Anything that even looked like a snake from then on frightened her—including even the bare rope. Here was this big killer eagle that was terrified by the snake she was supposed to attack. It was like a comical story premise straight out of a Disney film!

I finally got an inspiration for solving the problem. On paper I diagrammed the shots I needed—the eagle flying at the snake, landing on him, trampling him with her feet, and then flying off to the side while the boy gets the crutch to help out his friend, the eagle. Well, the first sequence was the hardest: a long shot of the eagle flying and landing on the snake. There was a way to fool the eagle, but I could use it only once.

I placed the snake at the base of a large rock, where the eagle couldn't see him from where she was sitting. Then directly in front of the snake and also just in front of the rock, I put a nice juicy piece of meat. The camera was set up and ready.

I whistled for the eagle as soon as the camera was rolling, and she flew toward the piece of meat, landing just where I wanted her to—on top of the rattlesnake. She was so surprised and panicky at seeing the snake underfoot and in such a hurry to get off that it looked as if she were trampling the reptile.

That was fine as a quick sequence, but I needed additional footage of her actually trampling the snake. I took Aguilar and held her just out of the camera frame, literally throwing her at the snake on the ground. Every time she would land on the snake, she would rise on her tiptoes like a ballet dancer to get off in a hurry, lifting her feet up and down, but looking as if she were trampling the snake.

After four of such sequences, Aguilar was hardly fit to work with anymore, but I had got the necessary footage.

I took the rough cut movie to the major film companies in New York City, and got a cash offer for it from RKO-Pathé for the original film.

The Boy and the Eagle was released, and without my knowing it, RKO submitted the picture as a contender for an Academy

Award. One day I received a telegram from the Motion Picture Aademy of Arts and Sciences, inviting me to attend the award ceremonies and to be prepared to give an acceptance speech. *The Boy and the Eagle* had received the most votes on the preliminary count of the viewing committee and was a potential winner.

When my father read this wire, he was thrilled, and he got a family party together. Everyone forgot his personal problems, including me in my rented black tuxedo and white tie. We went to the Pantages Theater on Hollywood Boulevard where the Academy Awards were then held.

As it happened, I didn't win, though I later learned that *The Boy and the Eagle* had come in second in the balloting. Dad was even more happy and proud than when he had received an Academy Award nomination for *Sergeant York*. Clapping me on the back, he said, "You see, Bill it runs in the family."

But all of this seemed relatively unimportant compared with the look of pride in Marge's eyes and the hugs that were her award.

My stock at home began to rise again—not only from the nomination for an Academy Award, but also from the money made by the film. Now there seemed to be a promise of far bigger and better things to come from my Hollywood film efforts.

12

Crisis at Notre Dame

Good things supposedly come in threes, but bad things seem to come in droves.

There had been more than a little friction in my marriage up to this time—mostly arising from my having been immature when I married and having failed to mature rapidly enough during marriage to assume a man's responsibilities.

A shortage of money is usually a rough sandpaper on the skin of a marriage, and my limited earning power while in the service and also at Swarthmore had been an abrasive and, even more, a constant reminder of my inadequacy as a provider. This friction seemed about to be relieved when—as a complete surprise—I received a phone call from an executive of the DuMont Television Network in New York, asking if I was available for a film assignment.

Would I be interested in writing and directing a seven-part documentary on the University of Notre Dame to be shown between halves of the Fighting Irish's televised football games?

"Yes," I said in the understatement of the year, and the man explained further.

The series' main objective was to show that non-Catholics, as well as Catholics, are welcome at the university as students and are an integral part of its multiple curricular activities.

What an opportunity, I exulted to myself. Like my father, I believed that after the typhoon, there's a period of delightful calm, and here was proof: first, *The Boy and the Eagle* and now this outstanding possibility.

The promised salary was excellent. More than this, it was my first opportunity to write and direct for a major company. Eager to comply with DuMont's requirements, I failed to consider whether the brief five-week schedule was realistic and signed their contract. Now I would be earning the kind of money that Marge and I always felt I should. Our marriage would improve, and my film career would advance into the hoped-for creative channel.

Well, that was what *I* thought.

On the eve of my flight's departure for South Bend, Indiana, the location of Notre Dame, where the series was to be written and filmed, I received a phone call from Bess, who was distraught because she had just learned that my father was keeping company with a young mistress. Bess was considering divorce as the only possible solution to their off-and-on marriage.

She asked me to her home on Saltair for a heart-to-heart talk. I told her of my assignment, saying I would see her for a few minutes on the way to the airport. No sooner had I hung up when the phone rang again. This time it was my father. He said he had a matter to discuss with me in the utmost confidence, and he was trusting me not to reveal this to my mother.

He told me he had met a beautiful young woman who shared his love of the motion picture business, someone who would accompany him to night clubs and who could be a real buddy to him. He knew I loved him and could only wish what was best for him. He asked me to meet with him and his wonderful new friend that very night. He was so enthusiastic and joyful that it was hard for me to tell him I had got the offer from DuMont and was leaving almost immediately.

"Why don't you phone me at Notre Dame?" I asked, and he agreed.

As I hung up, I felt totally inadequate to handle the middleman role.

All my life—ever since boyhood at the Santa Monica beach house—I had been constantly reminded of my parents having separate quarters, going their separate ways, living separate lives. I loved both of them and was completely distressed at being forced into a position of taking sides or of acting as an amateur marriage counselor. At this point, they both claimed that they wanted to go their separate ways to provide themselves with happiness. I felt selfish in wanting them to stay together.

How could I possibly handle this situation? Where could I turn for advice? Somehow I had to face this and at the same time face the huge challenge of my own—the many unknowns of any film project that requires first-rate writing and directing. I wondered how I could achieve both successfully.

Finishing my packing, I walked to the door with my two large pieces of luggage and said good-by to Marge. I hugged her and attempted to kiss her.

"Attempted" is the right word. We kissed, but there was a coldness in her response. I wanted to say something about it, but I knew that airplanes wait for no one, and besides, I had to stop for a few minutes at Bess's home.

Bess greeted me at the entrance way and asked me into the rose garden. It was here that she wanted this important heart-to-heart talk—among the roses, her closest friends.

"Billy, I know you're in a hurry, but I must tell you about your father. It's in the strictest confidence. For the past month your father has been acting very strangely. He seems guilty and embarrassed whenever we're together."

I began to feel embarrassed myself, as I thought of the information Dad had confided to me.

"You know, Billy, I want what's best for your father, but he's staying out every night until all hours of the morning. That isn't good for him. He is drinking more than he has at any time of his life. Recently he has had several accidents in his car. Only a few days ago, he got a speeding ticket from the Beverly Hills police.

"He can't keep up with a young companion. He has lost all interest in pursuing his work. Every time the phone rings, he races to get there before I can.

"Billy, you know I've been a good wife all these years. I've seen that his home has always been happy, bright, and cheerful, no matter what his life has dealt him. His home has always been a safe harbor. I, my home, and my beautiful roses are always waiting to receive him. And yet, all of this doesn't seem enough now. This young girl offers your father excitement, companionship, and a reassurance that though he is in advancing years, he is still desirable.

"I have a different way of showing this to your father, but my way no longer seems adequate. Perhaps he wants both—what I represent to him and what she represents.

"But, Bill, you see, I am getting older, too, and am beginning to think of my own personal happiness. It is true that there have been other men in my life. My personal loneliness has driven me to them. Perhaps if I were to give your father his freedom and realize my own freedom, there might be another person more right for me—someone who could share my love for my flowers and my painting in a more intimate way.

"Then, Billy, dear, there is the problem of finances. Your father and my situation is extremely rocky. We don't know what will be the outcome of the federal income tax situation. The small amount I have in separate bank accounts and my home and garden, I have earned. I have no intention of sharing this with your father's new acquaintance."

Now her voice took on a touch of harshness.

"If we are to go our own ways, he is going to have to start all over financially. I am not prepared to share."

She saw me looking deep into the heart of a red rose, as she stood beside me.

"Bill dear, what are you thinking?"

As I turned to her, I found myself thinking that she seemed less like a mother and more like a friend.

"Bess," I replied, "I was looking into the heart of the rose and thinking that I love you very much, but then, dear, I love Dad just as much. I really don't know what to say to you. I only know I have to get to the airport or I'll miss my plane."

She kissed me on the cheek.

"Yes, dear, I understand."

"Bess, I would like to talk to you more about your problems, and then maybe we could discuss mine. Marge and I have never been further apart. Everything is happening at once. I'll phone you from South Bend."

No sooner had I checked into my South Bend hotel when complications on the TV series began to arise. The cameraman was

With actor Yul Brynner, who played Pharaoh, and with an eagle trained by William Lasky. The previous film version of *The Ten Commandments* set a film industry precedent of presenting religious themes in motion pictures and was also directed by DeMille but produced by young Lasky's father, Jesse L. Lasky. COURTESY OF PARAMOUNT PICTURES.

Sergeant William R. Lasky, of the Medical Corps, during World War II, while he was based at Fitzsimmons General Hospital in Denver. With him are son Ronnie and wife Margery. PHOTO BY WILLIAM R. LASKY.

The remarkable likeness between father and son is indicated by this last picture of Jesse Lasky on a fishing trip in the High Sierras shortly before his death and the photo of William R. Lasky with Scylla, one of the very rare harpy eagles. He trained the bird, proving that even the fiercest bird of prey can be tamed by human love. BOTH PHOTOS BY WILLIAM R. LASKY.

William Lasky, president of the Beverly Hills chapter of the Full Gospel Business Men's Fellowship, with Christian friends. Above: Dean Jones, star of many films and a Christian witness, and his wife, Laurie. Below, left to right: Tom Lewis, film and TV producer; actress Rhonda Fleming, a Jesse Lasky discovery; William R. Lasky; and Bishop Michel D'Obrenovic, a leader in the Syro-Chaldean Catholic Church. BOTH PHOTOS BY JAN BLESSING YOUNG.

Two of the people who participated with William Lasky in the miracle of God's love. Susan Hayward and lay minister Gene Arnaiz, Lasky's Christian guide and Bible teacher. (HAYWARD) COURTESY OF WILLIAM R. LASKY; (ARNAIZ) COURTESY OF GENE ARNAIZ, JR.

not waiting for me, as I had been informed he would. I went up to my room, unpacked, and sat down in a chair.

I was tired from the trip, and an uneasy feeling began to grow within me. Could I do the job up to my standards of quality in the limited time allotted to me? Overeager to accept the challenge, I hadn't carefully considered the amount of time needed to gather information from the university's multitude of sources, assimilate the material, write the scripts, rewrite them, and then submit them for approval by the university heads, make changes requested by Notre Dame, then rewrite them, find locations and individuals to be filmed, and, finally, direct the shooting.

While one film was under way, other scripts would have to be prepared and run through all the steps.

Over and over again, I asked myself, "Why did I ever accept those terms? It's a ten-week job that has to be finished in five to meet the network's commitments for the football season."

The only solution seemed to be working night and day, but I was prepared to do this. If I worked almost continuously and if I received the proper co-operation, the job could be accomplished well and on time.

It had been my impression from the network that all the groundwork had been laid, that I would have a university contact man to help me at any time of day or night. One phone call corrected that impression.

I learned that the university contact man who was to introduce me around and facilitate my work on campus had many other duties, so I would have to catch him whenever he was available.

A feeling of apprehension began to rise within me. I don't know why, but I suddenly had an impulse to open the drawer of the lamp table next to my bed. What I saw was no surprise. I had seen Gideon Bibles in many hotel and motel rooms and accepted them as part of hotel decor. Yet now I had nowhere else to turn, so I turned to the Bible, picked it up, and scanned a few pages at random.

It was like a foreign language to me. I read "begat" and the word "love." In the back of my mind, I wondered how these two could come together, but I had no time to find out. The phone rang, and I put the Bible back into the drawer.

As I suspected, it was the cameraman. He was downstairs in the lobby. I invited him up. As we introduced ourselves, I experienced a new feeling of alarm. Unquestionably, he had the proper screen credits and qualifications, but I found he was a fresh import from France and spoke only a limited amount of broken English.

I will never understand why the network did this because it is of basic importance that the communication between director and cameraman be complete down to the most subtle and minute detail.

Even though I spoke conversational French, I knew my vocabulary was limited to a child's world. I could not possibly convey the nuances so important for quality results. My intuitive fears hardened into reality. The communications impediment immediately began to slow down the process and increase my level of apprehension, impatience, and irritability. This bothered me, because my cameraman was a fine and co-operative fellow, eager to please.

Added to that was the fact that certain key Notre Dame officials were not immediately available for interview. I had my schedule, but they also had theirs, and as my French associate often would tell me with a shrug of his shoulders, "*C'est la guerre.*"

The DuMont people had told me that a "must" segment of the series would deal with the Notre Dame football team, then in daily practice sessions under its legendary coach, the great Knute Rockne.

I consulted with the university's representative who was to help me.

"Father Carroll," I said, "I need footage of a typical practice session of the football team."

"Sorry, Bill," Father Carroll replied, shaking his head ruefully. "That's a tough one. Knute would never hold still for such a thing."

I soon learned one of the main reasons that Coach Knute Rockne had been characterized and immortalized in feature articles, books, and motion pictures. He had a "single eye" focus on winning. His Fighting Irish always had to be the greatest football team of that year and possibly in the history of football. Winning came first, and he had to have his completely secret and crucial practice periods to accomplish his end, and his ends justified his means. To accomplish total security, he had had a high wooden fence built completely around his practice field. No one could invade his private world of sweat and muscles.

No documentary film to be shown between halves of telecasts of his team's games was worth even a short interruption of practice sessions.

"Absolutely not," Rockne told me. "No matter what kind of commitment you have, my practice sessions are entirely private. Period."

I protested, as did Father Carroll, but Rockne was king, and his word was law.

End of discussion.

My contractual commitment meant nothing to him, but it meant everything to me and my future, and I was determined to fulfill it.

My cameraman, Pierre, and I tried every subterfuge to get past the guarded gate with our equipment, but his burly blond, sweat-shirted attendant said, "No chance, fella. Coach's orders."

We investigated every inch of the high fence for an opening, but the security was total and impossible for us to penetrate. I considered knocking out a knothole or getting a saw to do the job, but how could I explain that kind of behavior to Father Carroll?

I phoned the office of the chancellor, but the good father was away from campus on business, and his aide could not or would not try talking to the mighty Rockne for us.

Then I hit upon a possible solution that was then unorthodox but is commonplace in TV filming today. I hired the services of a helicopter that, in addition to the pilot, would accommodate Pierre, the equipment, and me.

In the midst of the practice session, we headed our chopper toward the Notre Dame campus, flying between the Life Sciences Building and the school library. The high fence around Knute Rockne's domain was no longer impenetrable.

With loaded camera pointed out of the rear window, we skimmed the ground, barely within altitude of the code, and as the fence loomed before us, we violated the sacred precincts of Rockne's Shangri-La. Rockne soon saw what we were up to and shook his fists at us, shouting imprecations that, due to the motor noise of the chopper, we were not privileged to hear.

King Knute Rockne had everything going his way at Notre

Dame, but, fortunately for us, he didn't have a private air force to shoot us down. Also, fortunately for us, he had to keep his practice session on schedule, so we got our footage.

The Rockne complication was only one of many that I faced daily.

There were endless departmental interviews, reports, books, and maps that had to be searched for pertinent data. I took a cram course in Notre Dame history, customs, and traditions that normally would have taken years. With the necessary research accomplished, I had to write scripts, get approvals, make changes.

Production problems, too, were complex—selecting locations, arranging for students and school personnel to be filmed at certain specific times of day or night.

Last was the filming itself. Half-hour segments for TV may be realistically filmed by a seventy-five-man crew in three days, but I was not allowed this sort of super budget.

I found myself often working all day and, many times, all night, becoming overfatigued, short-tempered, and nervous.

And then there was the phone calls from Bess and Dad in California.

Pierre tried to calm me down.

"Bill," he said, "a little scotch whisky will settle your nerves." Before I could protest, he poured me a straight shot in a water glass.

"Drink it down fast, Bill."

I had tasted little liquor in my life and disliked it all—especially scotch. I followed his instruction and began to cough.

"The second will go down better," he promised.

I downed the second. I felt guilty drinking, but in my stress it seemed quite all right and appeared to relieve my tensions.

As the days and nights ground away, and the schedule's tempo increased, I bought a bottle of my own scotch and sipped it with ice as I worked, often neglecting to eat.

Under the nervous strain, I couldn't sleep, and my nerves seemed to be inflamed. My legs seemed like heavy weights Fatigue had made me so bone-weary that I could hardly walk and keep my balance.

I don't know how many nights I sipped scotch and missed meals and sleep, but eventually my appetite vanished. Scotch became the substitute for food.

Despite this handicap, I somehow finished writing and directing five scripts and completed their filming. Five down and two to go!

It was at that time that I found myself oscillating between exhilaration and despair. Sometimes I felt I could finish. At others I was positive I could not. Exhaustion often anchored me to my chair. It was all I could do to move, let alone work.

My system often compensated for total exhaustion by uncontrollable elation and excitement.

I became like a machine running too fast to keep up with itself. My heart and mind speeded up. My speech doubled in rapidity, and even my breathing and heartbeat were faster than normal. I had difficulty getting enough oxygen. I was in a condition unlike any I had ever before experienced.

Desperately I turned to my cameraman for advice, counsel, and understanding, but his repertoire of help ended with one means—the bottle of scotch. There was no one who could share the depths of my desperation, misery, and frustration. Very late one night I remembered the Gideon Bible in the lamp table drawer. I took it out, paging and reading without knowing exactly what to read.

Only now do I realize that missing so many meals, combined with constant drinking, had caused malnutrition, and, as I read the Scriptures, strange visual sensations troubled my reading. The stresses of overwork, fatigue, and drinking were doing funny things to the printed pages. The lines began to waver and shimmer, as if they were water.

A lighted lamp across the room seemed to dim, shrink, and then brighten and expand to outlandish size and, in turn, became distorted from round to oval. It was as if I were seeing objects in the mirror of an amusement park's fun house.

"Crazy," I thought. "This can't be happening to me. It's really a nightmare."

A feeling of fear and helplessness came over me.

Blinking my eyes to make these visual images go away, I again started reading my Bible. I thought of it as mine, because I had written my name on the inside cover, had made notes in it, and intended to keep it always.

I found a passage referring to the Trinity of God—the Father,

Son, and Holy Ghost—and quickly flipped the pages at random to other parts, and everywhere it seemed that the number three would come to my attention. I began to sense that there must be a secret mystery behind the number three.

Once more the lines of print began to move like something human and slowly undulate like waves of water. Then they again settled back in place.

In the midst of my puzzlement and total self-absorption, the phone rang, shattering my introspections. It was the voice of my dad from California.

"Bill," he said, "your mother and I are discussing our divorce, but your mother is being very unreasonable. She says that if I am to have my freedom and happiness, I will have to start over from scratch financially. She doesn't intend to share one cent of anything we own. Will you talk to her for me?"

My head was overflowing with my own problems. I didn't need anyone else's, so the words came into my ears but not fully into my consciousness. I longed to get out of the confining room and into the night air where I could breathe. But finally, the agony of having to stay there listening to my father was over.

As I was about to leave the room, the phone rang again. This time it was my mother.

"Bill, you should know what your father is trying to do to me now . . ." she began. There was a torrent of words. For my emotional survival, I had to keep the words of conflict outside of my mind. "Will you talk to your father? Make him understand I only want what is best for him, but I have to be considered, too, and I have to be practical. My only source of income is my painting."

I have no idea what I answered. At this point all I wanted to do was to scream. "For God's sake lay off."

Then her monologue was mercifully ended with, "You promise you will talk to your father?"

I escaped from the room and into the night. Here was cold, fresh air to breathe. Amid the tall oaks and maples on campus, I could see a sad and waning moon.

How long I wandered I do not know. Then I became aware

that I was tired, more tired than I had ever been before. It was hard for me to put one foot in front of the other.

Suddenly I realized that I was in an unfamiliar part of the campus. The ground under me seemed to undulate, as if I were walking on rubbery waves.

"Oh, my God. What is happening to me?" I cried out to myself. "Where can I go for help?"

Something in my path made me stop. It had loomed up before me—a statue of a woman who looked familiar.

How unbelievably familiar she was!

In the flicker of an instant my memory raced back through the years to Mademoiselle Bernadette Branche and my childhood.

It was impossible to mistake her from the picture my beloved governess had given me. It was her patron saint, St. Theresa. I remembered something Mademoiselle Branche had told me, something to the effect that if I ever needed St. Theresa she would always be there to protect me.

Tears were welling in my eyes.

The statue appeared to soften to human flesh. The blue and white of her robes seemed like real fabric, rustling in the night breeze. And, most wondrous of all, she held a fresh red rose.

I couldn't keep my gaze away from her face. She looked down at me in tender compassion, and my distress seemed to melt away. I fell to my knees, praying out loud to St. Theresa.

Apparently I was there for quite some time, for I heard something dim, as if it were coming through a dense fog. A rich baritone voice, that of a priest in black vestments, addressing itself to another person. "A call has been placed to California for him . . ."

They were talking about *me!*

Then came a blur of events. I was back in my hotel room with several strangers. I was lying in bed. I don't know how much later, but Dad arrived . . . then an airplane flight to California.

13

Thirty-seven Shock Treatments—and More!

Things began to clear up a bit on the airplane.

"Dad, what am I doing here? My project isn't finished."

"Don't worry," he assured me. "They're getting another writer-director to take over for you."

I was too exhausted to object. It felt as if a tremendous weight had been lifted from me. I was going home and wanted to be at home. After the significance of this fact sank in, I remembered something I had hurriedly put into my luggage—something I wanted to show Dad.

Among the pads of started and finished manuscripts for the first five TV segments, I found my Gideon Bible. I removed it and, all at once, was aware that my father was watching me.

He saw my Bible and a strange look came over his face. He seemed embarrassed, but a new feeling of elation was filling me.

"Dad, for the first time in my life I have been reading the Bible. How could I have stayed away from this great book so long . . . ?"

I saw a note scribbled in my Bible about the Trinity.

"Dad," I said, "are you aware of the reality of the Holy Trinity and the strength of the number three?"

I tried to explain what I meant with an example that was inept and inappropriate.

"The Father, Son, and Holy Ghost make up the Trinity. This is the foundation of faith. You, Cecil B. DeMille, and Sam Goldwyn are three: the foundation of Paramount Pictures and the motion picture industry. Then there are you, Bess, and me—the foundation of our family."

He turned to me and simply said, "Yes, of course, Bill. I see what you mean, but how about your sister, Betty, and brother, Jesse?"

He had done it politely and kindly, but I felt crushed and put the Bible back in my luggage.

Little more was said before we landed, and soon I was between the clean white sheets of an exclusive mental hospital in Los Angeles.

Even the short rest, the release from tension, seeing Marge, Ronnie, and Bess for a brief time, made me feel better.

I was under the care of a Hungarian psychiatrist, and from a distance, I overheard him talking to Dad: "He needs more than psychoanalysis, Mr. Lasky. Ve describe his condition as 'high.' He vill require a series of shock treatments, starting right avay."

Shock treatments! The words sent chills clear through me. When I was in my teens, I had seen a film about shock treatments. Whether overdramatized or not, it had left a deep impression.

A lubricant had been applied to the patient's temples, and electrodes had been attached. Then a strong electrical charge had been sent through him, and he had thrashed and writhed, going through movements similar to those of an epileptic fit.

These thoughts made me tremble, and I began to feel sour digestive juices moving up toward my throat.

"If only they would let me alone to rest—away from stresses, from pressures. . . ." I longed to run, but there was no place to run, no place to hide.

Footsteps approached my bed, and there, in his white physician's coat, was the Hungarian psychiatrist. The muscles of his face moved into a mechanical smile: "How are ve today?"

Though fearful, I was irritated by his manner. He referred to me as if he and I were a team as he went on, "Now ve are going to do something together, Villiam. All right, now ve are going to roll over on our stomach and slip the needle in the spine."

My mind raced ahead. "A spinal first to render me unconscious and then an electric shock treatment."

There is no way to express my horror and fear at the prospect.

As a lab technician, I had heard a lot about spinal taps and the danger of them—the fact that they can cause permanent injury if badly administered. But all I could do was obey and turned over on my stomach, looking back over my shoulder. And then another chill went through me. I saw the hands of the psychiatrist, who, I later learned, was not even a medical doctor. The fingers were long and arthritis-crippled, curved like the talons of a bird of prey. He was barely able to grip the hypodermic needle between his fingers.

Although the room was cool with air conditioning, I began to sweat profusely. Then those bony fingers came at me with the hypodermic needle, which loomed larger and larger, like a weapon.

As he bent over, he said, "Ve are going to have sodium pentothal. Ve von't remember anything." I felt the prick of the needle.

"Thank God it's over," I said silently with gritted teeth, but it wasn't. His arthritic condition had made it difficult for him to direct the needle accurately. He had missed my spine. He tried again and missed, and in a cold voice, "Ve vill try again. Ve will get it this time."

A feeling of pure hatred circulated to every cell of my body. If he couldn't handle the needle properly, why didn't he get someone who could? Just when I was sure he would kill me, his rigid fingers aimed the needle at the right spot. I felt it puncture my skin, and then a door of my life shut, and blackness enveloped me.

When I woke up, I smelled burned flesh. The skin of my temples seemed tender, and I could feel a lubricating jelly on my forehead. My mouth was cotton-dry. I was bathed in perspiration and felt exhausted. My shoulders were sore.

I couldn't remember where I was, who or what I was, and I found myself not even caring as I fell asleep.

The shock treatments continued, and each time it would take several days for my memory to return. Following every treatment, the psychiatrist would materialize at my bedside. He had the same stock, cold impersonal question, "Vell, how are ve today?"

"Fine," I would say each time. "I want to get out of here. I want to go home and get back to work. I'm well. I don't need any more of this."

"Ha, ha," he responded. "Our last treatment is begining to vear off and ve're getting a little high, aren't ve? It's time ve have another treatment."

Then I was back in the treatment room again. Gnarled hands, and cold eyes, the pointed needle of the pentothal-loaded syringe . . . the same frightening picture. First the spinal injection, a jolt, and unconsciousness.

Something was different about my return to consciousness this time. Knifelike pains stabbed my shoulders, and pains seemed to be coming up from the lower part of my spine.

I was to learn much later that both of my shoulders had become dislocated by the convulsive reactions to the electric shock. A pressure on my sciatic nerve was to be painful for many years to come.

When I gestured to the doctor about this pain, he shrugged his shoulders. "It vill pass vith the next treatment," he said.

But the pain didn't pass.

After thirty-seven shock treatments, I had more difficulty than ever remembering anything about myself. The shocks were changing something in my mind—for the worse.

My growing hatred for this doctor was only exceeded by my fear of another shock treatment that might make me a complete vegetable. I became panicky about ever getting out. I had noticed certain patients in the ward who seemed in a state of sedation at all times—like vegetables. Was I to become a vegetable, too?

During my interim moments of lucidity, I felt the suspicion grow that this doctor wanted me as a permanent source of income.

Most of the time I was in a twilight zone between total concern and complete lack of concern.

One day Bess appeared by my bed. The instant I saw her, I cried out, "Thank God, you're here, Bess."

Her smiling face and auburn hair were the most welcome sight I think I have ever seen. Immediately I said, "Bess, you've got to get me out of here. There's nothing wrong with me, but these shock treatments are destroying my memory. If I stay much longer, I'll be a vegetable—useless even to myself."

She studied me for a moment.

"Bess, the hospitalization, psychiatric care, and the treatments are benefiting the hospital and the doctor—no one else. They must be costing you and Dad a fortune. The sooner you get me out of here, the faster I'll be well and working again. If I stay much longer, I'll become a zucchini."

She broke into laughter. We laughed together, but my sense of humor had made her realize that I was normal. Laughing made me feel even more so. It was the first time I had laughed in many weeks.

"Billy, you seem completely rational. What you say makes good sense."

So I was finally sprung from my psychiatric prison.

I experienced a fresh emotion—one of ecstatic joy—as I walked out the institution's iron gates. The joy mounted to tears as I heard the welcome song of a mockingbird. This "high" state would never come down to earth again, I felt.

How wonderful it would be to see Marge and Ronnie, I told myself. I walked up the driveway to the house, carrying my small bag of personal effects.

Truly it was wonderful. Yet, as soon as I stepped over the threshold, I realized that the happiness of my release had falsely colored my buried and forgotten marital problems. They had not changed.

Margery and Ronnie seemed glad to see me, but something was missing—the "welcome home" hugs and kisses. Whether it was an accurate or inaccurate appraisal, I didn't know, but one thing seemed clear to me: It was not a husband and father who had arrived home, but a discharged mental patient, received with reservations.

My joyous homecoming was quite one-sided. That point hit me hard when I saw my clothing, books, birds, bird paintings, record player, records, radio—everything I owned—moved to the opposite side of our house. My bedroom was now as far separated from Margery's as a small house would permit.

I had walked out of the sunshine into a living nightmare that I had always dreaded. Here within my life was mirrored the feared separation, as in the life of my father and mother.

Indeed, how deeply the present is rooted in the past!

The causes of Margery's and my separate bedrooms had started long before the crisis at Notre Dame, but now, inside me, was a deep feeling that we would always be separated.

No matter what dialogue I would start with Marge, no matter how much I searched for thoughts, words, or deeds to bridge the wide gap existing between us, it seemed hopeless.

Even more hopelessness weighed me down as the days—especially, the lonely nights—accented our separation. I began to lose confidence in myself. I felt rejected. I first felt sorry for myself, then frustrated, then angry with myself because whatever I tried to do failed.

I tried to tell Margery several times about having picked up the Bible in South Bend and finding it fascinating reading, but somehow everything was out of context.

My dad and now Margery seemed to use my newly born interest in the Bible as proof of mental instability.

Alone in my room that night, I opened my Bible and found my scribbled notation on the first page: "Father, Son, and Holy Ghost equals three. Cecil B. DeMille, Sam Goldwyn, and Dad equals three. Bess, Dad, and I equals three."

I thought about the last trinity—that of our family. With Betty and Jesse, Jr., it was five, not three.

Here in my own notes was proof that they were right about me. This evidence had to be destroyed. I threw the Bible into the incinerator.

Out of my conflicting emotional reactions grew a feeling that Margery was indeed right in keeping me at a distance, and I turned with full venom against myself as someone deserving rejection. Soon my self-accusations reduced me to nothingness in my own eyes. I began to lose confidence that I would ever be able to get myself together again enough to work for a living.

My rapid inner erosion finally reduced me to a fear that the phone would ring, and I would be asked to accept studio work.

My rapidly mounting marital problems motivated Bess to suggest a psychotherapist, who could professionally assess and evaluate my feelings of rejection and inadequacy. I poured out my problems to him—every feeling, every fear, my total loss of self-confidence, everything large and small.

He started speaking:

"From what you tell me, you are using your marriage as a substitute—an escape—instead of depending on yourself. As a child uses a parent to lean upon, you are leaning upon your wife. You use her as a mother, a parent, rather than as a partner, and this means that if you cling to your relationship with your wife—not a valid one—you will only further continue to disintegrate as a personality and a functioning individual.

"You must make your own decision, but it is my opinion that if you hang onto your marriage, you will eventually destroy yourself."

His words seemed to reverberate within my mind.

A number of times in my total futility, I had thought of doing away with myself, but I hurried to cut off such thoughts before they could grow into action that Margery, Ronnie, and I might regret.

Without a doubt, the psychotherapist had been right. I couldn't continue in a marriage that wasn't a full marriage. For the preservation of my wife, Ronnie, and myself, I would have to terminate the marriage.

How could I tell Margery of my decision?

I thought for hours and days about it and then, mercifully, one night, Margery came into my room and helped me to face the decision I was avoiding.

"Bill dear," she said, "we are no longer happy together. We are not helping our son, either. I think it would be best if we continued our lives apart."

So many times in the days that followed the legal filings—even in the chill atmosphere of our home—I hoped that some miracle would occur to fill the gulf between us, that would dissolve our often spoken and unspoken disappointment and bitterness, that would change us so that we would be right for one another as we once had been.

Instead of a miracle, there was cold, legal reality and the agreed-upon settlement. Margery would keep Ronnie, our home, and her car. I learned that she planned to return to work in the film studios. From what was said by both of us, I concluded it would be best for Ronnie—less upsetting to him—if I saw him only infrequently.

Almost all the acts of divorce and thoughts related to it bring varying degrees of pain, and there are many that I have buried too deep for memory to bring back. One day I found myself packing personal belongings—my books, my collection of treasured paintings of falcons and hawks, animal collecting gear and falconry equipment, as well as Mexican cages of birds.

Then high above my clothing in a separate closet area, I lifted down my sleeping bag, which started a rush of memories—of Crestline and the night under the pines where my love for Margery began. The sleeping bag was dusty and faded. It had been stored through five years in the Army, had been carried to Swarthmore and returned to California, but its travels were not yet over. It was to continue with me.

I took my butterfly nets, casting rods, nooses for lizards, and each one had memories attached to them. They came back faster than I could handle them.

Would there ever again be such glorious days with Margery and Ronnie?

I hurriedly packed my trout rods. They, too, sent me back into the past—to the Colorado Rockies on the Gunnison River, where I had first shown Ronnie, then a mere toddler, how to fly-cast. As my dad had told me and his dad had told him, I had passed on the Lasky family's fishing avice, "Always go to the top of the stream."

The rich memories—never again recapturable—and the bleak possibilities of ever having Marge and Ronnie back again made me blink back tears.

I was about to walk away from the past, much of which had been warm and beautiful, about to walk away from my life's greatest pleasures and from the plain fact that I couldn't stand to accept—my failure as a husband and father.

According to tradition, grown men are supposed to be too manly for tears at a time like this. I wanted to be manly, but as I walked away from the brightly lighted house to the darkness of my loaded Ford, I had to discipline myself strongly.

For the last time, I glanced back at the place that held the two most precious persons in the world to me. Completely empty, I entered my car and, as quickly as I could, drove away.

14

Love Is the "X" Quantity

A Hollywood-scarred veteran actor once characterized the economic uncertainty of a film career when he said to me: "Bill, I make fifteen hundred a week when I work, but if it's a bad year, I come out with less salary than a service station attendant."

This has been my experience, too. After a particularly bad period, I sometimes shared my home or apartment with a friend to cut expenses and also to have the companionship.

Through one of these sharings—this one with a young man named Henry, an accomplished pianist whose playing I enjoyed—I experienced the third mustard seed of my life.

Before Henry moved into my Malibu ranch home, I learned that he had been in a head-on auto accident and had suffered nerve-tissue damage in the fore part of his head. I didn't ask any questions about it. There was not even a prominent scar where he had been injured. I imagined that the hair had grown over the area, and I dismissed the whole thing from my mind.

About ten days after he had moved in, I happened to be reading in the living room. He was in the kitchen, preparing to cook a meal. Without a warning, I heard a crash and found him unconscious on the vinyl tile floor. The pot into which he had poured frozen peas had come clattering down on top of him. Luckily the contents had not yet been heated or he might have been seriously scalded. His accident was such a surprise that I was apprehensive. Just as I reached to feel if his heart was still beating, he began to revive slowly.

I must have looked as startled as I felt, for as he glanced up at me, he smiled and said, "Don't look so scared, Bill. I'm all right. I have these black-out attacks once in a while as a result of my accident."

Later that night he said, "I hope you won't be upset about what I'm going to tell you. The doctor says I have only a limited time to live. Toward the end of it, I will probably have to be hospitalized and medicated for the severe pain. I'm just living each day as it comes—as best I can. Please don't worry about me. What will be, will be."

In the year that followed, Henry's attacks slowly increased in number, duration, and severity. Soon he was having attacks at least twice a week, accompanied by excruciating head pains.

Sometimes I had to drive him home from the restaurant in which he worked. Once the attack was over, he would again be apparently normal, and often he would sit at his mahogany baby grand and fill the house with music, both semiclassical and popular. He would become so lost in his music, it was almost as if he didn't know I was even there.

After one of his sessions at the piano, he turned to me and said, "Bill, I guess I should have told you about my head condition before I moved in. I must be a real drag on you."

"No, Henry. Not a drag. An enrichment to my life—your company and your piano playing."

He looked at me for a long moment, saw that I meant every word I had said, and seemed reassured. He had no way of knowing that some kind of innate quality, something that must have come with me when I was born, made it impossible for me to look the other way when somebody was in trouble. How many dogs, cats, birds—injured or maltreated—had come my way for first-aid treatment, feeding, and nursing back to health. And there were some people, too, bruised inside, who stopped for a while. And when the animals, birds, or people were strong enough to go, they went.

The people and animals were healed, and so was I—in the manner of the boy and the eagle in my film.

But now, with Henry, I had no idea how I could help him. Perhaps by just being an understanding companion.

I began to see the pattern of Henry's illness. Severe headaches would be followed by the black-outs and fainting, and then he would be relieved and like his old self. It was as if the pressure would build up and then be released.

As the pain became more severe, he began drinking alcohol to lessen it. This pain caused me increasing worry until I could no longer sit by.

"Henry, we're going to a doctor. There just might be something that can be done for you."

Henry protested, but I finally got him to a specialist who had him X-rayed and then told us the bad news. If an operation were conducted and the brain entered into, Henry could only expect life as a vegetable.

So, in accordance with Henry's wishes, we lived only one day at a time. About the only event that we anticipated more than a day ahead was an old-fashioned German potluck picnic that was being given and shared by all the employees at the restaurant where Henry worked. Our food contribution was to be a big, hot, German potato salad.

A few nights before the picnic, Henry had been forced to come home from work following a severe attack and black-out—the most painful and longest period of unconsciousness he had ever sustained. That night he insisted on talking with me.

"Bill, I value your friendship more than I can say. No one else in the world would have put up with me and my problems over the past year. I want to prepare you for something that will happen. I have always known that I would die very young, but, somehow, I feel I have lived a full life. I'm going to die tonight, Bill. . . ."

"Henry, come on now," I interrupted. "You'll feel better tomorrow and we'll forget all about this."

"No, Bill, you've got to listen. I have some instructions. I have only two possessions—my car and the piano—and I'm making payments on both. My car insurance has already lapsed, but I'm not going to pay it. . . ."

I tried to talk, but he raised his hand, palm toward me, to let him continue.

"Let the finance companies pick up the car and piano, and don't feel bad about what I'm saying."

That night when we went to sleep in our individual bedrooms, I tossed for many hours, frequently getting up to make sure that Henry was breathing.

Next morning I woke up to piano music filling the sunlit house. Henry was not only alive but full of exuberance, and it was so reassuring to hear him alive and at the piano that I lay still, just listening to an Erroll Garner number the name of which I could not recall.

When I entered the living room, I said, "Henry, do you remember all that hogwash we talked about last night? You can see now it was just overdramatics on your part."

He stopped playing, turned, and looked me square in the eye in a manner too serious to be questioned, and said, "Funny, but I had a feeling I was going to die last night. I was so sure of it. I remember every word I said to you."

The subject was gloomy, and I had had enough of it, so I said, "Henry, we both need haircuts, and we have to buy potatoes for the picnic tomorrow. Let's drive into Santa Monica and get some things done."

"Okay, Bill, but I want to drive my car."

"No, Henry. You just had an attack yesterday and we both had a rough night last night. We'll take my car. After all, you don't have insurance."

"All right, Bill. We'll take your car, but I'll drive."

Tired from the night of insomnia and the emotional stress of our conversation, I gave in and agreed to let him drive my car.

As we casually drove down the Pacific Coast Highway toward Santa Monica, I put my head against the seat rest and dozed off. What happened a few minutes later, I was not to learn until I regained consciousness three weeks later.

A car coming toward us was being driven by a mentally ill aircraft worker. He had repeatedly stated that he was a devil worshiper and that he was going to make a sacrifice for the devil. He had begun ranting and raving on the job and threatening to make a human sacrifice to the devil and was finally taken home by company representatives.

As soon as they had left, he got into his car with only one thought—to do what he had said he would. He headed his car down the Santa Monica ramp leading into the Pacific Coast Highway, gaining speed until he was going over ninety miles an hour coming toward us.

There was an elderly woman driving an old Ford directly in front of us. His car came roaring toward the woman, crossing the center line. She saw him coming and sharply turned her car into the Santa Monica Beach Club parking lot and to safety. As she cleared the path, we were exposed, going about thirty-five miles an hour, and he hit us head on.

The impact was so sudden and severe—an impact of 125 miles per hour—that Henry never had a chance to turn the steering wheel. He was instantly killed and thrown out onto the pavement.

I was crushed by the dashboard. Twelve of my ribs were broken, puncturing both of my lungs with shafts of bone. It was a blessing that I had been asleep when the accident occurred. I was unconscious for three weeks, during which time my family attended to Henry's funeral arrangements and were fully prepared to face this eventuality with me.

My condition worsened due to the complication of double pneumonia, both of my injured lungs filling with fluid that had to be drained through my side.

One night I regained consciousness, and I saw the doctor standing beside my bed. He was speaking, and finally I began to make out the sense of what he was saying.

"Bill, you and I are going to have a serious talk. We've removed your drains and stopped most of your medication, because there's little more we can do for you.

"You'll have to know sooner or later that your friend was killed in the car accident. There's nothing more that we can do for him, but there is a slim chance for you. You yourself have got to want to get well."

He then asked me a question that I barely understood at the time. "Do you have any reason to want to live?"

I remember thinking, "I really don't."

He was suddenly speaking again.

"Just remember this, Bill. God has a plan for each one of us, but you have a choice—to live or to die. If you choose to die, you may never find out what God's plan is for you."

In that very instant, something was reborn within me. Perhaps it was curiosity to find out what God's plan could possibly be for me. From that moment, I recovered rapidly and marveled at the healing powers that brought me back to full physical capability. As those who have heard this story before have said, "You could, and probably should, have been dead after what happened to you."

Very likely that's true, and I would have been if the doctor had not filled me with curiosity about God's plan for my life. The doctor, like Mademoiselle Branche and Sergeant York, was another mustard seed in my life—the third.

But the third seed, like the others, lay fallow for some years. I was soon back at work in Hollywood—that is, until one of the bad periods when a great many films that normally would have been made in Hollywood were shot in overseas locations.

After a bad financial period, I fell back on what I loved best—my hobby of animals, birds, and flowers—even if they didn't and couldn't pay very well.

For many years, I had lived and maintained a large bird collection in a sparsely populated and heavily wooded area of Topanga Canyon, later moving to Laurel Canyon where I began the business of importing hummingbirds from South America.

My business plan was to custom-design and install aviaries with hummingbirds for homes of the wealthy in Beverly Hills, Bel Air, and Brentwood.

I had been trying to think up an appropriate name for the business venture. One night I woke up with some lines from *Alice in Wonderland* running through my mind. I've always loved the Lewis Carroll classic—ever since Mademoiselle Branche began reading it to me—even before I could fully understand it.

The lines kept repeating themselves to me:

> "The time has come," the Walrus said,
> "To talk of many things:
> Of shoes—and ships—and sealing-wax—
> Of cabbages—and kings. . . ."

That was it!

"Cabbages" would represent the orchids with which I would decorate my aviaries and "Hummingbirds" would represent kings. This was the name I had been searching for—"Of Cabbages and Hummingbirds."

I know it was a name that, once heard, would be remembered. I had business cards, letterheads, and my bank account made out in this Alice-in-Wonderlandish name.

My first Beverly Hills client had dealt with me a few years earlier when I had trained a falcon for him. His phone call to me presented a welcome challenge.

"Bill, can you think of an idea, something with living birds and plants? I'm having a fantastic party, and I want the highlight to be an exotic bird room. Don't be concerned with the cost!"

I surprised him with my answer, "Hummingbirds."

"Where are you going to get hummingbirds?"

I said, "Leave it to me."

A glass-fronted room in his den was to be the location for me to create the Garden of Eden, apples and snake not included.

He advanced what I needed in cash and I went to work redoing what looked like a zoological ghetto that had been haphazardly thrown together by an indifferent Noah—rabbits, guinea pigs, and dirty pigeons, plus a few noisy parakeets had chewed up and defiled some plastic vines and wire-stemmed poinsettias left over from Christmas past.

The assorted animals and birds went to neighbor kids and the room was stripped down to the walls. I first installed a rock-bordered stream and pool fed by water pumped over a splashing waterfall. Then, using huge, grotesquely shaped driftwood logs and mosses over rich, earthy loam, I began my setting.

A visit to the famous Armacost and Roysten Nurseries, then in Santa Monica, had given me an idea. There I saw twelve to fifteen greenhouses filled with hundreds of white cattleya orchids. I bought a thousand dollars' worth as well as ferns and other tropical plants.

Orchid plants were removed from pots where roots had been cramped and reset in a profusion of blooms along moss-covered logs. The sight and tropical aroma of the hundreds of white blooms, freshly and gently sprayed from a mist hose fitting, became the seductive home of several dozen imported feathered jewels.

White orchids, tropical greens, waterfall, and fiery flashing hummingbirds left my client breathless.

His prominent guests from politics and the entertainment field were so fascinated that much of the party centered around the bird room. Everybody crowded in to watch these tiny, animated hummingbirds that created miniature rainbows with near invisible whirring wings against the sea of white orchids and the jungle green.

That was the first job for "Cabbages and Hummingbirds." Each one that followed made me want to have my own at-home aviary at the Laurel Canyon Place. I took a whole back-yard area and converted it into a greenhouse with plastic roofing and aviary-wired sides.

I built my own rock-lined stream and waterfall and installed a rotating pump, fallen tree logs, ferns, bromiliad air plants with scarlet flowering centers, and dozens of rich fuchsias, which hung like little chandeliers amid the forest greenery. Then I introduced more than four hundred hummingbirds of every conceivable variety into my personal jungle. The hundreds of fuchsia blooms provided nectar filling stations. I could sit in this private jungle hideaway for hours, observing these beautiful little birds. I purposely would wear wild and colorful Hawaiian shirts which encouraged my bird friends to perch on my shoulders, head, or outstretched hands. It was so exciting I had to share it with friends, inviting them all to come in colorful shirts and dresses—among them Shirley Jones and her family.

A highlight of this creation was a late afternoon visit from Bess, who could no longer resist seeing the finished product.

As she walked into the area, a violet-throated hummingbird flashed for a long moment in front of her. She raised her hand, and the bird fearlessly settled on her outstretched finger. As it switched from her hand to a lavender orchid petal, she turned to me overwhelmed, her eyes moist.

For what seemed minutes but was actually seconds, she absorbed the whole scene: crystal-clear, tumbling waters over the rock-strewn streams, the myriad kaleidoscopic beauteous feathered jewels—blues, iridescent greens, flashy crimsons, every color of the rainbow—overlaid on a backdrop of dark green ferns, sun-dappled leaves of the tropical plants, and inlaid throughout with multicolored orchids of every shape and hue.

She was speechless—a painter with a love of beauty who had been served a palette full of colors.

"Billy," she said breathlessly—she had not called me this endearing name in many years—"you have reminded me that God is the Master Painter."

She turned to me impulsively.

"Bill, this is too beautiful a day to end so fast. Let's have dinner together."

"Sure, Bess. How about lobster at Moby's Dock?"

Our family had gone to Moby's Dock off and on since I had been a little boy.

"I'd love it."

Then she seemed to remember something. "Bill, I have a gift for you. Let's go by my home after dinner, and I'll give it to you."

As much as I enjoyed Bess's company and lobster, I couldn't wait to know what the gift was.

When we arrived at her home, she was like a little girl at Christmas. As she turned on the living room light, I felt a sense of beauty and peace that she had created in her home. The pure white rugs and pastel furniture offered a perfect setting for her magnificent landscapes and still lifes tastefully displayed on the walls. Beautiful flower arrangements had been lovingly placed on side tables and rare inlaid antique English lowboy cabinets. Everywhere her taste and artistry were evident.

She walked over to the concert grand piano and picked up a little ancient metal statue with inlaid gold and jewels and carried it to me. She said, "Billy, there's no way I can return the gift of beauty that you shared with me this afternoon."

I glanced curiously at the object.

"Billy, for many years I have treasured this little ancient Ming Dynasty Buddha. Its face reminds me of the way you looked when you were born. I have always intended to give it to you but was waiting for the right moment. That moment is now. Keep it always as a reminder of my love for you."

I am pleased that Bess shared my aviary when she did, for that was its very peak time.

The cost of the jungle and the birds had been astronomical for my dwindling budget, and little by little the flock thinned down as I used many of the birds to create miniature jungles for several clients.

Whenever I felt discouraged, I would go into my private retreat, and suddenly, as with the flock of wild geese passing over Fort MacArthur, I knew things would be all right again.

Then business slowed up, and film work was almost nonexistent. At this period, I began to realize that I was not finding sufficient satisfaction in living. There had to be something outside of me—something more to life. I was becoming aware that ego gratification was not the answer to self-realization or to happiness.

Reflecting back on my brief reading of the Old Testament in South Bend, Indiana, I had to face the fact I wasn't a Jew or much of anything else. Any resemblance between me and a real Jew was strictly coincidental. It was unpleasant to look candidly at my nothingness, so I turned away, trying to think of less disturbing things.

Being incredibly lonely—as only a person can who is deep in debt and having difficulty finding employment—I needed comfort, understanding, and hope, but there seemed to be none. A feeling of deep depression that daily grew in magnitude caused me to escape from daytime hours through sleep. I would stay in bed until late afternoon to make the day as short as possible.

I am aware now that this devastating state of affairs was caused not only by material disappointment but by an ever-growing spiritual void that was crying out to be filled.

Then a long sequence of disturbing events took place. I was unable to collect a bill from a client for an aviary that I had designed and constructed, and, further, I got stuck for a four-hundred-dollar bird that had been ordered for the same client and, shortly after being installed in his home, had died of unknown causes. On top of this, a cage holding four rare and expensive tropical birds, called scarlet cock of the rocks, was raided by a wild raccoon during his night foray. Their scarlet feathers were like my blood on the ground.

Film work was still unobtainable, and the future looked bleak. Then one morning I received a phone call that temporarily softened my problems and led to a unique experience.

The call was from Jerry Lindell, a film producer, who presented me with a fascinating challenge.

"Can you get a harpy eagle? I've run across a magazine story that will make a shocker of a picture. It's called 'Harpy.' CBS is interested in the property, but they won't buy it unless I can satisfy them about two things: Can I get a harpy eagle, number one? And, if I can, can the eagle be trained to do what the script requires?"

"Jerry, it might be possible to get one, but harpy eagles are on the endangered species list. They're very rare birds. But tell me, what does the eagle have to do in the script?"

He told me the gist of the story: A falconer-architect who loves his birds has divorced his blond wife and has fallen in love with a young secretary in his office. The ex-wife symbolizes the predacious nature of the harpy eagle. She determines to reacquire her husband not for love, but for her ego, and she will destroy anything that gets in her way.

The falconer has a young Indian assistant who loves the birds as he does. As the story progresses and the wife feels a growing frustration through her inability to get her husband back, she becomes inflamed with jealousy, enters his hawk and eagle house, and kills and maims several of his trained birds.

He is so furious that he orders his ex-wife to leave him once and for all. She teases him, saying he will never be rid of her, and furthermore, she will see that the young secretary doesn't marry him either.

Angry that the woman has killed the birds and now is threatening his boss, the Indian boy takes matters into his own hands and secretly trains the harpy eagle to attack blond hair.

Finally, the Indian boy releases the harpy, which perches in a tree over the road. As the eagle sees the wife in her convertible, her blond hair blowing in the wind, he attacks. She tries to avoid the eagle, plunges the car over a cliff, and is killed.

"Bill, that's the story in brief," the producer said. "Now can you get a harpy eagle and train him?"

I had my doubts about a harpy's availability, and I knew that the harpy is a ferocious predator, the biggest bird of prey, weighing about sixteen to seventeen pounds, with a seven-foot wingspread, and capable of killing a full-grown jaguar or deer. Very few of them had ever been trained.

"I'll start checking right away," I replied. "If I can locate a harpy, I'm sure I can train it to do what the script requires."

A research article in my files showed me that Stan Brock, a staff member of the *Wild Kingdom* TV series, had managed to train a harpy eagle. I wrote him a letter and found that he had a female harpy, a bird that had been imported from British Guiana in the Caribbean. He confirmed my information that harpy eagles are indeed rare, but he said that he would be willing to sell the bird for fifteen hundred dollars.

I took the letter to Jerry Lindell, who, in turn, presented it to CBS-TV. After a week of considering the matter, the network decided to buy the eagle, make the film, and give me a lucrative contract as the trainer.

The eagle was air-freighted from Chicago to California and temporarily housed in Jerry Lindell's garage. As soon as I saw this giant bird, I knew the job was going to be as rough a challenge as I had ever had, so I secured the services of Tom Cantella, a young falconer friend, to help me.

When we tried to enter the garage, the tremendous eagle attacked us and we had to retreat.

I had trained several golden eagles before, but they were much smaller. I knew that no matter the size or wingspread of a bird, there is only one way to train it—through affection and love. First, however, a period of conditioning called manning is necessary.

I admired the sight of this proud, arrogant creature. Every time I opened the garage door a crack, the eagle angrily raised her crest in challenge.

After a minor wrestling match with her, Tom and I managed to fit her legs with leather straps, called jesses, and tied her to a perch with a leash. Every time we approached her, we offered her bits of meat. At first she haughtily flung them back at us, but then, as we persisted—and her hunger increased—she accepted them.

In a short period of time, she was taking pieces of meat from our fingers and looking forward to our frequent visits for her rewards. Our friendship training proceeded, and, at its termination, I was able to trust this huge bird on my bare back, her talons gently resting on my shoulder.

I was only too cognizant of the risk, but I had to show

confidence and affection, even though I knew that if I moved too fast and the eagle panicked, she could sink those talons into my flesh and even crush the bones of my shoulder.

She was too heavy to hold on my wrist, the way falcons are generally carried. A special device would be needed to sustain her weight and to protect my arm in case she became nervous during filming. I consulted an orthopedist and told him exactly what sort of device I needed, even drawing a suggested design. Together we created an extremely heavy plastic sleeve to fit over and protect my arm. It was equipped with a metal joint to permit arm motion.

Now I had to solve how to accomplish the harpy's role within the screenplay. In the story, the eagle attacks and kills a wolf to establish for the film viewer the eagle's capability as a hunter and killer. To accomplish this, I had to make a decoy to encourage and induce the harpy to attack a simulated wolf. I attached two pairs of wagon wheels to a sawhorse. The scene in the movie called for the decoy to be pulled behind a horse, and the eagle had to attack it. I covered the sawhorse with fox fur from a pawnshop and tied strips of raw meat to the back of the decoy. Then I showed the eagle where she could feed. After many repeated attempts, the eagle learned to fly at the decoy.

The second major objective was to make another decoy that would teach the eagle to attack a blond wig. Taking an old mop, I dyed the end of it blond. I also attached the harpy's favorite meat to this, and it worked well.

At this point of training, I began to be concerned because we had no double for the eagle. If she should become sick or if an accident occurred, the picture couldn't be filmed. Further, we needed a stand-in eagle in certain scenes for lighting and to line up our cameras.

Through Marlin Perkins, zoo director and TV personality, I learned that the St. Louis Zoo had a harpy eagle for sale. This one was a male and somewhat smaller—a little over nine pounds.

We purchased him, and our two eagles and our growing collection of hawks to be used in the film were headquartered in the hospital facility at the old Griffith Park Zoo in Los Angeles.

We called the female Scylla and the male Charybdis, both names borrowed from *Ulysses*. The original Scylla was a rock on the Italian coast, and Charybdis was a whirlpool off the Sicilian coast. Both were characterized as female monsters, but we figured the male wouldn't mind our literary license.

It is imperative for a falconer training eagles and hawks to be almost constantly with his birds. Continuous association builds confidence between them. Training had progressed satisfactorily when a two-week period was reached in which the script was being finalized for shooting. There was also a rumor afoot that the production might even be canceled because of casting difficulties. Few actors could be found to work with vicious eagles.

During this period of inactivity, CBS ordered the two eagles to be taken out of training and placed in a large cage adjacent to the hospital.

Already I had grown to love Scylla, and I wanted to express this love for her in action as well as in feelings which she could sense. I rigged up a large platform for her and brought in a whole pile of sticks that had fallen from nearby trees. With great interest, she watched me work. The next morning, to my complete surprise, I learned that her interest was more than casual: She had lifted several large sticks from the floor of the cage and had shaped these roughly to form the outline of a huge nest. There were no records of harpy eagles nesting in captivity, and—for that matter—only a few records of any hawk or eagle so breeding, and I couldn't believe what she was trying to show me.

I lifted a large stick and, holding it in front of her, asked her, "Scylla, would you like me to help you build your nest?"

To my utter amazement, she gave a throaty cluck, which I interpreted as an enthusiastic "Yes." She took the offered stick, flew with it up to her nest, and placed it in a spot that she chose to further the nest construction. At this point, the little male watched his "two-timing" mate with only a slight interest. Nest building was not for him.

So we continued. I handed the female sticks, and she carried them up to the nest, placing them where she thought they would fit best. We worked together throughout the day.

The following day, I brought in a large pile of English ivy vines that someone had cut and discarded, and we continued to share nest-building chores.

It was as nice a co-operative effort as I have ever taken part in. I got the idea that the nest could use the ivy lining in the bottom. She thought it was great. It only seemed reasonable to set aside my human dignity and join her on a bird level in her nest. It was amazing that she would permit me such familiarity.

Then she began to bring over long strings of ivy, handing me pieces to tuck into place. Occasionally, she would walk over to inspect my work. Apparently, my work was not always perfect, for she would readjust the ivy until she was satisfied.

Through all of this, the male eagle watched in a detached sort of way. I got the feeling he was saying, "Okay, go ahead if that's what you want to do, but nest building is for women *only!*" He was a male chauvinist eagle!

In the happy, nest-building days that followed, mealtime became another proof of her increasing affection for me. I would bring in large pieces of meat for her. And of extreme interest to me, one day as she was hungrily eating, she tore off a strip of tenderloin and offered it to me. I took the food from her bill and she clucked in approval, continuing to eat.

Before I knew what was going on, I had become a part of an eternal triangle—a love object to the female. However, the male kept himself in her favor. When I left the nest, he would fly over to it and actually mate with her.

Scylla and I were working in the bottom of the nest one day, putting the final touches on its inner lining, when I decided to take the still camera around my neck and get a snapshot portrait of Charybdis on his bachelor perch some fifteen feet away. As usual, he was coldly observing the nest goings-on. The weather was a bit nippy, and I was wearing a leather jacket. Just as I pointed my camera toward him, he must have felt a wave of jealousy, and knowing that I was defenseless against him, he suddenly attacked without warning, his talons hitting me on the shoulder and ripping my leather jacket to the skin, drawing blood. In a fraction of a second, it was all over, and he never again attacked. My black-and-blue marks were ample proof of his physical prowess. I still have an excellent photograph of the eagle coming at me for the attack.

Intrigued by the events of the nest building, I asked permission of CBS and the city of Los Angeles, which supervised the Griffith Park Zoo, to breed this pair of eagles, promising to locate substitutes to train for the picture. Harpy eagles had never before bred in captivity, and here was a first chance to establish a scientific procedure for their breeding, which could lead to increasing the population of this endangered species.

I was turned down flat. CBS rightly maintained that the eagles had been purchased to be trained for the film and that I would have to take them out of the breeding cage, dismantle the nest, and put them back into training for the movie. It would not yield. Following filming, as per contractual agreement, the birds would be given to the zoo. Should the zoo decide to breed them later, that would be within its zone of authority.

But who really knew if a later time would produce the same conditions conducive to breeding?

The motion picture people couldn't understand my extreme distress in being forced to terminate this actual historical, zoological event. Nor could they understand my mixed feelings. True, I had agreed to accept a salary for a job, but, in my heart, I was a scientist embarked into territory as adventuresome and unexplored as the surface of Mars. It was like having succeeded in landing on another planet, and then ordered to turn back. Neither the salary nor the movie any longer seemed important.

And then I got an idea. There was one human being, an enthusiastic zoologist like myself, who carried enough weight and who might intercede—the renowned Marlin Perkins.

I phoned him.

"Marlin, I need your help. Our pair of harpy eagles has completed building a nest."

I felt constrained to omit my part in the event, but I detailed for him the contractual problems. "CBS purchased these birds as actors for a motion picture. Their possible captive breeding is an unexpected accomplishment. I know you understand its importance. Could you intercede for me?"

He promised to do everything he could, and he kept his word, but the city, the zoo officials, and CBS were all adamant. Nothing could change their minds, so I had to go through one of the hardest ordeals of my life, taking down Scylla's carefully constructed nest stick by stick. In a sense I was betraying the beautiful bird's trust.

CBS was angry about my pulling Marlin Perkins into the act. Their displeasure became increasingly evident when I was forced

—on sudden notice—to make the eagles perform and demonstrate their flight abilities to a degree for which they were not prepared. CBS stipulated that if the eagles could not fly a certain distance that very afternoon, then, all things considered, they were going to replace me and void my contract.

At this point both eagles had gained excessive weight from inactivity. There was not enough time to slim them down and to accomplish CBS's objectives.

I was amazed how the eagles rallied to my support, and they did perform way above my expectations, but my judges had seemingly prearranged their displeasure. Whatever the eagles did, they were not satisfied.

The following day came confirmation by phone: "Bill, we have decided to replace you with another trainer. You will be paid off to the end of the week."

It was already Thursday.

They would not permit me to fulfill my contract, which, actually, had a "no cut" clause.

How could I tell my eagle friends that we were no longer to be a triangle? With a heavy heart, I drove home from the zoo.

The film was completed without me, and I started suit against CBS. It took me three years to win the case and I got a nice financial settlement, but that was really no substitute for not being permitted the once-in-a-lifetime opportunity to breed these magnificent birds.

And yet, the story has a happy ending. I learned again the power of the greatest force in the universe—love. The birds were attempting to nest and breed in the zoo.

15

No Greater Loss

Despite his financial history with more extreme ups and downs than a skycraper's elevators, Dad continued to look for security in his earning power and dollars laid away in banks and investments —to the very last.

I don't mean to criticize him on this account, for we all, at some time in our lives, tend to lean heavily on the material world and consider it to be the only real world.

I've never ceased to admire Dad's courage in the face of financial disaster—especially the fact that he never became embittered by devastating experiences, and he had indomitable courage and faith that good always triumphs.

He had produced three pictures at Warner Brothers to fulfill his contract: *Sergeant York; Rhapsody in Blue,* the life of composer George Gershwin, starring Robert Alda; and *The Adventures of Mark Twain,* starring Fredric March. Each of these motion pictures was a box-office bonanza, and with his healthy percentages of gross earnings, he realized a tremendous amount of cash, which he put into banks, savings and loans, two large apartment buildings, several service stations, stocks and bonds, and life insurance to protect his family.

He used to say, "Well, Bill, now I can realize the goal of a lifetime. I can retire and not be concerned about money, work steadily on 'I Blow My Own Horn'—you know how long I've wanted to write the book about my life—get out in the sun, play golf, and you and I can even get in some fishing."

His eyes had a particular luster whenever he mentioned fishing.

There was only a faint resemblance between his fantasy-tinted picture of retirement and what actually happened. Dad's accounting firm had advised him he was in excellent shape financially for retirement. After conferring with Internal Revenue Service officials, they notified him that he was to be allowed a tremendous tax deduction, based on terminating his corporation and divesting himself of his holdings in these last three films. The premise for the tax benefit was the fact that he was going out of business into retirement and that he had no intentions of producing any more films.

Other top-bracket money-earners, too, were retiring and realizing the same tax shelter, but some began to abuse their privilege by later going back into business. Dad was not one of them. However, he always did live to the hilt, spending lavishly and investing in properties and projects which did not permit him to be financially liquid. Suddenly almost seven years later, the Internal Revenue Service reversed its decision and reclaimed the money Dad had been allowed to keep.

There was no way he could pay back this vast amount. He did everything to prove that he had not used the special IRS clause as a tax loophole, but it did him no good. He then decided to fight the case legally. The IRS did not back down and—for whatever reasons—decided to use Dad as a test case, possibly to set a precedent for other taxpayers.

During all the interchange of correspondence between Washington and Los Angeles, Dad remained confident that he would win because he had observed his tax dispensation with scrupulous honesty.

Then a human error by someone else complicated his case and developed IRS sentiment against him. A letter from the IRS addressed to him in care of his accounting firm requested that he be present at a hearing in Washington, D.C., to participate in a review of his entire tax situation.

A clerk or secretary in the offices mistakenly filed the unopened notification away with other papers in the Lasky file. Dad never saw the letter until he had heard from Washington that his ignoring the summons had placed him in contempt. Ignorance is no excuse in the eyes of the law, and his failure to respond to the summons only put him in a worse position. He was now in default, as well as in arrears.

Despite the numerous discouraging communications and meetings, Dad never had anything but an optimistic attitude when I discussed his situation with him. Some might have called him unrealistic and Pollyannaish, but I feel it was more than that. He believed in the goodness and fairness of everyone. Good just had to triumph. He would not even remotely accept the fact that the government seemed ready to strip him of everything he had.

Although the case had not been finally resolved, Dad was asked by the IRS to prepare and present an inventory of his entire estate and assets—real properties, stocks and bonds, business interests, savings, their home on Saltair, mother's furniture, antiques, jewelry, cars, and all his insurance policies on himself and us children. He was further requested to sign over these assets to the federal government.

Several close friends, including a superior court judge, Helen Sherry, advised him under no conditions to sign this statement. "Do it only if the final ruling is against you, Jesse," they strongly recommended.

"No," said Dad. "I love this country that has made it possible for me to do so well. I can't believe that the government would do anything that is not fair, honest, and completely honorable."

I remember the fateful evening when he gathered the family together and held a counsel to tell us he had made a decision that could affect each of our lives. It was very unusual, for seldom in his lifetime had he discussed business and problems away from his offices.

He began the meeting with, "Children, you know my situation with the government. I have decided to trust them entirely and to do as they have requested. I'm going to sign over to them a full inventory of my assets until such time as a final decision has been rendered."

Immediate protests came from Bess, Jesse, Jr., and Helen, the judge, who was present. All three begged Dad not to sign, and there were suggestions that he should disperse his holdings among each of us, as was his right.

Dad listened to everybody, but was unwavering in his faith in the government. He signed.

Then there was a long period of silence on the Washington end. Even with this suspense, Dad remained optimistic. He did his best to enjoy golf with his divot-digger buddies, but there was always the darkness hovering over him. Frequently, he said to me, "Bill, let's go fishing and forget about all of this." Unfortunately, I was working on some of my most choice Hollywood assignments at these times, and so we had to defer dates over and over again.

Between the times when we would get together to talk, I noted that Dad was beginning to show signs of aging. He was becoming increasingly forgetful and slower and less limber in the way he moved around, although he would never have admitted it. I said to myself, "I'll never forgive myself if we don't have at least one more great fishing trip to the High Sierras together."

Once my motion picture assignment was over, I initiated this fishing trip, and I'm glad I did. It was to be our last one together.

Fishing trips to the High Sierras have always been a thrill to me, not only because I love the adventure of new streams and the excitement of catching the big ones, but because these expeditions allowed me the luxury of being close to Dad and discussing the many stored-up subjects that we had to catch up on. More than that, they always presented a challenge. They became a Hollywood-type expedition and competition as to who would catch the first fish, the biggest fish, and the most fish. These challenges were always backed by large financial bets that nobody was ever required to pay. I had never beaten my father in any area of life, especially fishing. Perhaps this would be the time.

Since this was to be the trip of trips, I decided to share it with my lifelong friend, Fred Gates, whom I had hardly seen since we had been separated by military service.

Dad was then in his mid- or late sixties, and he said, "Bill, who knows how long I or anyone else will be around on this earth, so let's make this our biggest and best fishing trip. We'll spare no expense. We're going first-class!"

I couldn't remember when Dad traveled anything but first-class, but I wondered how, in the presence of imminent doom with the federal government, he could spend money with such a clear conscience.

And so we went shopping even before we knew precisely where we were going. Together we drove to Kerr's Sport Shop in Beverly Hills, and he bought us the best of everything: hundred-dollar Canadian quilt-lined fishing jackets, Arctic goose-down sleeping bags, European trout creels, and so many trout flies, lures, and decoys that I couldn't see how we could possibly use them all.

And then we had to face reality—the most difficult thing of all—exactly where were we going in the vast High Sierras?

Here's where Randy Rogers, Dad's lifelong personal assistant, came in. Dad asked Randy to make a thorough investigation of the fishing potential of the California Sierras. Dad kept repeating, "I don't care what it costs. Bill, Fred, and I are going to catch the big ones."

Following this, he began to come home with brochures, pamphlets, maps, and newspaper ads that promised the ultimate in piscatorial delights. Although Fred and I had been frequently consulted, Dad eventually made the command decision and revealed the chosen place.

Randy had arranged everything—an Isaak Walton paradise, almost inaccessible, and a guide and all the expedition's logistical details.

We three drove into the Sierras as far as Bishop, where we were to start our seven-day trip by horse and pack mules into the primitive and glorious golden trout wilderness called the Muir Trail.

We rendezvoused with the guide and his wife (the cook-helper) and the horses and pack train of five mules. The rendezvous point was at the foot of a gurgling stream, whose headwaters were in the near-impregnable mountains that we were about to invade. As the three of us stepped out of Dad's aging Cadillac, we were greeted by our guide and his wife, who told us it would be a few hours before the packing would be finished.

Dad couldn't wait. He took out his pole and creel. The enchantment of the moving waters had started their spell. In his inimitable way, he looked at me. Years had faded from his face. No more was there the threat of financial ruin—only the promised thrill of adventure. And then, "Why not start fishing right now?"

Before I could comment, Dad continued. "You boys can wait down here if you want to. I'm going after the big ones."

He indicated the stream and repeated the fishing information I had heard since childhood. "You know, if you want the big ones, you always go to the top." He pointed vaguely up the stream and said, "See you later."

"Hey, Fred," I said. "There's a nice pool right over there." I pointed my rod to a place not more than thirty feet from the car. "Let's have a look."

At the pool we did several double takes. Surely our eyes were deceiving us! Casually cruising around the bottom were twenty to thirty sleek, spotted beautiful trout—many twelve inches long or even more. Randy had certainly selected the spot of spots.

"Fantastic," I said. "What incredible fishing country! Why go upstream when the big ones are right here?"

We debated for a minute as to which bait to use, then lost no time rigging our poles with hooks garnished with Norwegian salmon eggs. No sooner had my line hit the water when, *smack*, with a tremendous splash, I had hooked my first trout.

While I was subduing my twelve-inch beauty, Fred shouted, "I've got one, too!"

Soon our creels were packed with beautiful, giant trout.

"Who needs bait?" Fred asked. "Even my bare hook caught me a beauty."

"Never in my life have I seen fishing like this," I told Fred. "This is actually boring. Here we're getting packed to go upstream and we've already got more than enough trout for several meals."

It was such an anticlimax that Fred and I put away our trout poles and assembled our butterfly nets in search of more challenging quarry.

Two hours later Dad came down from the mountain, tired, scratched, bruised, and dirty.

"I hoped you fellows did better than I," he said in a tone that really meant, "I hope *you* didn't catch any *either*."

Fred and I exchanged glances. We didn't dare break it to him suddenly, so we remained silent.

"Fellows, I didn't even get a strike," Dad confided. "I didn't even see a fish. The big ones must be *way* upstream. I just didn't go far enough."

"Dad," I said, "I've got something to show you."

Fred and I brought out our trout-packed creels. His reaction was indescribable as he looked at the fish with utter disbelief and unconcealed envy.

"How did you do it?" he asked.

"Sheer expertise and wizardry, Dad," I smiled smugly.

"That's the only explanation," Fred grinned.

Our guide who had witnessed this last broke into uncontrollable laughter and patted Dad sympathetically on the back.

"There's no question about it, Mr. Lasky. The big ones are way up beyond where you went. But before you accept the words of Bill and Fred about their wizardry, perhaps you and they, too, should know the real explanation."

We all turned to him.

"About fifteen minutes before your car arrived, the Fish and Game man dumped bucket after bucket of big, hungry, hatchery-bred trout right into that pool. There were so starved, you could have caught them with your bare hands."

It was one of the few times I had outfished Dad, and the explanation gave us both many a laugh—and me, another treasured memory of my father.

As the guide had promised, Dad caught many big ones at the top—more than Fred and I did—but he was bothered by the high altitude, which affected his heart and gave him daily distress. This distress envinced itself in petty forgetfulness that was even more vexing to Dad. First he lost his hunting knife, then it was his fishing hat, and then his package of flies. I substituted my identical package for his so that he wouldn't feel upset. Then his flashlight was mislaid, his fishing creel, and, finally, he lost his horse. That is a story that only Fred and I know.

Dad had started out bright and shiny, early in the morning. He planned this day to ride on horseback to a distant high mountain lake that possibly no one had ever before fished.

In high spirits, he ate a good breakfast and rode out of camp with the flourish of Richard the Lion-Hearted. The day passed quickly, but when dinnertime arrived and no Dad, Fred and I became worried.

What could have happened to him? This worry mounted as several hours passed. It was close to nine o'clock when we heard a tired voice penetrating the darkness beyond the campfire.

"Boys," said Dad, "come help me back to camp!"

We ran out to where he was standing and assisted him to the warmth of the campfire. He appeared totally exhausted.

"Where's your horse?" I asked him.

For the first time, I heard him make a confession. "I guess I must be getting too old for this sort of thing. I've lost my hunting knife, my fishing hat, my creel, my flashlight, and now—of all things—my horse, and I didn't even get to the lake."

"How could you possibly lose your horse?" I asked.

"Well, about a half mile past camp, I was riding with the style of a conquering king, and I came upon a German walking party. Every eye was on me as I rode through their camp, and then it happened. Just on the other side, I felt my saddle slip. I had forgotten to tighten the belly strap and, in a second, I was on the ground, and the horse took off without me, leaving me, my saddle, and fishing gear stranded. I continued on foot, trying to find my horse, and lost a whole day's fishing."

At this point, our horses gave a whinny of salutation as Dad's horse gingerly approached his trail mates.

I consoled Dad.

"Don't worry," I said. "We'll get your saddle in the morning, and tomorrow will be another day for fishing."

Through the shadows of the campfire, I saw the expression of weariness on Dad's face that gave confirmation to his words:

"No, Bill, I can't take this high country anymore. My heart has been real painful all day. Actually I've been resting more than walking. We're going to have to get out of the high mountains. I can't take this altitude anymore. Our last fishing trip is over."

Along with the ending of the last fishing trip, Dad's general condition continued to decline.

The night before his death, he came home late and did something very unusual. He entered Bess's bedroom, woke her up, and sat on the edge of her bed. It was an act that surprised her. She struggled to wake from a sound sleep. Many, many years had passed since the last time he had come into her bedroom, and she knew something very important must have happened.

He took her hands in his and said simply, "Bess, I'm home."

"Yes, Jesse," she said with an indulgent smile. "I see you are."

"No, Bess. You don't quite understand. I'm really home. Tomorrow I'm going to spend some time in your beautiful garden. I was noticing earlier today that your tangerine tree was heavy with fruit. I'm going to pick some tangerines and eat them fresh from the tree."

She listened with slight puzzlement. He hadn't picked fruit from a tree since his boyhood in San Jose.

"Bess," he continued, "isn't God wonderful? He puts fruit on our trees and roses in *your* garden. As I came through the living room, I was looking at your beautiful paintings. You are really a fine painter." The unexpected recognition left her speechless.

"You know, Bess, I really love you. I guess I haven't told you that in many years, but I want you to know how I feel."

"Jesse," she said tentatively, "something *has* happened to you . . ."

"Yes. It's all over between the young girl and me. Bess, she really didn't exist. She existed only in my imagination—an external wish for the fountain of youth. She never loved me at all. When I told her the terms of our marriage, that if I divorced you, she would have only me—no cash—to begin life over with, her entire expression and attitude changed. She made a remark I will never forget."

As he continued, Bess noted that his face seemed to sag, his shoulders to round, and his back to bend. Suddenly he appeared to be much older.

"Bess, she said, 'Jesse, I was counting on at least a fifty-fifty community property settlement.' "

Bess tenderly squeezed his hand. She understood.

Dad understood that she understood and had forgiven him. He bent over and kissed her tenderly. Bess later told me that it was a gentle loving kiss that took her back over the years to their early love at Long Lake in the Adirondacks.

"Bess, dear, good night. I have a busy day tomorrow. I'm to hear from the Internal Revenue Service. This will be the final decision on our tax situation. I know they'll be fair with me. I'm also giving a talk to a woman's club at the Hilton—mostly to give a little publicity push to my book." He glanced down at her with a smile. "If they ever make a movie of *I Blow My Own Horn*, they'll have a difficult time finding an actress as lovely as you."

The next day I was working at Warner Brothers on the set of the *Maverick* TV series. Our company had broken for lunch, and I was eating alone in the cafeteria. Suddenly the loudspeaker system boomed out my name:

"Bill Lasky . . . Bill Lasky, you're wanted on the telephone."

I picked up the phone and heard the strained voice of my sister-in-law: "Bill, prepare yourself for a shock."

I knew what the message would be even before she continued: "Your father is no longer with us. After speaking at the Hilton Hotel, he walked down to the entrance for his car. As he lifted a foot to get in, he fell to the pavement. Bill, I don't think he ever knew what had happened. He was dead before the ambulance could arrive. Your mother asked me to phone you. She needs you now. Please go to her."

In a daze, I drove back to the set, and mumbled to the director that my father had just died. Before I could continue, he said, "Bill, you'd better go home."

As I drove out of the Warner Brothers Studios gates, I seemed to be entering into a new world—a world that wouldn't be the same without Dad.

My car radio was on and suddenly I heard a newscaster's voice. The words became personal: "We'll all miss him."

Before I realized it, I was pulling into the driveway of my mother's home, and she was in the front waiting for me. I didn't know what to expect, but Bess, as always, was composed in time of emergency. She hugged and held me for a long time and said softly, "Your dad never felt anything. It was just as if he opened a door and walked out of one room into another." When she released me, I saw her face, and she was crying softly. I had not seen her cry very often.

"Billy," she said, "what am I going to do?"

Then she shifted to another thought. "I had never before heard your father talk like he did earlier today when the tax decision came through. Always there had been hope, always the promise with a new day for a new opportunity, but this final blow had hit him so hard that he had forgotten how to hope. Your dad's simple words told it all. He said, 'Bess, I've got very bad news. This is the very end. The government is going to take everything—even our home, cars, and the life insurance for the kids. I have nowhere to turn.'"

Bess had answered in the only way she knew how. "Jesse, just come home. We'll have your favorite—corned beef hash and poached eggs. You can pick some of the tangerines for dessert. Remember the flowers in our garden are still blooming, and, you'll see, we'll work it all out together."

But my dad's voice was wavery and low.

"No, Bess, this *is* the end. There is no way."

Then he tried to summon up his last bit of courage. "I have to give my talk first, Bess. Then I'll be home."

That was all.

I held my mother in my arms. "It will be all right, Bess. You'll see. We'll work it out together."

Those were my father's words, not mine. They were the words that my father would have wanted me to say.

After Dad's death, even the Saltair home belonged to the government, but Bess decided it wouldn't for long. Although she had a small annuity saved up from the sale of her paintings through the years, this was only enough to sustain her daily living. Helen Sherry came up with a solution.

She struck upon a method of buying the place back. Thanks to good friends, it worked. Representing Mother, Helen asked Sam Goldwyn, Cecil B. DeMille, producer Sol Lesser, Y. Frank Freeman (former president of Paramount Pictures), legitimate stage producer Gilbert Miller, and San Francisco financier Louis Lurie to take a mortgage on the home.

The amount on the home would satisfy the federal government. Bess could live in the house for the remainder of her life, and after her death, these men or their estates would be paid back the principle plus their interest through the sale of the house.

Some people give the impression that they will live forever, that they just might look a wee bit older as time goes by, but that they'll always be here. Bess was one of these. She had been exuberantly healthy all her life, so far as I knew, and that was why when sickness came to her, I could hardly believe it.

For several years, she had been secretly under the care of Dad's heart specialist. One day he took the liberty of phoning me and said, "Bill, I don't like to tell you this, but your mother has had diabetes for a long time. I've been keeping it in check with medication. The diabetes is complicated by a heart condition, about which she's very concerned. It could be serious. She hasn't wanted to alarm you!"

But this did not stop us from weekly lobster dinner dates at our favorite restaurant, Moby's Dock. Ever since Dad's death these dinners with her had become very special occasions.

Neither did it stop her from attempting to pursue her favorite pastime. Periodically she would try to capture on canvas the flowers in her garden, but it was like my dad's last fishing trip. She even asked me to set up her easel in front of the lily pool, where a large Egyptian lotus had just burst into bloom. She said, "Stay with me, dear, as you used to when you were a little boy." But after merely a charcoal attempt to capture the blossom on canvas, she made an admission that I had never heard her make before. "You know, dear, I guess I'm not as young as I used to be. I think I'll go inside and just lie down for a little while. We can try again another day."

Only then did I become aware that she looked older, that her hand had trembled as she held the charcoal.

On the previous Mother's Day and on a number of other occasions since, I had given her a white cattaleya orchid plant. Now she had six or seven around the house, and she loved them almost as much as her roses.

Several months passed, and her condition worsened, but, even then, when I arrived at her bedside, no matter how weak she was, she would rise and say, "Come on, Billy, let's take a look at my roses."

It was always a thrill to me to see what roses did for her. No matter how tired she would be, I could see a touch of youth come back in her eyes and facial expression. Dad with his trout; Mother with her roses.

"Oh, how I would love to paint some of the roses again," she told me.

"Bess," I said, "let me make you a flower arrangement."

Then the enthusiasm faded and again she looked her age. "No, Billy, I will never paint again."

A sinking feeling entered my heart.

I tried to convince her that she could, even if only to reassure myself, but she seemed to have deeper knowledge.

Then a number of weeks later her condition worsened and she fell into a deep coma. The doctor told me that she would probably never again be able to talk or even be aware of what we were saying to her.

I visited her often. On rare days, she would come out of the coma and say just a few words. "Billy, you know I think I'm going to be well enough to have one more lobster dinner with you. Perhaps you *can* make that flower arrangement for me."

We never did have that last dinner together. Almost immediately she sank back into the coma and never regained consciousness, and soon the doctor insisted that she go into a hospital where he had all the facilities to care for her.

On the last day before we moved her I walked from the living room to her bedroom and felt a chill. It was not from the cold. It was for another reason. There was not a single flower in the house, only empty vases. The last of the white cattleya plants were neglected on a coffee table. At the base of the pot was a fallen, wilted bloom.

I had a feeling that I would never again see Bess alive. I had to do one last thing for her. I went into her garden and picked every flower I could find—armfuls of beautiful roses, zinnias, asters, Canterbury bells, irises, and gardenias.

Then I went into the kitchen cupboards where most of the vases had been put away. Filling each of them with water, I made the arrangements. It was as if I had brought her garden indoors, but I brought only roses into her bedroom and placed a large, single red rose beside her bed.

The nurse who looked after Bess said, "Mr. Lasky, why are you doing this? Your mother can no longer see. She doesn't hear what we are saying. She hasn't been able to talk for weeks. What's the point?"

"A very good point," I said. "She knows they're here."

"But she has been unconscious for weeks."

"She knows," I insisted.

As the nurse left, shaking her head in disbelief, I had to acknowledge to myself that Bess had not been able to communicate for weeks. I knew she was near the end, and I wanted to say one last good-by to her and know that she had heard me. Perhaps she couldn't see—or, in her unconsciousness, even hear—but there was a way to communicate with her.

I took the vase with the large red rose into my hand, bent low over her, and put it near her.

"Here is your rose, Bess," I said. "I have filled your room full of roses right from your garden."

I could see no response, but I went ahead anyway.

"Bess, I have a feeling that this is to be our last visit together. I know I have to say good-by to you. It's the hardest thing I've ever had to do."

She lay still, her face white and not a sign of life except shallow breathing. She was curled up under the bedding like a tiny doll.

"Bess, dear," I continued, "do you remember the most beautiful rose I ever found for you when I was a kid and you were so busy painting? Do you remember that glorious butterfly who used to visit you every day under the jacaranda—our butterfly? Do you remember your first visit to my aviary and those beautiful hummingbirds among the white cattleya orchids?"

I studied her face for even the slightest sign that she had heard, but there was none. I couldn't bear the thought that we would not be able to communicate again.

"Bess, I won't say good-by. You see, you will always be with me. Every time I see a beautiful red rose, a sunset, a hummingbird, or a butterfly, no matter where I am, I know you will always be there."

Still I could see no reaction.

"Bess," I said, "let me know you have heard me. Let me know that you understand. Please give me some sign."

Again I studied her expressionless face and was about to turn away, when something attracted my attention. A tear began to form in the corner of her eye.

"Thank you, dear," I said, kissed her on the cheek, and left my Bess and her roomful of roses. It was the last time I saw her alive.

16

Out of the Tunnel, into the Light

At the age of forty-seven, I became aware of a strange paradox in my life. No matter how high the score of activity and achievements, the total added up to zero. As I thought back, nothing had any value to me. A life of an accumulation of experiences and achievements and learning had arrived at a total void.

As the feeling grew, so did my feeling of distress, dislike, and disappointment in myself. What good was it all? I asked myself if I had ever achieved happiness or peace of mind, and my disheartening answer was negative.

Certainly I have always searched for truth, but what truth? It seemed as if everything I had learned had taught nothing. One more question, and the most distressing of all, I thought. Have I ever experienced love? This was too heavy for me to contemplate further.

There was no way of my knowing it as one evening I headed my car down Ventura Boulevard in the San Fernando Valley, but I was following a plan and heading in the direction of an answer.

My thoughts were interrupted by the sight of two young boys hitchhiking in the dark. They were dressed in blue jeans and white T-shirts and appeared to be about eight years old. It has always bothered me to see youngsters hitchhiking. I believe parents should assume the responsibility of transporting their children. These two were headed for a destination near where I was going, so I invited them in. They climbed into the back seat. I scolded the boys for being out alone at night, but it seemed to roll off of them. One towheaded surfer type said, "It's cool, dad."

The other joined in. "Hey, dad, you want to come to a groovy happening?"

Over my shoulder, I said, "No, thank you."

My mind couldn't encompass what kind of a groovy happening two eight-year-old "teeny-boppers" would invite me to. Picking up their hipster jargon, I surprised them with the question, "Young dudes, what's the gig?"

After recovering, the first boy gave me a hipster kudo.

"Dad, you're real cool. We're going to a Buddhist meeting. It's a real groovy gig. You go down on your knees . . ."

The second boy cut in. "And, yeah, man, you rub your beads and chant."

Somehow I couldn't picture myself on my knees and chanting, but then came the shocker. The first boy said, "Oh, come on, man. It's a real groove and, besides, we don't turn on to smack anymore."

As I looked back over my shoulder, he lifted his arm, showing me the unmistakable hypodermic needle scars.

My mind slipped a few cogs in coming to the realization that these grade school kids had used heroin.

"I'm glad you're off that stuff," I replied, thinking that Buddhism had to be an improvement.

"Dad, why don't you come along with us?" the first boy asked.

"No, thanks," I replied.

The second boy said, "You haven't lived until you've tried Buddhism."

I chuckled. Here was the worldly wisdom of eight years telling forty-seven years he hadn't lived.

We reached the street where the boys wanted to get out, and I said good-by with a further caution about their hitchhiking.

As my car traveled into the night, the dialogue of the kids stayed with me. Maybe the kids were right. I just didn't belong anywhere or have any religion, but soon after that the incident faded out of my mind.

A few months later, I was working as an assistant director on the set of a TV series at Warner Brothers Studios and was asked to host a student visitor who was studying motion picture making at the University of California, Los Angeles. He commented on the large number of studio personnel on the set, some apparently doing nothing. I explained that they all had intermittent functions and were subject for call at any minute.

"Directors don't hold still for unnecessary delays when they're ready to shoot. That's the reason for what appears to be idling."

As we chatted, he suddenly turned to me. "I've been studying something lately that might interest you. It's modern-day Buddhism."

Without blinking an eye, I took him completely by surprise with, "Oh, you don't turn on to smack anymore?"

In total confusion, he said, "What do you mean by that? I have never turned on to smack in my life."

I explained with the story of the two hitchhiking youngsters, and he laughed, assuring me that not all Buddhists are dopers and that there is great wisdom in the philosophy of Buddhism.

As we parted, he made a prediction that I thought entirely unlikely. "It's been nice to meet you, Bill. Maybe you'll try it sometime."

It is strange how often in my life things appear in threes, but a third event was about to take place, specifically directing my life.

A few months later, I was working at Universal Studios, and the star of that TV show was Tommy Rettig, former boy lead in the long-lasting *Lassie* TV series.

"Bill," said Tommy, "my wife and I would like you to come over for dinner next Sunday. We've got a surprise planned."

I liked Tommy—and particularly surprises—so I accepted the invitation.

After dinner I was about to relax in an overstuffed chair, when Tommy said, "Come on, it's time for the surprise. We're taking you somewhere in the car."

We drove to the beach front of Santa Monica, where we entered a small, broken-down beach house. I was instructed to take off my shoes. As we walked into the living room, I paused for a second in total disbelief of what I heard and saw.

Directly in front of me were several dozen people on their

knees, rubbing beads and chanting in a strange language, and I had a quick recall of the "teeny-boppers."

This was a Buddhist meeting!

I had no intention of joining what was going on. The only time I had gone on my knees had been before the statue of St. Theresa at Notre Dame, so when Tommy indicated that I could just sit on the floor, I felt relieved.

For a half hour, the group chanted a phrase that was incomprehensible to me. Then the speaker got up and said that the chant I had been hearing, "*Nom myo ho renge kyo*," was translated, "I devote myself to the mystic play of cause and effect through sound."

He continued, and what he said made sense to me.

Our lives resemble a charging lion who always takes one step backward before taking three steps forward.

He explained that Buddhists did not concern themselves with an afterlife, but the entire focus of their religion was making good causes in this life which would promise good effects in the next. This was called karma, the law of cause and effect.

I was fascinated by everything I heard. I had never experienced any discussion or explanation of a religious philosophy before, and, besides, I realized how hungry I was for anything that would bring me closer to truth.

After the meeting, Tommy turned to me, "How about it, Bill?"

I heard myself saying words I could hardly believe. "I'll try it. Maybe I'll like it."

I agreed to go to the Buddhist Temple in the grape-growing community of Etiwanda. Following an impressive service there, I received a prayer scroll, called a gohonson, and was assured that I had become a Buddhist.

My Buddhist leaders told me that this was my most priceless possession. I gazed at the gohonson and the writing on its face. It was all meaningless. The hieroglyphiclike symbols were in the long-since-dead language of Sanskrit.

We had been instructed to keep a branch of fresh evergreen in front of our small shrines that held our gohonsons.

I studied the philosophy deeply and sincerely, as I do all things. This went on for five years, and at fifty-two, I found myself right back where I had started.

For five long years, I had been as faithful as a human being could be about Buddhism. I had studied all I could get my hands on, and, oh, the countless hours I had knelt before my gohonson, chanting, chanting, chanting endlessly and rubbing my black and shiny beads.

One day, I knew I could do this no longer. Five years of Buddhism had concluded in emptiness for me.

I had been instructed to keep a branch of fresh evergreen in front of my shrine, but mine was withered with neglect. We were further instructed to keep a little cup of water to symbolize the essence of life, but my cup was dry.

It was plain to me now that what I needed most in life, true love, was not present in the dry cup, the dried branch, or the ink-inscribed piece of paper. I felt sick at heart. Instead of the promised happiness and fulfillment, my life seemed filled with so many problems that no piece of paper could help me solve.

In the weeks that followed, everything seemed to climax. I learned that one of my closest friends was a heroin addict.

Then I was bitten by a poisonous copperhead snake and suffered indescribable pain. Right after returning from the hospital, my landlord told me that my rented home and yard containing my orchid and hummingbird collection—which had become almost as neglected as the pine branch in front of the gohonson—were to be sold out from under me. And I was still depressed from my mother's death. I had cut myself off from all but one of my closest friends, and I couldn't even find companionship with other Buddhists. I felt uncomfortable with them. My much-loved hobbies no longer interested me.

I had been in a long period of unemployment and was heavily in debt. I hated to answer the telephone or open my mail to receive the dunning letters of creditors.

One disappointment after another had hit my little bird and animal business, "Of Cabbages and Hummingbirds," and my bank account had become such a mess that the banks closed it with my promise to make good my arrears within the next several months.

Finally, a check that I had expected to help me buy food was not backed by sufficient funds and had to be returned to its maker, who had skipped town.

I sold off all of my prize hummingbirds, and, with this money, had just enough to pay the first month's rent on a small unfurnished apartment at the foot of Laurel Canyon at Hollywood Boulevard.

Moving day was bleak and wet. It was the season's first rain—a continuous downpour. Two kids had volunteered to move me in their open truck for twenty-five dollars, but I had to help. There wasn't even a tarp to cover my furnishings, so we moved as best we could. By the time the boxes, clothing, and furniture were unpacked in the apartment, everything, including bedding, was soaked through. Even my two green parakeets were wet.

My entire worldly belongings were in the middle of the living room floor. As the truck pulled away, I felt alone in the world. Exhausted and hungry, I wanted something to eat. Turning my trouser pocket inside out, I found only my keys and six cents.

Occasionally in times past when the income was limited, I had fed my pets discarded outer leaves of lettuce from the large galvanized metal garbage cans in the rear of supermarkets.

Maybe I could find something there for myself.

The idea was so repellent that nausea almost overwhelmed me. I drank glass after glass of water just to fill my stomach, but, again, in a few hours I was hungry.

Then I decided to take a walk and found my footsteps leading me to the rear of a supermarket. Within a garbage can, I found the usual outer lettuce leaves and—windfall of windfall—some apples with only a few spots of decay. I put the apples and lettuce leaves inside a clean cardboard box and hurried back to the apartment, where I vigorously washed the lettuce and the apples, cutting way the rotting portions, and ate.

This routine went on for several days, accompanied by a new low in depression. Continuous rain and the low-wattage lighting in the apartment brought no cheer. My thoughts crowded in on me. I had lost my wife and treasured son, Ronnie, through divorce, had lost both my dad and mother. I was still low about having lost my best friend through heroin addiction. Loss. Loss. Loss. That was the story of my life.

I had lost my business, my Laurel Canyon home, my hummingbirds, and, now, even my dignity and pride.

When I entered the kitchen for a glass of water, I saw a film of grease on the old-fashioned gas range, which had a slow leak, and my mind flashed back to the contrast of our mansion at 609 Ocean Front. Five Rolls-Royces . . . a private railroad car . . . twenty-seven servant's rooms . . . Academy Award nominee William R. Lasky, for *The Boy and the Eagle*. The son of Jesse L. Lasky, cofounder of Hollywood! If they could see me now!

Suddenly I no longer wanted to live. In one of the soggy boxes directly in front of me was my Academy Award nomination certificate, framed in black—an appropriate color.

"If there's anything less than nothing, that's what I am," I told myself and went into the kitchen and quickly turned on all the gas jets, breathing deeply until all of a sudden a peculiar thought came to me.

"The escaping gas will kill the birds—and maybe others in the apartment building!"

My trembling hands quickly shut off all jets.

That was the wrong way to do it.

I remembered sleeping pills left over from a doctor's prescription. Maybe there would be enough to finish the job. I hurriedly opened the vial. Ah, eight left. That should be enough. I filled a glass with water and put all the pills into my mouth, but I couldn't swallow them.

The thought of my son and the fact that he would have to live his life with the memory that his father had committed suicide stopped me for an instant. I tried again, raising the water glass. Suddenly my parakeets began to chatter madly as if they were fighting.

I spat out the sleeping pills and ran to see what was the matter. All was peaceful in the cage, and I could not understand the reason for their warlike chattering, but as I looked at my green birds, I realized they had saved my life.

Starting from the parakeet incident, an idea began forming in my mind. Why not try to get a job in a pet shop? At least that would mean food money.

Just the thought of modest employment among my friends the animals and birds took the black thoughts from my mind, and within a few days, I did have a pet shop job.

For many weeks, I worked in the happy atmosphere of animals, birds, and snakes. The store even had some exotic pets from South America and Africa.

I had no way of knowing that the job wouldn't last. A couple came in to buy a dog collar for their little dachshund and to price a parrot. The woman reminded me of Mademoiselle Branche. She was direct, sunny, and warm. The man was tall and broad, a Nordic type with a heavy beard. He reminded me of the Vikings of old, and yet, in contrast, he was jolly and ingenuous as Santa Claus. I liked him immediately. They asked if there was an appreciable difference in the quality of the highest and lowest priced collars. I replied in sincerity, "No, there isn't."

They bought the lowest-priced collar.

The lady then said, "We're considering buying a parrot, but yours seem way high-priced. Couldn't I do better elsewhere?"

The parrots were very much overpriced. "Yes, you can," I said in honesty.

"Thank you," they said and started to leave. But even before they were outside the door, the owner of the store jumped me.

"You're fired," he stormed. "You lost me the parrot sale. Those people would have paid anything for what they wanted."

The rapid pace of events left me in a semi-daze. Within a few minutes, I was out on the parking lot, getting into my car.

"Hey, wait a second," someone called. It was the couple who had been in the store.

"We're the Winters," said the man. "My wife's name is Harmonne, and my name is Richard Erik. We couldn't help hearing that you were fired for being honest—and on our account."

"What's your name?" asked Harmonne.

"Bill Lasky," I replied.

They invited me to their house in the Barham area of Burbank for a cup of coffee and questioned me until I bared my soul about my problems, including the fact that I was too down to go back to my depressing apartment.

To my amazement, Richard and Harmonne invited me to share their home. They served as brother and sister and foster parents in one beautiful, big, and generous package. Never once did it seem that I was an inconvenience to them. They always treated me as if I were a member of the family.

Still heavily depressed, I set aside job-hunting, and they understood without questions. I visited my own apartment every two or three days only to feed and water my parakeets and clean their cages. It was more than I could stand to stay there for more than a few minutes.

All the clothing I had was a pair of army suntan pants, a sport shirt, and a pair of sneakers. Each night when I went to bed, Harmonne would wash my clothes and have them clean and ready for me in the morning. I had no interest in myself or the physical world. What did I have to live for? What was happening to me? I was in a state like walking dead.

One evening at about eleven o'clock, I was driving back to the Winters from a visit with one of my friends, Ken Paradise. I saw a figure standing by the side of the road next to a lamppost in a sparsely populated residential area on the Hollywood side of Barham Boulevard.

In the weak light of the lamp, I saw it was a young man. I said to myself, "He'll never get a ride. Not enough cars."

I stopped my car and opened the door. Then, just as I did this, I saw the glint of the street light reflecting on a shiny pistol. At that very instant, I saw a round circle of fire.

I didn't hear the shot because I guess I was in a state of shock. Instinctively, my foot hit the accelerator, the car shot forward, and the door closed with a slam.

At that moment, I got a look at the face. It was a strange kind of face such as I had never before seen. The dark beard and hair came together in a circle, and the hair seemed to come to a point on the center of his head. I have never seen such cruel, cold eyes.

It must have been a blank cartridge, I thought. Probably a practical joke, but the car's rapid acceleration by now had moved me a few blocks away. Suddenly my back felt wet. That's funny. Without giving the matter much thought, I put my hand on my back and brought it forward. I could see that it was covered with blood.

"I *have* been *shot*," I said to myself and drove quickly the remaining few blocks to the Winters' home, hurried inside, and tapped on their bedroom door and entered.

"Harmonne, Richard, wake up! I've got something to tell you. Don't be frightened, but I've been shot."

I was bleeding profusely, and they held a towel to my back. Richard hurriedly bundled me into his car and drove me to the police station from where I was rushed to the Presbyterian Receiving Hospital's emergency room.

I was operated on and a bullet removed from under my left shoulder blade.

"Very lucky," said the surgeon. "A few inches in either direction, and the bullet could have gone through your lungs or your spinal column. I guess it just wasn't your time!"

The police report stated, "Attempted Manslaughter," but the person who fired the gun was never found. Investigation revealed that no one had seen anybody in the area who answered the description.

During the healing period, I wondered why my life had been spared for the third time—first the car accident, next the poisonous snake, and now the gunshot. Certainly my life had no point, no meaning. Why couldn't the assailant have aimed more accurately? Why couldn't he have done to me what I had been trying to do to myself?

In a few days the stitches and adhesive tape had been removed, and the doctors declared me well, but I had reached the absolute bottom of despair. Surely there must be some way I could end my misery.

I couldn't do it in the Winters' home. They were too wonderful people. How could I possibly bring them grief in return for kindness and generosity?

I got into my car. I tried to drive over the double lines in opposing traffic, but I couldn't do that and hurt innocent people.

Then I thought of the freeway. I could aim my speeding car at the concrete support in the center, but what if it bounced off and caused an accident killing somebody else?

In a daze, I drove back to the Winters' and entered my bedroom and shut the door. I had seen many motion pictures of perfect crimes. Maybe some clever methods would get the job done for me in a way that wouldn't look like suicide.

Then the perfect plan came to me. A friend who was an animal trainer owned an Indian hooded cobra. I could use the pretext of wanting to rent the cobra for a film, then antagonize the snake. One bite, and that would be it!

As I was phoning the trainer, I seemed to run into a stop signal in my mind. If the snake did bite and kill me, my friend would feel guilty, as if he were a party to my death.

No, I couldn't do that to him.

I had thought of or tried every possible way. Now, alone in my room, I found nowhere to turn. Never have I known such despair, such utter hopelessness. I couldn't bring myself to die, and I didn't want to live.

In that moment, I remembered Mademoiselle Branche and my childhood, her last good-by, and the little ivory statue of the baby Jesus, which she had given me, and what she had said about the Jesus child loving me. And then I remembered the whole world was in his hands.

I was on my knees. I prayed out loud in the only prayer I knew how: "Now I lay me down to sleep. I pray the Lord my soul to keep. If I should die before I wake, I pray the Lord my soul to take."

Then, looking up, I heard myself saying, "*Jesus, help me!*"

17

Born Again

An instant on my knees asking for Jesus' help had accomplished more than a lifetime of traveling a thousand dead-end streets.

He must increase, but I must decrease.

This bit of wisdom was becoming very real to me.

Why had it taken fifty-two years for a simple act of submission?

Now I could not understand why I had made things so hard for myself. I was able to move back into the same apartment that had depressed me so, and, although the day was gray, sunshine seemed to be flooding the rooms. It was clear to me that many of us have to hit the bottom before we can go to the top.

In the months that followed, an increased awareness grew bit by bit, hour by hour, that I was not empty as before, but more than this, where there had been a void and a craving for love, there was a sense of fulfillment and peace.

French physicist Blaise Pascal had a special term for the hollow that exists in all of us, whether we are cognizant of it or not. He called it the "God-shaped vacuum." Even before I had heard of this, I had regarded myself as one half of a circle. Only God's love, through Jesus, could complete the circle.

With the prayer to Jesus to help me, there came more than the feelings I have described. My financial depression, too, came to an abrupt end. The phone rang in my newly arranged apartment, and a voice that I did not know said, "Mr. Lasky, we need an experienced assistant director on an unusual assignment. Would you be available to start immediately? You can anticipate a year's steady employment."

I was hired by Columbia's Screen Gems to work on the TV series *Police Story*.

My two little parakeets appeared glad that I had returned and showed their happiness by starting housekeeping and laying eggs, but this was only the beginning.

A new desire was born inside me, one that was totally unexplainable within context of the past and so totally foreign to my nature that it would only be God-given: simply, I wanted to go to church.

More than wanting to go to church, I *had* to go to church. So every Sunday I headed my car down a street and went inside the first church that appeared. In the several months that went by, I visited Baptist, Episcopalian, Catholic, Lutheran, Congregational, Presbyterian, and others. A person conducting a sampling of existing Christian churches couldn't have covered a broader range.

I felt peace and happiness in each church, but my desire to participate in services that I couldn't understand left me confused and frustrated.

Why were they all so different? My abysmal lack of church knowledge and experience gave me the impression that they should be more or less alike. Some were heavily decorated with Gothic art and statues while others were as plain as a hospital room. Some services were in Latin, others in English. In some the parishioners genuflected and crossed themselves. In others they did not. There was even one church where the congregation raised their hands above their heads. All these variations gave me a greater desire to learn and understand.

I knew that I needed one church to call home, but which one? Where did I belong?

Four months slipped by and slowly there was dawning in me a new need, call it fellowship, companionship, or brotherhood. I needed somebody to go to church with me, someone to guide me through the wilderness of the Bible text, someone who could answer my questions about the differences in the various churches and their services.

On one particular Sunday, I stumbled, without even knowing it, upon the church that was to be my church. Initially, I found it a strange and slightly embarrassing place. Although everybody was friendly, I heard for the first time someone speaking in tongues.

My reaction to this was a desire to find a logical explanation for such illogical behavior. I quickly concluded that it must be some Far Eastern language. I was startled and confused when someone not even near the person who had spoken translated the words into English. The latter person had to be a relative who had sat in a different part of the church.

How could this foreign language come from obviously American people?

On top of all this, the pastor asked for each person in the congregation to worship the Lord in his or her own way. This was really something—free-style worshiping. With everybody doing his own thing in his own way, I didn't know what was expected of me, so all I could do was repeat my initial prayer, "Jesus, help me." Amid all this confusion, I really needed help.

Then Pastor Leroy Sanders invited those who wanted to receive Jesus into their lives to come forward and kneel at the altar, and it was as if I were being lifted up by a host of husky angels and transported to the front of the church, where I found myself on my knees at the foot of the cross. The angels may be an extravagance of my imagination, but there is no explaining the speed with which I traveled from the rear of the church to the front.

And then I felt hands on my shoulders, and the pastor was praying in the background. I don't remember all of the details, but the essence of prayer that I said will never leave me.

I repeated after the pastor that I asked Jesus to forgive me of my sins and then, as I knelt, I prayed within myself, "Jesus, forgive me for being a Jew."

I completely forgot that Jesus was not only a Jew but the King of the Jews.

I said, "Jesus, I want to make you a deal." My eyes were shut in prayer. "If you will send somebody to go to church with me, someone who will pray with me and instruct me in the Bible, I will serve you for the rest of my days. You will own me, body and soul."

Then I opened my eyes and realized that people were all around me. Members of the congregation had come forward and laid hands on me. I thought, "It's funny, again no clap of thunder, no bolt of lightning."

As the following week crowded in, I totally forgot about my

prayerful deal, but Jesus hadn't. He had heard and was getting ready to answer my prayer. On the following Sunday, I was tying my tie before going to church when the phone rang. It was an old studio friend, Ron Nyman, who said, "Bill, we're going to have breakfast at the International House of Pancakes on Santa Monica Boulevard at La Cienega. Can you join us? There will be some friends of yours and also a person who wants to meet you."

There was nothing I wanted to do less. I am a punctual person, and getting to church on time had become a ritual.

"No, Ronnie, thanks a lot," I said. "I'm rushing off to church."

"Bill," he replied, "just come by and have some blueberry pancakes. We won't mind it if you eat and run."

With the words "blueberry pancakes," he had me.

"Oh, all right," I replied, "but will you order and have them ready? I'll only have ten or fifteen minutes with you."

So I joined the breakfast group, and he introduced me to the person who had wanted to meet me.

"Bill, this is Gene Arnaiz, a lay minister visiting from Stockton."

I learned later that Gene had been campaigning for the Lord in Texas. I looked up from my pancakes and heard the words "Gene wants to go to church. He has nobody to go with. Can you take him?"

Between finishing the pancakes and my impatience to leave for church, I hardly looked twice at Gene, a slender, darkly handsome young man whose family, I later learned, were descendants of Spanish land-grant holders in California and Mexico.

"Oh, sure, Gene," I said. "Come on along."

Often our minds are blunted when they should be acute. Only when we got into my car did I remember my prayer when I had asked for somebody to go to church with. Half jokingly I said to Gene, "Are you the answer to my prayer?"

"God always answers prayers, Bill," Gene replied. "Of course, I am." Then he took me by surprise by asking, "Are you the answer to *my* prayer?"

I glanced sharply at him and almost ran a red light.

"What do you mean by that?"

"I feel the Lord has called me to Hollywood to help someone in a special need."

He looked me squarely in the eye.

"Bill, you are walking out of God's permissive will into God's perfect will, and I sense the spirit of the Lord is guiding you into an unusual ministry."

I knew intuitively that Gene was going to help me in my Christian growth. Our meeting had been an accident—one of those accidents that God carefully plans. At this point, I second-guessed God about his selection of Gene for me.

Honestly, I had expected someone my own age to introduce me to the wisdom of the Bible. Instead I had met a young man—less than half my age and yet seemingly with many times my understanding.

As we came up to the impressive stone front of an old Presbyterian church in Hollywood, I said, "Gene, I haven't yet told you what my prayer was. I prayed for someone to go with me to church and to help me with the Bible."

Gene answered me in a totally unexpected way, but in a manner to which I became accustomed over the following months. "Bill, no Christian ever goes to church alone. First, he has Jesus, and, second, he has the entire body of Christ—the whole congregation, of which he becomes a part."

"Oh yes," I said politely, "but I still need a particular person and one who will help me select a church. I've been to so many different ones."

Gene smiled, and as we walked toward the church, he made a remark that I couldn't understand.

"You baby Christians are all alike. Yet with soft food and tender care, you will grow. One day, very soon, the table may be turned, and, who knows, you may become my old man in the Lord."

This first church service together was unforgettable. An odd occurrence brought me back again to my childhood dream of the dark tunnel and the bright light. As I sat next to Gene, I silently prayed to my new friend, Jesus, thanking him for accepting me, for answering my prayer, and for the numerous blessings he was showering upon me.

Then I gradually became aware of a strange phenomenon. It seemed that Gene and I were bathed in a cone of white sunlight. I looked up to the source, and high up under the church's vaulted ceiling, I noted that sunlight was streaming through a small opening in the stained-glass window. How incredible it was that with a church full of people, Gene and I were key-lighted from heaven.

This was the first of many signs from heaven that could not be ignored.

Following the church service, Gene and I went back to my apartment, and we had a first lesson in Bible study. We used Gene's Bible because I had none. Before we started, he instructed me to pray for understanding of the words—the way Jesus wanted me to understand them—and so my learning began.

As we talked and became better acquainted, we felt a strong bond of friendship beginning to develop. In the hours that slipped by, Gene questioned me about my family. I answered as best I could and gave him hundreds of questions about churches, doctrines, and Christian concepts.

I told Gene of my background of Jewish parents and was surprised when he observed, "Bill, you were born a Jew, and you will die a Jew. This is a rich heritage. You are one of God's chosen people. I envy you. Consider me with my gentile background. When I accepted Jesus, I literally became a grafted-on Jew—a non-Jew who became grafted onto the body of Christ. You, in accepting Jesus Christ, do not become any less a Jew but, rather, a completed Jew."

It was the first time I had heard this term.

Soon I was to learn from reading parts of the Old and New Testaments more and more of my Jewish heritage. I later said to Gene, "For the first time in my life, I'm proud I am a Jew."

As the days went by, Gene and I became more aware of the answer to our prayers, and also that we both had a decision to make. One night over lobster bisque at Alphy's, I suddenly heard words coming out of my mouth I seemed to have no control over. "If I'm to continue learning about the Bible and God from my wise old man teacher, it makes sense for you to live in Hollywood rather than Stockton. Why not move into my spare bedroom? We can share living expenses and our unique expertise."

Gene smiled and said, "Why not, except for one thing."

That piqued my interest. "What?"

"Bill, the Bible definitely forbids idol worship and cautions that we should have no gods before him. So, before I move in, your Buddhist shrine has to go."

Although I had lived with my Buddhist shrine for years, it had grown dusty with neglect, and I had hardly thought of it. The shrine had been a deeply ingrained part of my past life and home, and I had never really considered the possibility of taking it down.

As a Buddhist, I had been cautioned, time and time again, that to deface or to mar the paper gohonson would in some mystical way cause the same injury to my own life. No one is even allowed to touch the surface of the gohonson with his hands under threat to injury to its owner, so I answered, "Couldn't we kind of leave it up for a little while?"

"Bill, that represents your past, not your present or your future. You must cut away from the past cleanly. Take your choice. It's the gohonson or me."

So I carefully rolled up the scroll and gently wrapped it in a lavender silk Thai handkerchief that my mother had given me. Then I put the gohonson carefully away in a top drawer of my dresser, gently closing the drawer. Just as carefully, in case I should need them later, I put into a small box the little water container, the dried evergreen branch, incense burner and candleholders and candles, and a little bell that punctuates prayers.

That was not all. I remembered one more item but decided to overlook it—a little ancient statue of Buddha, the memento of my mother's and my day of the hummingbirds.

This little statue that she had treasured for many years was now my only physical remembrance of her aside from photos. All furnishings, antiques, statuary, and paintings had been sold to pay off creditors.

As Gene walked around surveying his new home, he paused in front of the statue and said simply, "I cannot share a house with a graven image." He had no way of understanding what the statue meant to me. The statue joined the gohonson in the dresser drawer.

Gene moved in, but in my heart I felt the problem had not been permanently solved. And so the baby Christian began to grow.

When he asked me if I wanted to drive up to Stockton with him, I said it would have to be a long weekend "if my back will take the trip."

Then I told him my history of shoulder and spinal injuries that had started with the shock treatments, had been compounded by the head-on collision, and were now reactivated by hours on the hard pavement in the *Police Story* series.

His plan was to get the rest of his clothing to move to Hollywood. He had come to Southern California only for a brief visit, but the week had stretched into months. About that time, *Police Story* phased out, so the time was right for a trip before a new series got rolling at Universal. Gene wanted to show me the magnificent mountains a few hours' drive from Stockton. We decided to drive up in my car, although my spine continued to bother me.

On the drive, Gene commented:

"Young man in Christ," he said, "it is time for you to follow the Lord's commandment to be baptized. We can combine the trip back home with a mountain visit, and you can be baptized in my church, the Calvary Tabernacle Assembly of God Church in Stockton."

The winter cold and the seven-hour drive aggravated the pain in my back and shoulders to such an extent that by the time I arrived at the little Stockton motel where I was staying, I was so crippled that Gene had to help me out of the car.

Alone in my room, I wanted to find a postcard. Opening the desk drawer, I paused in surprise. Here was an old friend—a brand-new Gideon Bible. I opened it and read the message:

"This Bible has been placed for your use by the Gideon Society, who would be most pleased if you would take it with you."

I didn't own a Bible. I felt this Bible was meant to be mine, and I determined that this time nothing would get me to part with it. I wrote my name in the inside of the cover.

Curled up in bed that night, I read *my own* Bible for the first time since the Notre Dame crisis. I opened to John 14, and as my eye traveled down the page, it stopped at the fourteenth verse. I read:

"If ye shall ask anything in my name, I will do it."

I said, "Dear Jesus, you answered my prayer for a friend to pray with, someone to go to church and read the Bible with, and now I pray that you heal my back and shoulders so that I can be baptized and be able to get out of the tank."

The following day, Gene and I took the promised drive through the Mark Twain country, although my pain had increased and hardly permitted me to enjoy the trip. He had phoned his church and made arrangements for my baptism, which was to take place that night upon our return.

As we drove down from the snow-blanketed mountains and approached the beautiful church, I suddenly felt an intensifying of my pain. It was so excruciating I had trouble getting out of the car.

Gene helped me into the little dressing room where I took off my clothes and put on the white baptismal robe. The pain continued.

"Really, Gene. My back feels as if half a dozen knives are stuck in it. Just suppose I get down into that tank and can't get out?"

Gene's smile and answer were not too reassuring. "Bill, you are following the Lord's commandment in being baptized in water. I'm sure the Lord knows what is in store for you."

I wish I could have shared the Lord's information.

All I could do was join the line of new converts. One of them was saying he had heard that the water in the baptismal tank was heated. It had better be, I thought. After all, it was winter and it occurred to me that Stockton's water supply came from snow in the mountains.

When it was my turn, I slipped down into the tank and gasped in shock. Only a polar bear would have been comfortable in what seemed to be near freezing water.

The pastor lowered me quickly and expertly beneath the surface, and as I shot upward, my arms went up and I shouted, "Praise the Lord."

The miracle of forgiveness was coupled with a total healing of my back and shoulders. No sign of pain was left, and I needed no help out of the tank. Nor have I ever since had pain in three years.

A triumphant trip home was slightly dampened by a question from Gene as we came to our apartment door. "By the way, what did you do with your gohonson?"

Filled with the new courage of baptism, I faced the truth that if destroying the prayer scroll meant dying, I would trust the Lord in this just as I had in the tank. Then I had a joyful thought. What have I got to fear? I had read in the Bible that we must die before we can be born again, so why not die as a Buddhist to be born as a Christian?

"Gene, I still have it—but not for long."

I went to my bedroom dresser, took out the gohonson, carried it into the kitchen, and under Gene's curious gaze, I tore it to shreds, took a match, and set it on fire, then washed the ashes down the sink disposal and turned on the electricity to finish it off.

This act of faith gave me new strength in my new life, but that was not all. There was still the box for the gohonson and its accouterments—bell, water glass, incense burner, candleholders, candles, even the dried pine bough. As Gene watched, I put them all in the trash can.

One last step remained: disposing of the ancient statue of Buddha.

I thought of the night Bess had given it to me. Truly, it had been given to me in love, but my mother's love was, in reality, no part of an ancient statue. No matter whether inlaid with gold or jewels, the statue itself was an inanimate object. It was a symbol of her love for me, but it was not her love itself.

I invited Gene for dinner at Moby's Dock, explaining to him it had been our favorite family restaurant. Following a fine lobster dinner, made even more wonderful by memories of my mother, I said, "Gene, I've got a surprise for you. I want to show you something at the end of the pier."

Fog began to roll in as we walked to the end of the pier. At the railing, with nothing but black ocean in front of us, I reached into my jacket and removed the statue, showed Gene what I held in my hand, and said, "The love that I hold for my mother is not contained within a statue. It's in my heart." Then I threw the statue as hard and as far as I could into the ocean.

As we heard the splash, Gene turned to me with a smile, "Bill, you're on your way."

18

Answer to Prayer

When we returned home that night, I had a feeling that my apartment without its Buddhist symbols had been cleansed and rededicated to Christ, and this dedication carried over into my spiritual awakening. Now, more than ever, I felt a need for a church home where I could realize spiritual revitalization and food.

Gene had made it clear to me that as a baby Christian, spiritual nourishment such as studying the Word and fellowship with other Christians were absolutely essential.

But where?

Gene said, "Why not look in the yellow pages to find out where the First Assembly of God churches are located?"

The closest one to Laurel Canyon was North Hollywood, so the following Sunday, we headed there, not realizing that it was there that I had prayed for someone to go to church with.

I have since learned that God is extravagant in his answers to prayer and instead of just sending me Gene, he was now extending the fellowship of the entire body of this church. Soon I realized that the church of Christ that I had joined was not just a building, but the entire body of believers.

I was surprised during my second visit to North Hollywood that there were quite a few Jewish members of the congregation. What were they doing in a Christian church? No sooner had I asked the question when I knew the answer: the same thing I was doing.

There were many qualities of the Assembly of God Church of North Hollywood that I liked. The congregation seemed proud to be Christians. I liked that. I had met so many persons who hid the fact that they were Christians—anonymous Christians. I was proud of being a Christian and wanted everybody to know it.

I joined and have been a member ever since.

Word soon got around the church that I was Jewish, and many members of the congregation came over to embrace me and welcome me into their church family.

Often the conversation would be: "When did you receive Christ?" or "When did your conversion take place?"

Gene had impressed upon me and I would answer:

"I'm not a *converted* Christian. I'm a *completed* Jew. I was born a Jew. I will die a Jew."

Frequently, I was asked another question.

"Complete Jew? What's that?"

"A Jew who has accepted Christ as the Messiah," I would answer, and I knew this was right, for Jesus Christ was the King of the Jews. "Aren't Christians really people who have accepted Judaism by accepting Jesus as their Messiah and savior?"

As months passed by, other facts struck me with impact. My life in the B.C. period had been like that of tens of millions throughout the world who search for self-fulfillment, for their identity in activities, attainments, people, places, and things. Only the specific areas of seeking—consciously or unconsciously—were a little different. I had looked to natural beauty in flowers and creatures for God, and I could gain only hints of the ultimate because these forms of life, like ourselves, are creations of God, not God himself.

With constant prayer and Bible reading, I gained new perspectives every day and began to see myself and others more clearly. It became plain to me that, like myself, millions of people in all parts of the world are seeking God in places where he can't be found: in the occult (ESP, numerology, astrology, spirit communication, automatic writing, tarot cards, Ouija boards), in superficial samplings of exotic religions, paganism, in endless narcotizing TV, in incessant travel, in constant additions to the wardrobe, eternal academic or social climbings, frantic career efforts, adventure, thrill-seeking, new sexual mates and expressions, alcohol and harmful drugs—"uppers" and "downers" that often make them "downers" and "outers."

There is nothing wrong in seeking, in trying to know the ultimate, for the ultimate is there for the knowing and must only be sought. Not to seek is not to find. The tragedy is in never letting the truth in, that the things of the world belong to death and that the things of our Lord Jesus belong to life—eternal life. The tragedy is in ending the search with earthly things when reality and the ultimate truth are beyond such things, ours simply for the asking.

Not a day goes by that I do not thank and praise Jesus for permitting me to see behind the stage sets of the earth to reality and to abundant life. I also thank him for his perfect casting in sending to this middle-aged man a "child in Christ," young Gene Arnaiz, an "old man in Christ."

How our Lord deals in humor and paradoxes! Who could possibly outguess him and how he works? Who would have bet a cent that the fisherman and farmers he recruited as disciples—uneducated and simple men—would have amounted to anything? Yet these twelve men changed the world.

Another thing became clear to me: why I have always been intrigued by the individuality of my pets—hummingbirds to eagles, butterflies to snakes, roses, orchids, and even the snowflakes that made me press my nose to the cold glass of our New York City apartment in wonder.

All of this had been a preview to learning about the individuality that God designs into every one of us—an individuality sometimes lost in society's efforts to turn us into numbers.

Our individuality is uniquely important to God. His body, of which we are a specialized part, has need for each of us. As we grow in faith, so we grow in understanding of what part of the body we fill.

As we are unique in all things, so is God's plan for our lives uniquely suited to each of us. If we diligently search, we find his purpose. We will learn who we are in his image, why we are on earth, and how we are to serve him. We are dependent on God through Jesus for life and salvation. And yet God is also dependent upon us. He created us as companions for himself, but gave us freedom of choice. We can choose him or not. We often try to reach God in our way. He would like us to come his way. Good works won't do it. They're not good enough. No matter how righteous we think we are—or sinless—we're not good enough.

I know that my identity crisis began dissolving the moment I turned to the Lord. By losing myself in him, I found myself in him.

God gives us enough knowledge of his plan to carry us from day to day. It is only when we gaze into the past, like a rearview mirror, that his plan becomes evident.

First, my beloved governess, Mademoiselle Branche, had made me aware of the little Jesus child—Mustard Seed Number One.

Second, Sergeant Alvin York and his life story had given me a new dimension of spiritual insight—Mustard Seed Number Two.

Third, the medical doctor treating me after my head-on collision had told me of my choice to live or die and had made me curious about God's plan for my life—Mustard Seed Number Three.

I marveled at the many starts and stops in my life, the dead ends, the doubling back, the false starts, the twists and turns, the ups and downs. This seemingly inefficient course became a direct path to totally giving my life to Jesus.

Our Lord does not waste one single incident in our lives—all of the good and the bad he uses in his specific plan.

The rearview mirror shows clearly how events in my parents' lives, how their character traits, how even my mother's selection of my governess, became a meaningful part of God's plan for me.

And, above all things, I remembered the Paramount Pictures logo. The snow-covered mountain against a royal blue background, encircled by white stars, symbolized our family tradition in the advice passed down to me by my father—"Always go to the top"—which is exactly where I went when I fell to my knees in the Winters' home.

How paradoxical, too, that my dad—a man with both feet in the material world—had handed down to me the best possible spiritual advice without even being aware of it.

Even though I was intrigued with beginning to see God's plan in my life, I wanted to carry out that plan as quickly as possible.

I wasn't content with a Christian walk. I wanted it to be a Christian run, but so far Jesus had wanted it to be a walk, and he runs my show.

For a number of years I had driven an old Camaro, which had developed battle fatigue. One day it gasped its last breath when Gene and I were about two blocks from the apartment. The transmission and motor were shot. The car sputtered and coughed, and we knew that retirement time had arrived.

Just then a cab driver stopped and asked what was wrong with the car.

"It has had it," I replied.

"Want to sell it?"

"Sure."

"My son needs a car that's just a skeleton to learn the mechanic trade. I'll give you four hundred dollars for it."

I was envisioning twenty-five dollars for junk.

I gasped in surprise. "It's a deal." He paid cash for it the next day.

I said to Gene, "This is really a challenge from God. I'm not going to buy another car for a while."

Gene glanced quizzically at me.

"In a city like Los Angeles, many people take public transportation and never even own a car. This will be a real adventure."

"So far, so good," responded Gene.

"If this is a test of God, I want to pass it. I'm going to hitchhike everywhere. Think how many chances I will get to talk about the Lord to strangers who pick me up, people I would normally never get a chance to meet."

Gene suggested we put it into prayer.

So that's what we did.

As I lead a busy life and travel throughout Southern California, I would always say a little prayer for my safety and, "Lord, you take this trip and use it."

Every driver was a new challenge. Every time I was picked up, I would start with a shocker: "I'm a completed Jew who has accepted Jesus Christ as my Messiah."

The startled reactions of drivers was an assurance that I had got their attention. I would ask if they had ever heard the term "completed Jew."

Invariably they would say no, and I would have an excellent excuse to witness to them about the Lord, who began to present me with some amazing opportunities and experiences, as well as explanations and answers.

One day a dark-haired young Jewish boy, whom we will call Mike, picked me up in the San Fernando Valley. I asked if he would drop me off at Ventura Boulevard and Laurel Canyon so that I could get another ride through the hills into Hollywood.

"I don't like to see you hitchhiking," he said. "It's like having my father out on the street. I'm going to take you all the way home."

The short trip gave me little chance to witness to him that I had received Christ and was now a completed Jew. He appeared mildly interested as I stepped out of his car. I suddenly got the impulse to give him my business card.

"If you ever need help, give me a call," I said and forgot the incident.

About two weeks later, I got a phone call during the daytime.

"Mr. Lasky," a faint voice said, "I'm Mike, the fellow who gave you a lift home a couple weeks ago. You said if I ever needed help, to call you. I need help. I wanted to kill myself a few minutes ago. I took so many sleeping pills, I'm passing out. I'm scared and don't want to die. Please help me!"

"I will," I hurriedly said. "Are you conscious enough to answer a question?"

"Yes," he said.

"Do you want to receive Jesus Christ right now?"

"Yes, anything! How?"

"Just ask Jesus' forgiveness for all your sins."

There was a pause on the other end of the line, and I became fearful that he had passed out. Then . . . "Jesus, I ask forgiveness for all my sins."

"Now, ask Jesus to come into your life," I gently instructed him.

"Jesus, please come into my life. I need you."

Another interval of silence. I tried to rouse him but failed.

"Hang up, hang up," I yelled, "and I'll get help for you right away."

Again there was no response. Finally I heard the click of the phone cradled into place.

Remembering I had no car, I quickly phoned my church in North Hollywood, got Pastor Ray Escalon, and asked him to rush over to Mike's house, which was not far from the church.

The pastor phoned to tell me had found him in bad shape and barely succeeded in reviving him.

"Let me bring Mike to your house, where you can watch him," he said to me. "Call Suicide Prevention immediately for instructions as to what to do."

"Bring him over," I said, and phoned Suicide Prevention.

Soon Mike was installed in Gene's bedroom where we alternately watched over him through the night. The next day he woke up bright and shiny. The sun was pouring through the windows, and my two parakeets filled the apartment with their chatter. "Am I glad to be alive," he said.

Mike's spiritual growth progressed steadily, and his problems that had led to his suicide attempt began to diminish. Soon he joined our church.

Things improved for me, too. A number of excellent Hollywood assignments came my way, and, eventually, I bought an excellent used Mazda at a reasonable price, thanks to a young minister, Robbie Walker, of the Shekinah Fellowship. But I was temporarily distressed because I would no longer be a hitchhiker. Then I laughed aloud. That was no problem. Now I could evangelize to hitchhikers. Sure enough, just about everyone I picked up was lonely, lost, or confused and seemed hungry to hear about the missing dimension in their lives.

I had been invited by Norm Rogers, program director of radio station KHOF, in Glendale, to appear on the Tim Berends all-night spiritual talk show to give my Christian testimony. I had finished answering the open phones around 3 A.M. and was driving homeward, when I saw a hitchhiker. I had some misgivings about picking him up. After all, I had been shot once. However, I quickly prayed to Jesus for protection and stopped. A middle-aged man, beginning to gray and puffy and red under the eyes, climbed in. In a second, my car was permeated with the overpowering smell of aclohol.

"Oh boy," I thought. "What have I got?"

I always keep a cross hanging from my rearview mirror. Even in his drunkenness, the man immediately noticed it, pointing a trembling index finger toward it.

He surprised me by asking, "Do you believe in Jesus Christ?"

"Yes, I have given my life to him."

"I'm a Catholic," he volunteered, "but back-slidden so far that my life is going down the tube."

"It doesn't have to, you know."

"I know it," he confessed. "I'm so miserable I didn't know where to turn. A few minutes ago, I was praying on the bus stop bench for a miracle—that *someone* would come along and lead me back to the Lord. Will you pray with me?"

"Sure," I replied, "but will you make a decision? Will you consent to be born again in Christ and invite Jesus into your heart?"

Never in my life have I seen a change come over a person so fast. Now he was completely sober. "Yes, please, I will," he accepted the Lord amid tears of joy.

Sometimes my gratitude to Jesus for what he has done for me builds up to overflowing. Once in a state of extreme exuberance to be of service, I confided to Gene, "I love Jesus so much that I would like to do something for him in return. I want to pray that he will send me someone to minister to who is totally unlovable, someone I must help just because of Jesus' love. I would like the chance to minister to someone who is totally repulsive and despicable to me."

Gene grimaced. "Bill, you'd better be careful what you pray for. The power of prayer passes all understanding. In God's permissive will, if you specify someone like that, that is exactly what you'll get."

"Gene, I don't know much about that, but this is the kind of experience I want. Maybe it's kind of a martyr complex, but that's what I want. Okay?"

"Don't say I didn't warn you, Bill," Gene replied, looking more serious than usual.

"Lord," I said, "you promise us anything that we ask in your name. I am asking for the opportunity to minister to someone who is totally repulsive to me."

Literally twenty minutes after the prayer, the phone rang and a strange voice said, "Does Gene Arnaiz live there?"

"Yes, he does," I replied.

"I phoned his home in Stockton and his mother gave me this number. Is he there?"

"Yes," I responded and turned to Gene. "A friend of yours."

Gene came to the phone, but he didn't get much chance to talk. I could see he was very much concerned.

"But, Joe, isn't there anywhere else you can stay?"

I could hear fast talk but none of the words. Finally Gene said, "Well, I guess we could. All right, Joe, we'll pick you up at the airport."

As he hung up the phone, Gene turned to me with a deep sigh. "Well, Bill, your prayer has been answered."

Now it was my turn to be a bit apprehensive. What had I got myself into?

"Gene, what do you mean?"

"This guy is trouble," Gene replied, shaking his head dubiously. "He's been in all sorts of jams with people and the law. I tried without much success to minister to him in Texas."

All the way to the airport I found myself growing more upset. Sure enough at the appointed gate, there he was—a six-foot-four giant with brown tousled hair. His clothes appeared as if he had slept in them for a long time.

His long, lean, high-cheekboned face had a saturnine expression. The sideburns down to his jawbone gave his face an even longer and more evil expression.

"Is that your friend, Gene?" I asked.

It seemed that the word "friend" was not exactly on target, but Gene nodded.

When Gene introduced us, Joe was abrupt in acknowledging the introduction, as if he wanted to get the unpleasantness out of the way. I was favored with a smile that was more of a smirk. And when back in the apartment, I said, "Joe, about the only place we have for you to sleep is on the living room couch," he glanced at the couch in mild disapproval but said nothing.

"While you and Gene catch up on what's been happening, I'll cook dinner," I said, "or maybe you'll want to watch TV."

"No. I'm an artist. Give me some paper and a soft lead pencil."

On top of my TV set, I have a painting of Jesus. Joe seemed to be looking in the direction of the painting, studying. Once I had given him the art supplies, he appeared to be copying the face of Jesus.

"Well, that's constructive enough," I said to myself. He picked up the painting and resumed his seat on the couch.

Soon dinner was ready, and I came into the living room to serve. Joe was still working away. From where I stood, the drawing appeared to be quite professionally done.

But when I took a closer look, I felt a cold chill. It was not the face of Jesus at all but the face of the devil. The face of Jesus from which he had copied had a sweet and innocent appearance. That of Joe's drawing had an evil, long, thin, smirking face. Instead of the soft brown hair in the painting was black hair and the sideburns connected with the beard.

For a frightening instant, I thought I was looking into the face of the man under the dim street light who had shot me. The black hair was even tufted up in the center and looked like horns.

"Who's that?" I asked.

"That's Jesus," he replied curtly. "Who else?"

"No, it isn't," I contradicted.

"Look," he said, "I know what I'm doing."

I thought back to the prayer I had made not too many hours before, and again wondered what I had got myself into. Was it possible to pray in reverse?

Just then the phone rang and Gene answered.

"Oh, hi, Mom," he said.

I listened intently.

"What kind of emergency, Mom?" he asked. Now several wrinkles of concern showed on his youthful forehead.

"How can I come right away? I don't even know if there's still a plane I can catch to Stockton."

My heart began to act a little strange. Was I going to be left all alone with Joe?

"All right, Mom. I'll throw something into the suitcase and get Bill to rush me to the airport."

On the way, he said, "Bill, I'm sorry to leave you alone with Joe, and I wouldn't if I didn't have to." Then he half-smiled. "You asked Jesus for this kind of assignment. Now you will have to minister to Joe by yourself. I think you will learn the power of prayer."

Never had Gene spoken truer words!

When I returned to the apartment, I found Joe fast asleep on the couch. It was Saturday night and I went right to bed. I woke up early the next morning for church, wondering whether I should invite Joe to go with me, but he was still asleep, snoring loudly.

I felt relieved as I drove to church and even more so when I arrived early enough to talk privately with Pastor Sanders.

"Pastor Sanders," I said, "I prayed for someone to come into my apartment—someone undesirable to minister to. My prayer was answered—and then some. Now I'm a little afraid of the man. What kind of protection can I get?"

"Bill, do you know anything about pleading the blood?"

"No, what's that?"

"Well, if you plead the blood of Jesus, you will be protected against anything of the adversary. If things get really bad, just plead the blood."

Joe must have been exhausted, because when I got back to the apartment he was still snoring loudly. The picture he had drawn of the devil was face up on the table next to the couch. Something seemed to draw me closer to it. It looked most alive with evil.

Then I got an inspiration. I hastily turned it over and wrote on the back of the picture, "the blood of Jesus."

I thought I would read the Sunday papers in bed and possibly take a nap. So I took off my clothes and put on my old bathrobe. I was just dozing off when I was startled by a loud curse.

It was Joe.

I jumped out of bed, quickly tying the belt of the bathrobe, and walked into the living room to see what was the matter. There he stood shaking, the drawing in his hands.

"Who wrote this on the back of my picture?" he yelled. He was livid with rage.

"I did."

"What does it mean?"

"It is the blood of Jesus."

"Why did you write it?"

"For protection. I'm afraid of you. I think you are the devil. The picture you drew is not of Jesus but of yourself."

"I'll show you who is the devil," he snarled and let loose a torrent of profanity and four-letter words. "I'm going to kill you."

He dropped the drawing and came at me, his hands reaching out to grab me. I started to back away. Suddenly he grasped my bathrobe and forced me backward into the kitchen.

"I haven't told you anything about who I am," he shouted. "I used to push heroin in New York—not to adults, just to kids. They're easier victims."

I thought, "Oh boy. This is what I prayed for!"

"They ran me out of New York. I went to Texas, and they ran me out of there, too. I beat up my wife and left her bloody for the ambulance to pick up. I threw her TV set out of the living room window and tore up everything she had. I'll show you who I am."

I started to repeat, "The blood of Jesus," as his hands tightened on my bathrobe and he pushed me backward. My heart was pounding. For an instant I broke away from his grip, but there was nowhere to retreat. He had me with my back to the kitchen window.

"The blood of Jesus," I repeated over and over. And then with a rapid shove of his hand he pushed my head through the window glass. I could hear the broken glass shatter on the sidewalk below. I brought my head up through the shattered pane, still repeating, "The blood of Jesus, the blood of Jesus."

He seemed stunned as he stared at me wide-eyed. Then he turned on his heels, grabbed his suitcase, and raced out through the front door. I hurried into the bathroom to check the back of my head and neck, which was covered with glass splinters, and it suddenly occurred to me why Joe had appeared so surprised.

My head had gone through the windowpane and had come back in again without a scratch.

Shortly after this experience, I felt a desire to become more deeply involved in evangelical work. Perhaps I should try to become a lay minister.

My first impulse was to laugh. "Me, a lay minister? Why, I'm just beginning to learn the Bible."

Then another thought came to me. Many plain, uncomplicated people have lived lives of effective witness for the Lord. Maybe I could, too. I prayed to the Lord to use me further.

I was invited to attend a meeting of the Full Gospel Business Men's Fellowship International, Beverly Hills Chapter, where I heard a moving testimony for Jesus. I felt I had to be a member of this organization, but I didn't know how to join.

I didn't have to. The meeting ended, and the chapter president approached me. "Bill," he said, "would you consider taking over my position as president of this organization? I have gone through a difficult time and feel that new blood is needed to make this chapter grow. With your Hollywood background and professional experience, you will be able to lead and build it for the Lord. Perhaps it can serve as a Christian oasis in this largely non-Christian area."

I wanted to say, "It's too soon."

I felt inadequate, too inexperienced in Christian affairs to assume the immense responsibilities that I imagined the position entailed, but the words came into my mouth, "If it's the Lord's will, I will accept, but it will be He, not me, who will head your organization."

Clarence Keller replied, "That is as it should be, Bill."

One way the Lord gets us to learn how to swim is to introduce us to some pretty deep waters. Maybe we won't ever qualify for the Olympic swimming team, but we come out better swimmers than we ever imagined.

I was elected president and was more than pleasantly surprised when the organization slowly climbed out of debt and its membership grew.

My prayers for increase have led to an attendance of as many as four to five hundred at monthly dinner meetings. Further, the doors have been opened to me to come in close contact with Christian leaders who serve as our speakers.

Through my new responsibility, I have come to know and be associated with such persons as Demos Shakarian, founder and president of the Full Gospel Business Men's Fellowship International, and his two sons, Steve and Richard; Brant Baker, youthful minister of the Shekinah Fellowship healing ministry; the Reverend Michael Esses, author and staff member of David Wilkerson's Melodyland in Anaheim; Pat and Shirley Boone; actor Dean Jones and wife Laurie; Tom Lewis, producer of the *Loretta Young Show* (the last three men are board members); Mary Dorr, executive directress of the Association for Religion in Media; Madame Bilquis Sheikh, wife of a former Prime Minister of Pakistan; Margaret Jenkins and the Ladies of Song (formerly with Mahalia Jackson); actress Rhonda Fleming (one of Dad's discoveries); Bishop Michel D'Obrenovic and his lovely wife, Jennifer Holt (daughter of my father's former Paramount contract star Jack Holt); Bishop Albert R. Cody, he and Bishop D'Obrenovic being leaders of the Syro-Chaldean Catholic Church; Jane Russell; concert pianist Dino and his wife, Debbie; Carol and Jimmy Owens, composers of popular Christian musical plays; Nora Lamm; Los Angeles Mayor Thomas Bradley and his lovely wife, Ethel, who has accompanied me to Christians in Government prayer breakfasts; former California Governor Ronald Reagan; Corrie Ten Boom; and many others.

Each day my lay ministry seems to be spreading beyond anything I could possibly have expected or predicted. I give testimonies before other Full Gospel Business Men's Fellowship chapters throughout Southern California, before Christian Business Men's Committee International chapters, breakfast clubs, dinner clubs, women's clubs, prayer breakfasts, lunches, and dinners of city, county, and federal employees, before church congregations of as many as twelve hundred individuals, over radio and TV—some taped for national and international syndication.

Even that isn't the end. One day in church, I met two young men who told me a motion picture studio was available, and they thought I would be, as they put it, "an ideal person to resurrect the place for the production of good, clean, entertaining films."

What a natural of an idea! Here I had had the training in motion pictures—more than a thousand screen credits for anything from animal training to assistant directing, directing, writing, and producing. Why not?

While there are such fine organizations as Billy Graham's World Wide Pictures producing some great Christian films, there would have to be many companies—not just the one I plan—to make upbeat and constructive motion pictures to counteract the ever-growing tide of negative film fare.

I discussed the thought at length with Gene Arnaiz and Pastor Sanders, and both have agreed that the Lord was indeed using me to initiate the project.

Pastor Sanders reminded me of the big letters in the hills just north of Hollywood. He said, "Bill, it's worth a good try. Why can't you work toward changing that name 'Hollywood' to 'Holywood'?"

Suddenly the task seemed to be taller than Annapurna, and just as suddenly I seemed at the very bottom of the climb, but a little voice within said, "No task is too big for the Lord."

And then I remembered my dad's start at the very bottom and the many times he had started again after numerous devastating experiences.

At this writing I am not sure that acquiring a studio to implement a production plan is the proper course inasmuch as $10 million would be involved, but launching a motion picture production company does seem the proper route to travel. And I would like the firm to be called "Lasky Productions" to honor both of my fathers in heaven.

For several months Gene continued to live with me, and his companionship and firm guidance will always be appreciated. On several occasions, he had asked me to join him in watching a TV program featuring a lady who at the time was a total stranger to me.

In those days, I was turned off by the late Kathryn Kuhlman's early Hollywood dramatic style—her Katharine Hepburn gowns and her overenunciated speech. So when Gene saw in the paper that she was to appear at the Shrine Auditorium in Los Angeles and announced, "We're going to see her in person," I resisted. But Gene was adamant and led me grudgingly to what I knew would be a fully wasted Sunday.

It was bad enough to have been semi-coerced into going, but it was sickening to face the sea of parked cars in every parking lot within a telescope's range and thousands of people gathered on the sidewalks and streets around the Shrine.

Has everybody in Los Angeles lost his mind? I asked myself. As if reading my mind, Gene said that many of these thousands would be turned away for lack of seats. This rocketed my optimism level skyward. There was an excellent chance of our being rejected.

Then Gene proposed a plan. He said that at each service, Miss Kuhlman admits ministers through a special entrance. But Gene had never been ordained and he was sure he couldn't get in by this means. I thought and hoped we wouldn't have a chance. However, to my dismay, we were greeted at the door as though there was some God-made plan for our admittance. And there was, though I didn't know it.

We were ushered inside and started to climb stairways. At each level we were told we would have to go higher. Just when the oxygen was almost too rarefied to breathe, we arrived at the top, edging our way to the center for two vacant seats.

From where we sat, the huge stage looked like an architect's model and those on stage like brightly colored ants. As I sat down, an electrical surge of excitement made my spine tingle and my entire body quiver. Within seconds, a magnificent choir of voices seemed to go right through me, and, to my utter disbelief, tears started flowing from my eyes. When the choir finished, I wiped my cheeks in embarrassment. Pianist Dino, a tiny ant at a mini piano, began, but as the notes welled up, the sound was out of proportion to the visual image as it soared and swelled and permeated the tremendous hall. The tears continued to flow again, and an indescribable emotion came over me. Yet even as I felt it, I rationalized that it would disappear as soon as Miss Kuhlman came on.

Instead of this, however, her mere presence on stage started the tears again. She was like a little white angel through my veil of tears as she moved across the stage, seeming sometimes to defy the law of gravity and float as angels are wont to do.

The tingle of electricity made me aware that a greater presence than she was in this archaic building. God himself in the form of the Holy Spirit filled the room.

Her message, "I Believe in Miracles Because I Believe in God," was spoken directly to me. Tiny as she appeared, it was as if we were holding an intimate two-way conversation.

Her questions and challenges found answer in my heart. When she invited all those who wished to receive Jesus Christ in a personal way to come to the front of the auditorium, my spirits were so high and I was in such a state of unworldly rapture that I had to restrain myself from using the imaginary wings of the birds and flying down from the balcony. The illogical, at that moment, seemed logical.

I turned to Gene and, in a voice choked with emotion, was able to get out, "Gene, you're absolutely right. She is a beautiful and wonderful lady, and she's brought me into a closeness and reality with God. Come on. Let's go down to the front with the others. I want to get closer to the stage."

As we went down the back stairs, slowed by the thousands of people jamming the approaches to the stage, I became aware that my contact lenses underneath my glasses were bothering me. I wrote it off as a reaction to excessive emotion, but when I came home, I had to remove them. I couldn't stand them any longer. With my contacts removed, it seemed my vision improved.

I tested this in my Bible, and for the first time, I was able to read perfectly normally without any aid. Several weeks later, I wanted to find out if I had truly received a healing of the eyes.

Dr. Morton Greenspoon, my eye doctor who had first fitted me with contact lenses fourteen years before, checked me carefully and said, "Bill, it appears that your eyes have sustained a dramatic change. Your close-up reading vision has become completely normal. You can discard your contact lenses. Likewise, there has been a change in your distance vision. I'm going to weaken a prescription for new glasses. It may be that your vision will correct itself totally in time."

It had really happened. I, too, believe in miracles because I believe in God.

I was so enchanted with Kathryn Kuhlman and her service that I determined that, with the Lord's help, I would meet her in person. Gene assured me that this was impossible.

But I insisted and we prayed on it.

I phoned her office and spoke to her secretary. She promised to convey my message to Miss Kuhlman. I would be notified in the auditorium if this request could be granted. Her instructions were that Gene and I should go through the ministers' door.

Weeks rushed by, and Kathryn Kuhlman arrived in a flurry of anticipation. Would I have the expected face-to-face meeting with this incredible servant of the Lord? At the ministers' entrance, we were surprised to find that our names were on a special guest list, and, as a gentlemen escorted us to what he called "The Nest" (a miniature balcony directly above the stage), we found ourselves to be within touching distance of those on-stage. Then a stranger came over and whispered into my ear, "Miss Kuhlman will meet you after the service in her dressing room. I will be here to escort you."

My prayer, as always, had been answered.

Following this beautiful second service and a repeat of joyous tears in acknowledgment of ministries of both Dino and Miss Kuhlman, Gene and I accompanied our escort backstage, where Miss Kuhlman was standing, no longer in her white stage gown but in a smart, tailored, brown traveling suit.

"Miss Kuhlman, I had to meet you."

Her answer was a big warm smile. "Bill, I had to meet you."

I introduced Gene, and it was as if we were talking to a dear sister and friend. I told her how I had first attended her service with not only skepticism but distaste, and she reacted with youthful laughter and amusement, saying, "You know, Bill, so many people have that same reaction to me."

There was one little secret that I didn't divulge to Miss Kuhlman. As much as I loved and admired her, under no conditions was I going to be "zonked" by the Holy Spirit and bounced off a cement floor.

I vaguely remember Kathryn raising one of her childlike hands to the appropriate area of my forehead, and I believe she said something like, "Bless you in the name of Jesus Christ," but her words were blurred by an indescribable sensation. For a second, I had left the confines of the room and was in the presence of the Holy Spirit. Despite my secret determination not to be "zonked," I found myself on the floor.

As I picked myself up, the tiny hands were again raised and, again, the voice repeated the blessing and, again, I was zonked. I had rationalized that to be slain in the spirit, of course, Miss

Kuhlman had to push over the person to whom she was ministering. This rationalization was as reasonable as a butterfly knocking an elephant off its feet.

I have since had the great pleasure of meeting Miss Kuhlman on several occasions, and I am joyful to call her "friend."

In the Lord's time, Gene's ministries took him out of my apartment and into a home of his own. We both felt that the time had come for me to turn directly toward the Lord. Ever present were a number of new Christian friends to share and learn with. Among my most treasured Christian brothers is the Reverend Brant Baker, whose relatively new ministry, Shekinah Fellowship, is growing from a humble Long Beach-centered beginning to an ever-extending nationwide ministry.

For a month, I traveled with Brant to his services, often witnessing with him, and I learned the devotion and dedication that he has for our Lord.

One additional benefit. For three years, I had had an aggravating skin malignancy on my right eye temple. This skin tumor periodically became angrily inflamed. I was advised that I should have cobalt treatment but decided to turn it over to the Lord in prayer through Brant's ministry. At a meeting of the Full Gospel Business Men's Fellowship meeting in Beverly Hills, where Brant and his young people were our guests, Brant called out a healing of a skin growth in the area of the head.

With some hesitancy and considerably mixed emotions, I stepped forward to claim this healing. He laid hands on me, and in a matter of days this skin growth disappeared and has never recurred—another proof of God's answers to prayer.

19

Anyone Can Pray

Thank God that in two out of three Hollywood lives, I was in the right place at the right time and listened to the still, small voice within and—equally important—did what it asked.

Sometimes we're all a little late on our timing. We can easily miss that precious and enchanted moment to offer encouragement, forgiveness, a spontaneous gift, or a word of love that might have helped to turn a life around—or even have helped it to become eternal.

I worked with Marilyn Monroe on her motion picture *Bus Stop*, and, like most of the members of the company, my relationship with her was one of embarrassed self-consciousness. I've tried to analyze in the past years why she was one of the few actresses and actors whom I was unable to come close to among the many stars with whom I had an easy rapport—Katharine Hepburn, Spencer Tracy, Gloria Swanson, Bette Davis, Gary Cooper, and others. I believe therein lies a key to the tragedy of her death.

On numerous occasions, I had the opportunity of showing her little kindnesses and considerations that seemed to embarrass her, and her embarrassment caused me to be embarrassed. It was as if she could not accept any gesture that could be interpreted as love.

This is the way it is with me. Sure, that's why I see in Marilyn Monroe a parallel to much in my life. I have always felt a lack of love regardless of whom I was sharing my life with. But this lack of love is not exclusive of self. By this I mean the causes and effects of our lives are inseparable, as I learned in my years of studying Buddhism. If the effect of our life is insufficient love, then the cause is our inability to give sufficient love.

I do not feel we can separate physical and spiritual love. Love is the greatest need of every human being, whether he be a Marilyn Monroe or a Bill Lasky. The Bible tells us that if we simply open the doors of our lives and invite in the love of the universe—*agape*, the total love of God—we will be healed of this haunting feeling of insufficiency.

Marilyn's rejection and embarrassment caused a similar reaction in me, and I felt myself to be equally embarrassed and rejected in her presence. I feel that her tremendous need for love—this Hollywood-dubbed "Goddess of Love"—may be more than a casual clue into the tragedy that was to conclude her life.

It was no secret in Hollywood that Marilyn, for several years before her death, was in extreme emotional distress and under psychiatric care. She required a lightproof bedroom and still suffered acute insomnia, dulled only by excessive barbiturates. She was frequently tremulous and jittery, feeling caged and "ready to jump out of my skin," often claiming that nobody loved her.

Knowing that she required something more than medical doctors, psychoanalysis, sedatives, and human attention, understanding, and comfort that the material world could provide, several ministers tried to contact her to make her aware of the opportunity to receive the love that is Christ into her life.

Among them was international evangelist Billy Graham, who had met her previously. While he was in Los Angeles, he had heard that she was not well. Hoping to be of help, he telephoned her home, asking for an appointment. The request was turned down. Her secretary informed him that she was too busy and that she would consider it at a later date when her schedule would permit.

Not too long after this last opportunity to receive Christ, she was dead. Newspaper reporters, TV and radio commentators in all parts of the world tried to piece together the story and mentioned the great loss to the entertainment world that her passing had brought.

Yet no one talked about the personal loss that the turn-down to Billy Graham had meant to her!

An incident during her final weeks on earth is more revealing as to the emptiness of her life than entire books about her could tell.

Marilyn was in a well-known Newport Beach restaurant and

wrote in the Travel Guest Book, which routinely requested each person's name, home address, and destination.

In the appropriate place for "Name," she signed "Marilyn Monroe." In the space allotted for home address, she scribbled, "No place." In the space for "Destination," she wrote, "Nowhere" and underlined it.

Shortly after that, she was dead.

It was my privilege to know two other Hollywood personalities well enough to play a part in their life dramas: Susan Hayward and Edward G. Robinson, Jr.

There were few similarities between the life and death of Marilyn Monroe and Susan Hayward, but the ending of life on earth for Susan was a far happier one.

Susan Hayward, to me, was a courageous and glorious human being—one of the finest persons I have met in my entire film career. I was happy to become a personal friend of hers a few decades ago, when, as an assistant director, I worked with her on her much-acclaimed Metro-Goldwyn-Mayer film *I'll Cry Tomorrow,* based on a best-selling book on the life of singer-actress Lillian Roth. This film graphically portrayed all the intimate details of Lillian's battle with alcoholism.

It was coincidental that Susan was deeply engulfed with her personal problems at the time she was offered the prized Lillian Roth role. She had just divorced her husband, actor Lex Barker. Susan's despair over the failure of her marriage and her divorce—even though her love for her husband still existed—caused her to attempt to take her life. This attempt was publicized in all the media.

Under severe personal stress, she began the filming of *I'll Cry Tomorrow* only a couple days after the near tragedy, and she insisted on a closed set—no visitors. This was not because of a lack of love or consideration on her part for would-be visitors to the set, but was based on her all-consuming involvement with every role that she ever played.

For reasons that at the time I was unable to determine, we had a warm friendship. There were certain similarities in our lives.

I had experienced the tragedy of divorce, as had Susan, and the love for my wife, Margery, was no less than was Susan's for Lex. In this case, our mutual lack of love and our need for it, as well as our failure to give and receive love in our marriages, gave us an unexpressed affection for each other.

Combined with her rare physical beauty were harmonious and contrasting personality traits: warmth, sensitivity, strength, forcefulness, a businesslike manner (when circumstances demanded), a rich sense of humor, and the quintessence of femininity with undertones of deep sadness.

Added to the gnawing of her own thoughts and emotional reactions to the divorce and suicide attempt, she daily experienced total involvement in her role, Lillian Roth's living death as an alcoholic.

As an example of her involvement with her role, she volunteered, prior to the picture's filming, to go to Los Angeles' Skid Row and spend time on the streets at night with winos, derelicts, and prostitutes, as Lillian Roth had done.

She wore no make-up, bought herself a used dress at the Goodwill Store, and walked the streets to observe and understand the setting and the life. She confided to me that there were several times when she was glad the studio had sent a bodyguard to follow behind her, for on quite a few occasions, she was accosted by men, and when she refused their advances, they became antagonistic and ugly.

Motion pictures may be make-believe to some, but to Susan the making of them was a reality. In numerous films, she refused to use stunt women or doubles to perform hazardous scenes for her. She wanted everything to be genuine. Each dramatic sequence had to be perfection with her. Anything less was more than she could tolerate. One of the major scenes of *I'll Cry Tomorrow* called for the costar, Richard Conte, who played Lillian Roth's husband, to beat her up.

Stunt doubles, often hired for fight scenes, can protect the faces and bodies of stars that they double by simulating blows and punches, but Susan would have none of that. She insisted that, for total realism, Conte actually fight with her in the bar, drag her outside, and hit her with the full force of his fists. When she reacted emotionally for the camera, she wanted it to be true reaction—perfection, not near perfection. Conte was reluctant to do it, but Susan won her point. It was agony for those of us on the set to watch.

And the following day, Susan came out of it black and blue. Even today when I see that motion picture on TV, I never fail to thrill at an actress completely dedicated to the perfection of her performance.

During this film, Susan also developed a close friendship with Don "Red" Barry, who played the role of one of her boyfriends.

Both Don and I were concerned by her sadness and came up with a little plan calculated to cheer her.

Every morning before the start of shooting, Don would bring her a package of her favorite cigarettes. And, prior to heading for the studio, I would drive several miles to my mother's home and pick from the rose trellis at the entrance way, a single pink Cecil Brunner rosebud. I would tape the rosebud to the package of cigarettes and leave them on Susan's make-up table in the Make-up Department.

She was very touched by this daily thought and said to me one day: "Bill, to me you'll always be 'the Rosebud Kid.'"

We started talking about her twin sons whom she so dearly loved and she told me that their hobby was rock 'n' roll music. I asked her if she had heard of Bo Diddley, who was quite popular at that time. She hadn't, so the next weekend, I went to Music City and bought a Bo Diddley record, and the following Monday morning, the record joined the cigarettes and the rosebud.

As Susan came on the set from the Make-up Department, she said, "Somebody left me a record with the cigarettes and rosebud."

I confessed and she said, "That was very thoughtful of you, Bill. I don't have any money on me, but tell me how much it is and I'll pay you for it later."

After her bitter experience in marriage—the feeling of rejection—it was hard for her, due to pride, to accept anything, even the small gift of a record.

I guess I looked at her in utter amazement.

"But, Susan, it's just a little gift. Anyway, it's for your kids."

Her eyes welled with tears.

"Bill, you shouldn't be buying me or my boys gifts."

I was stunned when, in recent years, I heard the news that

Susan Hayward was seriously ill and had had a diagnosis of brain cancer. It was said to be terminal.

I was a brand-new baby Christian then and beginning to be aware of the power of prayer. It was impossible to get Susan and the news of her illness out of my mind. I was then working at Universal Studios on a TV feature film, *Tramway to Death*, which we were shooting on location at the Palm Springs Tramway and at the studios.

Susan was dear to me, and I wanted to express my love for her in some way. It was impossible to reach her. I tried and tried by phone. All I knew was that somehow I had to make her realize that however devastating her condition, Jesus loved her and that whatever his plan was for her, there is love, peace, and joy in knowing him. I had to communicate to her the information that we never walk alone unless we choose to.

Something had to be done, but what? I prayed for an idea, and it came immediately: *a prayer luncheon!*

Nothing of that kind had ever been done before at Universal Studios, but I was able to get permission for a prayer luncheon to be held in the commissary. Then I personally invited the group, setting up a reservation for eighty-five people, including everybody in the *Tramway to Death* company. I phoned Gene Arnaiz and asked him to say the prayer for Susan. After all, he was a lay minister and could do the job better than I. It occurred to me that I should be the one to handle it, but I rationalized that I had done very little public praying and that, after all, I was too new and green a Christian to do the job properly.

"Gene," I said to him on the phone, "we're having a prayer luncheon for Susan Hayward and a lot of the studio personnel will be there. Will you come over and lead the prayer?"

"Great idea," responded Gene, "but, Bill, are you certain that you shouldn't lead the prayer yourself?"

I assured him we needed his expertise and would he come?

"Yes," he said. "I'll be there."

The time of the luncheon arrived. I hadn't heard from Gene again and I began to be concerned.

More than eighty-five people started to take seats at our specially set-up tables—among them, Stefanie Powers, Bobby Sherman, Ruth McDevitt, Nancy Malone, Ross Martin, and the director, producer, and others on the production staff, as well as extras, grips, electricians, and carpenters.

Most studio personnel are on a forty-five-minute lunch period, so, in my anxiety for Gene, I wore out the clock on the wall with anxious glances.

It was 1:15, and still no Gene. Those in attendance began reaching for dinner rolls and drinking water. That bothered me, because I didn't, at that time, even believe in permitting a sip of water until grace has been said.

And Gene was nowhere in sight.

The pressure was on so hard that I began to feel that I would have to do it myself. And I prayed for wisdom and for the words to say.

There was so much noise in the commissary that it was difficult to get anyone's attention. And then the idea struck me. I took my knife and hit my drinking glass like the J. Arthur Rank Productions' gong. The noise gradually died down until the silence was terrifying. All of a sudden I was on stage. The only prayer I really knew was for kids: "Now I lay me down to sleep." That was not going to be any good here.

And then the Holy Spirit took over.

"Will you please bow your heads with me," I heard myself saying in a new voice. "We are going to pray for Susan Hayward."

I heard myself talking simply, with strength and assurance:

"Lord, we ask blessings on our meal, blessing for everyone here, and we ask special blessings for our sister, actress Susan Hayward, whom we not only admire as a performer but love as a person.

"It has become general knowledge that she has cancer of the brain, and we ask you, God, in the name of the Lord Jesus Christ, to give her a special miracle. We know that, in you, all things are possible. So, please, Jesus, touch her, move her, come into her life so that she will come to accept you as personal Savior and Lord and that her healing will be in your time."

It was anything but a masterpiece of prayer, but it did come from my heart and I felt confident that Jesus had heard the prayer with so many gathered in his name. Two things happened then. I saw Gene in the back of the room, a kind of self-satisfied grin on his face. He had been listening all the time. And Stefanie Powers began crying audibly. A few others started crying, and suddenly

Kleenex and napkins were meeting many eyes. Even the actors who play tough-guy roles and the four-letter-word experts among the grips and electricians had tears in their eyes. Stefanie later expressed what she felt were the sentiments of most present: "Bill, this is the most beautiful luncheon I have ever attended."

I wanted to tell her and the others to thank the Holy Spirit, because Bill Lasky on his own couldn't have uttered the appropriate words, but there were many who would not have understood.

I was too overcome to be upset with Gene, who happily explained that his prayers had revealed to him that he should keep his promise of attending the luncheon but that he should come late so that I would gain the experience of prayer leadership and would be enriched and strengthened in faith, ability to pray, and in compassion and love for people.

So that Susan would gain encouragement and support by knowing that the Universal Studios group had prayed for her, I passed on the information to her son Tim, now a mature man, also asking him to arrange for me to see his mother.

Tim got back to me later. He had told his mother, and although she was thankful that her friends had prayed for her, she said she was really not well enough to have visitors. She hoped to see me in the very near future. That's the way she was. She didn't want anybody to see her in a less than perfect physical state. She didn't want to burden anyone with her problems.

But there are many ways of communicating with people who can't be reached directly. Gene came up with the idea of buying and sending Susan a copy of Kathryn Kuhlman's book *I Believe in Miracles.* We did and wrote inside the cover, "We, too, believe in miracles," and signed it, "Love in Jesus—Gene Arnaiz and Bill Lasky, the Rosebud Kid."

I went to my mother's house on a sudden impulse of the Lord. She had been dead now for a year and I had not been back since. Her beautiful rose garden was unloved, dried, unwatered, and unattended by the new owners. However, the Cecil Brunner vine seemed to know of my coming, and even though the leaves were parched and brown, there remained one perfect pink rosebud. I picked it and attached it to the book. Then I delivered the book and bud in person to Tim's office.

A miracle occurred all right, but it wasn't the kind Gene and I had planned on. It was the kind God planned for Susan and us.

Not a word of response came from Susan. We had heard she was living in Florida and had begun to travel in Europe with the other twin son. We hoped that the healing had taken place.

Shortly after, I saw this beautiful lady for the last time at the annual Motion Picture Academy Awards ceremony. Gene and I had ended up in the last row of the Music Center's balcony. We had got our tickets late, and the last row was all that was available. As we were watching through the monitors, I was very much alarmed when I saw Susan Hayward, beautifully gowned and groomed—every inch the great star—reach out to support herself, as if in intense pain.

Seated next to Gene and me was John D. Barrymore, one of the two sons of the late movie idol John Barrymore. John had noted that a well-known radio commentator was interviewing celebrities in various parts of the audience, and unhappy with his seat and hoping for a chance to be interviewed on national radio, he went downstairs.

In the Lord's humorous planning, as John disappeared down one flight of stairs, the radio interviewer for whom he was searching came up another with the intent of talking with anyone in the very last row. He saw the seat vacated by John and sat down beside Gene and me.

When he learned my identity, he interviewed me on my plans for starting a film production company. Before leaving he asked, "By the way, how come you are in the last row of the balcony?"

I laughed and said, "These are the seats nearest to heaven, and, besides, they are the only ones that were available."

Later I went backstage, but in the confusion and crowd, I couldn't find Susan. I learned that she had been rushed away in her private limousine. Shortly after this, there were newspaper headlines about her death.

Strange, unexplainable things often happen when one has invited Jesus into his heart and lets him run his life according to his Plan. That is how I heard about the last act of Susan Hayward's life.

We had prayed for her at the luncheon and many times since, and now we were to learn that our prayers had been answered.

Someone I didn't know came to me unexpectedly, a gentleman who just happened to be a friend of the nurse who was at Susan's bedside those last days.

"By any chance, did you know Susan Hayward?" he asked me.

"Yes. Yes, very well," I replied.

"Did you know that she died a Christian?" he asked.

Before I could answer, he continued, "Yes, she did receive the Lord, and on her last night on earth, she asked the nurse to put a cross in her hand. She died peacefully in her sleep. Her last words were 'No matter what, keep the cross in my hand.' "

He looked at me for a brief instant and added something he could not know the significance of: "She *did* die with the cross in her hand, and one thing more: On the night stand beside her bed was a well-worn copy of Kathryn Kuhlman's book *I Believe in Miracles*."

20

Anyone Can Serve

Miracles are made in heaven for us on earth. All that's required of us is faith and patience. Even though I've seen quite a few miracles happen, I sometimes wonder how the Lord, in his infinite wisdom, seems to select unprepared and untrained individuals for certain roles in his miracles.

As far as the "Edward G. Robinson, Jr.," drama is concerned, I felt that the Lord could have been a better casting director and have chosen a real veteran Christian to handle the Bill Lasky role. But maybe he knew more about casting than I thought.

About six or seven months after I became a completed Jew, I awoke one morning at four o'clock with the strange thought that I should phone Edward G. Robinson, Jr., whom I had known as a child, although we had not been in touch for years. Our mothers had been fine painters and close friends. I had heard that Mrs. Robinson died tragically in a mental hospital.

For quite a number of days I continued to wake up in the morning with the feeling that I should call Eddie on the telephone.

But then, again, I asked myself, "Why should I? His mother and father are dead. So are mine, and our parents were the only ties between us. Maybe I should because I'm a new Christian. But what difference would that make to him? And, besides, there was the incident of the cat."

Three weeks went by and I began to think of him in the daytime as well as during the nights and early mornings, and it seemed to me I should call him, but I continued to resist, even though all I had to do was to call the Screen Actors Guild for his agent's name and get his phone number.

One Sunday I was faced with a dilemma. It was during the period of gasoline shortages, and I had failed to fill my tank at the appropriate time, so I didn't have enough fuel to go to my own church. But I was determined not to miss this weekly joy. I had begun to realize how much I needed the recharging of the spirit which I always get from Pastor Sanders' sermons. Now this was impossible. I decided to walk down Hollywood Boulevard and go into the first church I came to. It happened to be an Episcopal Church, which I had never before attended. I enjoyed the simplicity and beauty of the Episcopalian service. As I was about to leave, I was surprised when a well-dressed gentleman came over and introduced himself, saying he was with Phoenix Mutual Life Insurance Company. And then he asked, "What's *your* name? I've never seen you here before."

"William Lasky," I replied. "I've never been here before."

"Oh, *Lasky*. Are you, by any chance, the son of Jesse L. Lasky?"

"Yes, I am."

"Fantastic, fantastic," he said. "Do you happen to know Edward G. Robinson, Jr.?"

I felt a sudden chill, and the hair on the back of my head began to rise.

"I knew him casually as a child," I replied.

"Do you have his phone number?"

"No," I said. He reached into his pocket and drew out a small piece of scratch paper on which a phone number was scribbled. I put the paper into my pocket, and as I turned to go, he said, "Now promise me, Bill, you'll phone him right away. He needs you."

Questions kept popping up in my mind.

What could be so important? Why does he need me? Does he know of a motion picture job for me? Really, this whole business is ridiculous. We haven't spoken to one another since we were kids.

I returned home, became involved in the usual Sunday afternoon happenings, and forgot all about the phone call.

Now, God works in many wondrous ways, but it has been my experience that he generally uses three means of communication with us. First, we have an all-encompassing feeling that there is something we should do. If he fails to reach us in this way, he tries the second way. He sends someone to carry his request to us. If we ignore the first two methods, then, as a last resort, he speaks to us in a manner that we are unable to ignore. I don't mean that the voice comes in like a Cecil B. DeMille voice in *The Ten Commandments*, but when I have heard his voice, there's no doubt in my mind as to its origin. And so it was in the Eddie Robinson affair.

As I had ignored the first method, he had used the second. I firmly believe our Lord has a sense of humor, which was again evinced in his modus operandi. I had failed to respond to the first two methods, so the Lord used the third means of communication. He spoke to me directly.

It was eleven that night, and I was ready to retire when I heard it loud and clear.

"Call Eddie Robinson, Jr.!"

This was an order that had to be obeyed, but I began to argue, not realizing that I was resisting God.

I remember thinking that I can't phone somebody I hardly know at eleven o'clock at night. Besides his wife—if he has one—will be upset at a call so late.

Then, once more, I heard, "*Call him.*"

I reached in my pocket, took out the paper, and dialed the phone number.

The story becomes more interesting when you know the truth: Edward G. Robinson, Jr., was to die at 1 A.M. There was only about an hour and a half left for him on earth.

A woman's voice answered: "Hello."

"Hello. Is this Mrs. Robinson?" I asked.

"Yes," the voice answered. "My name is Nan."

"Well, Nan, I'm Bill Lasky, and I'd like to talk to Eddie."

She asked, "Are you the son of Jesse Lasky?"

"Yes," I replied.

"Fantastic, fantastic," she repeated. "Eddie needs you."

The same words that had been uttered by the man in the Episcopal Church!

I started to say things and couldn't as Eddie's voice came on the phone.

"Hello . . . *Bill?*"

"Yes, Eddie," I said.

"Bill, this is so fantastic that you should call me. I need you. I need you desperately."

Again those same words!

"You need me?" I asked. "You're the third person today who has used those identical words."

"Bill," he said, "did you know that my mother died in a mental hospital and that she had lost her reason and will to live because my father couldn't give her enough love?"

"Yes, Eddie. I do."

Information poured out of him to fill in the past.

"Bill, did you know when my father died, he cut me out of his will? Did you know that I begged him on my knees before he died just to tell me once—only once in my life—that he loved me? He said he couldn't do that. Remember, he was brought up in the slums of New York. He *was* Little Caesar. And Little Caesar couldn't say he loved his only son. It would have been unmanly."

"Eddie," I said, "I understand completely. I feel as if I want to say something on the phone to you. I don't want it to wait until we see one another. I hardly even know you, but I want to tell you I love you."

There was a moment of silence. Then he began crying gently and his voice became husky.

"Bill . . . I'm not worthy of anyone's love. Do you know anything about my life, some of the things I've done?" he asked tentatively.

"Not very much, Eddie, and that doesn't really matter now."

"Do you know that I'm an alcoholic?"

"Yes, Eddie."

And then came a whole confession of his weaknesses, faults, misdeeds, and sins.

It was now just about midnight. We talked and talked, and every subject bridged the span of years and dissolved personal differences that had separated us.

"Eddie, there's something new that will probably be of interest to you, because you could be an important part of it. I have plans for organizing a film production company—possibly even trying to acquire an existing studio. How would you like to be our first contract actor, just as your dad was a contract player in my dad's era? I want to take a part in the rebuilding of Hollywood."

"Oh, Bill. That's great."

I felt a new excitement in his voice. Then I told him we had a specific blueprint for the kinds of pictures we want to make—films with a constructive base—and that there are hundreds of stories of this kind available and more to be written.

He couldn't hear enough about the plan.

I mentioned that we were raising money for the project and how much it meant to me personally that Hollywood should experience a rebirth. I told him I believed in its birth and mentioned what Pastor Sanders had said: "Why not *Holy*wood?" rather than Hollywood.

Abruptly he cut in:

"Bill, I've got a question to ask you."

"What, Eddie?"

"*Are you happy?*"

"Oh boy, Eddie. I sure am."

"*Why* are you happy, Bill?"

It wasn't I who was directing the conversation any longer.

"Eddie, it is because I have accepted Jesus Christ as my personal Savior. It is because I know Jesus loves me."

"Bill, does that mean you are a Christian?"

"Yes, Eddie. That's what it means. We use the term 'completed Jew.' You know how proud we Jews are!"

"Bill," he said, "I have always wanted to know Jesus—especially in the last several months."

I remembered that my first urge to phone Eddie had come several months before.

"Bill, how can I become a Christian?"

Now, remember that there was not much time left in his life.

"Well, Eddie . . ." I began to feel uncomfortable and stall. "Eddie, I'm just a new Christian . . ."

I wanted to suggest that he go to church next Sunday and let the minister do it. And the Lord spoke to me for the last time.

"*Now!*"

Right then and there I learned something with the clarity of a lightning flash. All of us are ministers. The many inner urgings to call Eddie Robinson had not been for the purpose of referring him to an ordained minister. The urgency of the situation pressed upon me for a reason I couldn't then understand. There was no time to call in the first team. I, Bill Lasky, was on the field.

So I started again. "Eddie, I know that you can personally invite the Lord into your life and receive him in your heart. I received him all alone in my bedroom. You can welcome him in wherever you are. And on the telephone is as good a place as any. You're supposed to say a sinner's prayer. So let's say it together. Jesus, come into my heart."

Eddie repeated: "Jesus, come into my heart."

"Fill me with all the love that is you. Forgive me of all my sins. Make me as clean as new-fallen snow. Wash my sins away forever in the great ocean of your mercy. Please come into my life. I wish to be born again in your Eternal Love."

He repeated the words after me, and I could sense a radiance through his tone of voice. Then he said, "Bill, it's so incredible. I feel as if I'm a newborn baby."

"Eddie," I replied, "you can't understand it now, but you are."

"Bill, it is so wonderful that you would even call me up."

I wanted to confess that I had used every form of evasion, every trivial excuse and rationalization, to do everything but that.

"Bill," he was saying, "why not phone me on Wednesday? Let's go down to the beach. Let's sit in front of the ocean and just talk. I need a friend. I need a brother. You'll never know how much."

"Eddie, you have a friend. I am your brother in Christ."

"Well, how about the beach?"

"Sure, Eddie. I'd love it."

"Will you phone me tomorrow morning, Bill?"

"Sure, Eddie."

We hung up and I went to sleep and slept soundly until around nine the next morning. Then I dialed his number, and Nan came on the phone.

"Hi, Nan," I said. "Bill Lasky calling. Can I talk to Eddie, please?"

Her voice was cold. "No, you can't."

"My God, have I said something wrong? Is something wrong, Nan?"

"Nobody can *ever* talk to him again!"

"Nan, what's happened?"

"Don't you read the newspaper, watch the news on TV, listen to the radio? He's dead. He's dead!"

She began crying.

"Nan, how could it be? I spoke to him just a few hours ago . . . ?"

"It happened," she said stolidly. "Last night after talking with you, he hung up the phone and came to my bedroom. His eyes were shining. His face . . . I've never seen him look like that before. He was beautiful. He said, 'Nan, I'm so happy. Imagine, Bill Lasky called me up! And do you know what he told me? Bill told me about Jesus. Bill had me say the sinner's prayer. Nan, I asked forgiveness for my sins, and I am forgiven all my sins. I'm a new Christian. I have never felt so clean inside and happy in my whole life. You know . . . and then, it's funny—an old habit—but I'm going to have a drink.'

"He went into the bar, poured himself a full tumbler of vodka, and drank it down. He said, 'I'm so exicted, I can't sleep. I'll never sleep again in my life. I'm so excited with everything—my new life, Bill's plans for the film company. He tells me I may even be a part of those plans. We're going to meet on Wednesday and go to the beach. Bill's going to be my new friend.'

"He went to the bathroom and took some Seconals. I don't know how many. Nobody knows. He called out, 'Nan, I'm hungry,' went into the kitchen, took out a roast from the refrigerator, put a piece of meat into his mouth, choked on it, strangled, and died."

But he had accepted the Lord in time.

Edward G. Robinson, Jr., did not die in vain.

As proof of Christ's promise of eternity, this story will be told and retold, and many have known, and will come to know, the Lord because of it.

Marilyn Monroe, Susan Hayward, and Edward G. Robinson, Jr., taught me a great deal. This lesson is indelibly recorded on my mind.

"It's never too early to be a Christian witness."

Never again will I hesitate for a day, an hour, or even a minute to tell someone about Jesus.

We are all ministers, and we have to be ministers *NOW*. Later can be *too late!*

21

End and the Beginning

A particular Bible truism commonly experienced in all our lives is that a prophet is without honor in his own home town. Frequently, each of us is least honored by those who know us best. There is a reason for this. Those closest to us know us in the bright light of our human failures and weaknesses. These failures and weaknesses obscure the transformation and metamorphosis of our Christ lives. We are equally aware that our loved ones know us through the evidence of our past selves and this tends to keep us from reaching them in Christian love. We fear a judgment always, and if we are honest with ourselves, we know this judgment is merited. So it was with me and my son, Ronnie. Divorce and separate lives had accented my failure to be the kind of father that I wished to have been to my son.

In one area I truly feel that I have not failed. Whenever possible, I have shown my love for him.

My son had patiently observed my five years in Buddhism and he had not judged me. Only after a period of growth and maturing could I tell him. "Your dad is no longer a Buddhist but is now a Christian."

Furthermore, Ronnie had completely broken away from the indolent religious background of his parents and grandparents and had grown in awareness in his birthright of Judaism. He had married a lovely young Orthodox Jewish girl named Yvonne, who had spiritually guided him.

So, rather than upset my son and his wife's religious relationship, I had simply told him on the phone that I had given my life to Jesus, who is the promised Messiah of the Jews.

Ever since I had invited Jesus into my heart and life, I not only wanted to spread the Good News to everybody I knew, I wanted to shout if from the housetops and the mountaintops, even to people I didn't know.

Since my rebirth, it had been my deepest desire that Ronnie, the most precious member of my family, should give his heart to the Lord Jesus. As I had learned to believe in the power of prayer, I had decided to claim Ronnie for the Lord a year earlier. Typical of me, I had forgotten about the prayer.

Following my prayer, I had found several Jewish-Christian tracts, which I sent to Ronnie and Yvonne. I had no reaction from them until one day when I phoned Ronnie and asked him directly, "Did you read the last little tract I sent you?"

Its theme dealt with the sacrificial blood of Jesus and its analogy with the blood left on the doorsteps of the early Jews, representing the forgiveness of God. The intention of this practice of sacrifice was so that God would pass by their houses and not kill their first-born.

Quite a parallel exists here that involves the Passover service and relates to the blood of the lamb—Jesus being the sacrificial lamb, the final atonement for all of man's sins, the forgiveness of God in each of our lives. The tract indicated that there is no more sacrifice necessary on our part beyond submitting our sins, ourselves, and our lives to Jesus, for he made the final sacrifice for us on the cross.

I had never seen such a clear expression of the close parallel between the old Jewish concept and the Christian one, so I was anxious that Ronnie and Yvonne would read it. Then I hoped we could discuss it.

Yvonne had studied the Old Testament in depth, and she knew the Passover (Jewish "Pesach"). I really didn't know if she had knowledge of the New Testament and the parallel between Jesus' sacrifice and the early sacrifices of our people.

Yvonne must have overheard Ronnie, saying half apologetically that he had had too little time to do more than scan the tract on the blood sacrifice, because she came on the phone.

"Dad," she said, "I wish you wouldn't send us any more Christian literature. We're not reading it. Besides, we want to hold to tradition and remain Jews. We don't want to be converted. We're studying Hebrew at our temple. Ronnie is learning to be a Jew. You seem to be trying to confuse us."

"Yvonne," I said, "my purpose is not to confuse but to clarify. You don't *change* anything that you are. Remember that Jesus was a Jew, and all the early Christians were Jews. Mary and Joseph were Jews. The apostles were Jews. Both the Old and the New Testaments were written by Jews. Jesus said in his lifetime, 'I do not come to change the laws of the past, only to clarify them.' The reason I sent the tract was to show you that the so-called Christian doctrine is Jewish. Like you and Ronnie, I, too, am studying to become a better Jew. I have completed myself in the awareness that the prophecy of the Messiah has come true in Jesus Christ. In doing this, I have lifted a veil of disbelief from in front of my eyes. I can see all this clearly now.

"Any Jew who can see this is not going to be changed when he accepts Christ as his Messiah. He simply accepts the prophecy in the Old Testament which becomes completed in the New Testament. In the life of Christ, you complete yourself as a Jew. You are born a Jew, and you'll die a Jew. You always stay a Jew. In fact, many gentile Christians with depth of knowledge in the Bible acknowledge that they themselves are grafted-on Jews. So Christians who follow Jesus Christ, a Jew, are really Jewish."

This was something she was not quite ready to accept. She listened courteously and lovingly but still firmly held to her original request: "Dad, please don't send us any more tracts."

That seemed to be the abrupt end of my efforts in Ronnie's household—at least on the human level.

I was asked by Mary Dorr, executive directress of the Association for Religion in Media, to tape a thirty-minute Christian testimony for a new program entitled *Faith* to be aired several weeks later on CBS-TV in Los Angeles.

Victor Webb, the show's producer, had called a meeting to discuss the show's content. I had been cautioned by Mary not to use any controversial religious material. This was a CBS station policy, and I was to talk in generalities, avoiding specifics such as being a completed Jew.

Once again, the Lord opened a shut door, and, in the first five minutes of the meeting, I noticed a change in Victor. His attitude, when we began the discussions, was one of tolerant submission to the job at hand.

And then it happened. As I began to witness, pulling out all the stops, Victor's eyes began to shine. He interrupted and said, "Mr. Lasky, I've never said this to anyone on this program before, but I want you to have unprecedented carte blanche and say anything that comes into your heart."

I will never forget the expression on Mary's face. The production meeting was a tremendous success and a further witness to the miraculous overwhelming power of the Lord. A few days later we taped the program.

During the interview, I had mentioned the power of prayer—an expression of God's love—to work miracles and, I smiled visibly, remembering how *he* had moved the producer of the show. I told the story of Susan Hayward and Edward G. Robinson, Jr., mentioning the inability of Eddie's father to tell him that he loved him.

I told of the personal joy of becoming a completed Jew—a Christian—and how this had changed my life entirely, how I had been born again in Jesus.

Love was a dominant theme in the testimony. I mentioned never having remarried after divorce from my wife. I had said I still loved my wife and that I felt all marriages were made in heaven, and, even though people were separated, they are, in essence, still married in the eyes of God. I told the viewing audience of my love for my son, Ronnie, for his wife, Yvonne, and my grandson, Ian, and granddaughter, Sarah.

A few days before the program was to be shown, I suddenly had an impulse to telephone my son to alert him to my TV appearance in hopes that he would watch the program, which was to be shown at 11:30 A.M. Sunday. I was hesitant to ask him to watch on his day off, and I prayed that God would help him to find it convenient to listen to my telecast testimony.

Well, finally the program was shown, and I waited all day for a phone call from him. But the phone refused to ring, and I didn't have the nerve to call him.

Another day passed. It had been full of strenuous activity, and I was tired and went to bed early. I was sound asleep when the phone rang. It was only about 10:45, but I had been sleeping so deeply that I was hardly coherent when I said, "Hello."

It was Ronnie.

Everything started in a matter-of-fact way.

"Dad, this is very hard for me to tell you . . ."

Immediately I started to be apprehensive. He continued, "There have been differences between us in the past—many things about the divorce from Mom, things about you. And I'll never forget my keen disappointment in you on the weekend you had promised to take Ian to Disneyland and then, a few hours before the time, canceled out."

He paused, and I found nothing I could say to this.

"Dad, the older I get, the more I begin to understand how we all fall a little short of the persons we want to be. I certainly understand you better now. It occurs to me I never did thank you . . ."

I wondered, "For what?"

"You know, Dad, you have given me so many things that are important in my life, things I've grown up with—beautiful memories. Remember how we used to go out butterfly collecting, snake hunting, noosing lizards, fishing together and trying to get the big ones at the top of the stream, like Grandpa and Great-grandpa. Remember the day on the golf course when we got up at dawn to find our lost falcon, Danny, and how excited we were when we heard his bells and saw him fly gracefully back to us. Wonderful memories, Dad, and I've never before thought to thank you for them. I only hope that I'll be able to give some of the same memories to my son."

There wasn't a word I could find to say.

"Dad," he continued, "there's something I really want to say to you. I've never said it to you before, and I don't know exactly how to say it now. Dad . . . I love you."

I tried to respond, and the lump in my throat was too big.

It would have been impossible that Ronnie could have told me he loved me unless the Lord was working in him. No human effort could have brought this about.

Our phone conversation was nearing an end, and a new thought occurred to me.

"Ronnie, this coming week there's a meeting of the Full Gospel

Business Men's Fellowship at the Holiday Inn on Wilshire Boulevard in Westwood Village. You know, I'm the president of the Beverly Hills Chapter, and I would like you to attend as my dinner guest and to sit at the speaker's table next to Michael Esses, our guest speaker."

"Dad, who's Michael Esses?"

"He's a Jewish rabbi who has accepted Jesus Christ as his Savior and Messiah. He's a very popular Old Testament teacher and scholar at Melodyland School of the Bible in Anaheim near Disneyland. He has written several best-selling books, among them *Michael, Michael, Why Do You Hate Me?* and *The Phenomenon of Obedience*. He comes from a long line of rabbis—some forty generations. . . ."

Ronnie appeared to be interested.

"Dad, if I'm able to come, I'll probably be late because when I leave work it's already about seven o'clock."

"Fine, Ronnie," I replied. "Don't worry about it. I'll have them keep your dinner warm for you."

He hung up the phone.

Thoughts of my marriage flashed through my mind. I loved my wife, and she loved me, but, without God in our marriage—without his agape love—there was an insufficiency of love, and nothing could take the place of that in a marriage. A marriage without God's love is a marriage without a soul.

The days slipped by quickly, and the big evening arrived. We had a tremendous attendance—about five hundred—for buffet dinner. Around 6:45 P.M. I stepped to the microphone and asked the chapter's chaplain, Glen Adkins, to say grace. Then the guests started through the food line.

I had a little fun with Michael Esses when he came back to the table from the buffet. His plate was heaping.

"Oh, Michael, you have a wonderful dinner there," I said.

He looked at me, smiled, and winked, "After all, I am your guest."

Another completed Jewish gentleman named Richard Cohen, of Lamb Ministries, passed by the speaker's table and kiddingly nodded toward the bountifully supplied plate and remarked, "Michael, I see you're not fasting tonight." Then he looked closer at Michael's plate, and exclaimed in a loud voice that everyone at the speaker's table heard:

"Michael, you're not eating salami?"

Dr. Esses looked up smiling, and replied, "Pray for me, brother."

Ronnie hadn't arrived yet. Michael was eating heartily and I kept wishing that the empty seat next to him would be filled by my son. I whispered to Michael, "I know how it feels for a person to leave nine hundred and ninety-nine sheep and go look for the one that's lost, I feel like I want to go find my son and forgot all about the meeting."

"No, Bill," Michael replied. "We'll just pray on it, and he'll be here."

So we prayed together and claimed that Ronnie would arrive safely at the meeting. About forty-five minutes went by. We had also been expecting an actress-evangelist, Elaine Edwards. Brant Baker and I have a little private joke. We refer to Elaine as "the late Elaine Edwards," because she invariably arrives about forty-five minutes late for our services.

I wanted to stall for time, so I opened the meeting by telling those present the story of how Ronnie had seen my TV appearance, had heard my testimony, and had phoned to tell me he loved me. I also mentioned how much it meant to me for Ronnie to attend this meeting.

Another forty-five minutes went by, and I began to get a feeling that Elaine and Ronnie just were not coming. And, then, sure enough, Elaine made her entrance with a movie star's flourish and, on the mike, I commented to the audience, "Here comes Elaine Edwards. You know those movie stars—always forty-five minutes late." And just as I said that, I saw my son right behind Elaine, and announced, "And here comes my son, Ronnie."

Every eye in the banquet room was on him, and there was a ripple of applause as he came to our side at the speaker's table.

"Ronnie," I said, "this is our speaker, Dr. Michael Esses."

The two shook hands. I continued, "Why don't you get your food, Ronnie. It's late."

"No, Dad," he said. "That isn't important. I just want to get on the microphone for a minute. May I?"

"Why not eat first?" I asked.

"No, Dad. I want to tell them something."

"Well . . . all right," I replied tentatively, because I had no idea what he had on his mind. He took his place at the mike and said:

"I'm Ronnie Lasky, Bill Lasky's son. I want to tell you people a story."

He repeated word for word his account of having seen me on TV and how he had phoned to tell me that he loved me. Then he paused for a few seconds.

"You know, when I told my father I loved him, *it was at that precise moment that Jesus entered my heart.*"

A silence settled over the vast dining room. Everyone was so moved that it would have been impossible to find a dry eye in the place.

Then Ronnie sat down next to Michael Esses, who prayed the sinner's prayer with him, and Ronnie reaffirmed the Lord in his life.

What a happy day to see my prayer answered. But even this was not the end of it, for so it is with love.

Not long after that, I appeared on the stage with Brant Baker and the Shekinah Fellowship at the Four-square Church in Long Beach. I told the Eddie Robinson story and that of my son telling me that he loved me and of his accepting the Lord.

At the conclusion of the service, Brant invited me to join him in the prayer line for individuals to come forward for prayers and healings.

A handsome, tall, blond young surfer of about twenty came up to me. His face was peeling from the effects of salt and sun.

"Mr. Lasky, when you mentioned Edward G. Robinson, Jr.,

"Sure," I said. "Let's go over to the side."

He began to unburden himself of a weighty problem, pausing many times self-consciously as he proceeded:

"Mr. Lasky, when you mentioned Edward G. Robinson, Jr., whose father could never tell him he loved him, it really got to me. And then when you mentioned your son telling you he loved you . . ." His eyes became moist. "I really need your prayers. You know, I never once told my father I loved him, and now it's too late. Last week my dad died of cancer. I didn't even know he was sick. Now he'll never know how I feel about him."

He averted his face so that I wouldn't see the tears that were trickling down his cheeks. "Lord, help me to help him. Give me the wisdom and the words!"

Then I heard the words coming out!

"You can still tell him you love him. It is very easy. Will you pray along with me?"

He bowed his head and we prayed together:

"Our Father, who art in heaven . . ."

Now he no longer tried to hide his tears.

"Son, you have two fathers," I heard myself saying. "One you knew on earth, and the one you will know in heaven. And your Father, God, whom you can reach through Jesus, hears everything we say. Jesus will make sure your message goes to both of your fathers in heaven. . . ."

He threw his arms around me. In that warm, brotherly embrace, I learned a profound lesson. How provincial we are in giving and receiving love. How we tend to reserve our love for ourselves, for the immediate family, when agape love cannot be bounded by four walls, our immediate circle of friends or acquaintances, our communities and nation. It is universal.

There is an eternal quality to love that is not limited in geography and time. True agape love is not to be hoarded but to be given freely.

As I said in the beginning, the past has a powerful influence on the present—as my father's and mother's lives had on mine.

Human life and love may die, but God's life and love (agape love) are eternal. It is true that my experiences with Susan Hayward, Edward G. Robinson, Jr., my son, Ronnie, and my new son in Long Beach—through God's love—are now in the past.

These experiences had a special meaning and beauty all their own. Their significance was directed to my life, but, as we are all one in the Lord, so are they significant to us all.

These experiences gain an eternal quality in the telling and retelling.

Historical records will say that Susan Hayward and Eddie Robinson, Jr., are dead. Don't you believe it! They live in every retelling of their stories, for these stories are woven from God's love.

Others will find eternal life through these stories as they find their way to the only meaningful experiences that anyone has on earth, finding God and themselves in the process through our Lord Jesus Christ.

No matter what scientists tell you about the world in their long and impressive words, the world is held together with agape love. We all enter the kingdom through the love and sacrifice of Jesus, and we do not die because, through him, our lives are eternal. He is the only answer to any and every question that we may have.

We can't merit God's love, but through his grace, we can have it for the asking. Yet we have to take the step and ask.

In his Love: THE END AND THE BEGINNING.

How to Receive Christ

Many times I have been asked, "How can I receive Christ?"

For me three little words sufficed: "Jesus, help me!"

These three words represented my total personal submission to Jesus, the opening of the door to my life and heart to permit the mercy and love of Jesus to enter.

It is clearly stated in the Bible that God must increase within each of us and that he cannot until we decrease. We must humble ourselves to the realization that until we have his love, we have nothing.

Here is an easy prayer for receiving Christ: "Jesus, come into my life. Fill me with your love. Forgive me of all my sins. Make me the kind of person you would have me be."